The Age of Napoleon

Recent Titles in
Greenwood Guides to Historic Events 1500–1900

The Dreyfus Affair
Leslie Derfler

The War of 1812
David S. Heidler and Jeanne T. Heidler

The Atlantic Slave Trade
Johannes Postma

Manifest Destiny
David S. Heidler and Jeanne T. Heidler

American Railroads in the Nineteenth Century
Augustus J. Veenendaal

Reconstruction
Claudine L. Ferrell

The Spanish-American War
Kenneth E. Hendrickson, Jr.

The American Revolution
Joseph C. Morton

The French Revolution
Linda S. Frey and Marsha L. Frey

The French and Indian War
Alfred A. Cave

The Lewis and Clark Expedition
Harry William Fritz

The Second Great Awakening and the Transcendentalists
Barry Hankins

The Age of Napoleon

SUSAN P. CONNER

Greenwood Guides to Historic Events 1500–1900
Linda S. Frey and Marsha L. Frey, Series Editors

GREENWOOD PRESS
Westport, Connecticut • London

Library of Congress Cataloging-in-Publication Data

Conner, Susan P. (Susan Punzel), 1947–
    The age of Napoleon / Susan P. Conner.
        p.   cm.—(Greenwood guides to historic events 1500–1900, ISSN 1538-442X)
    Includes bibliographical references and index.
    ISBN 0–313–32014–4 (alk. paper)
        1. Napoleon I, Emperor of the French, 1769–1821.   2. France—History—
    Consulate and First Empire, 1799–1815.   I. Title.   II. Series.
    DC201.C64   2004
    944.05—dc22   2003060132

British Library Cataloguing in Publication Data is available.

Library of Congress Catalog Card Number: 2003060132
ISBN: 0–313–32014–4
ISSN: 1538–442X

First published in 2004

Greenwood Press, 88 Post Road West, Westport, CT 06881
An imprint of Greenwood Publishing Group, Inc.
www.greenwood.com

Printed in the United States of Americ

3 1984 00216 6831

The paper used in this book complies with the
Permanent Paper Standard issued by the National
Information Standards Organization (Z39.48–1984).

10   9   8   7   6   5   4   3   2   1

Copyright Acknowledgments

The author and publisher gratefully acknowledge permission for use of the following
material:

Excerpts from "Supper in Beaucaire" by Napoleon Bonaparte. Reprinted by permission
of Peters, Fraser, & Dunlop Limited, on behalf of Sir Christopher Frayling, ©: as
printed in the original volume.

"To Joseph Bonaparte, Paris, June 22, 1792," "To Citizeness Bonaparte, April 3, 1796,"
"Constitution Making, September 19, 1797," and "Continental Blockade, January 10,
1810." Copyright © 1998 by Prion Books Ltd. Reprinted by permission.

CONTENTS

A photo essay follows page 110.

ILLUSTRATIONS

SERIES FOREWORD

American statesman Adlai Stevenson stated that "We can chart our future clearly and wisely only when we know the path which has led to the present." This series, Greenwood Guides to Historic Events 1500–1900, is designed to illuminate that path by focusing on events from 1500 to 1900 that have shaped the world. The years 1500 to 1900 include what historians call the Early Modern Period (1500 to 1789, the onset of the French Revolution) and part of the modern period (1789 to 1900).

In 1500, an acceleration of key trends marked the beginnings of an interdependent world and the posing of seminal questions that changed the nature and terms of intellectual debate. The series closes with 1900, the inauguration of the twentieth century. This period witnessed profound economic, social, political, cultural, religious, and military changes. An industrial and technological revolution transformed the modes of production, marked the transition from a rural to an urban economy, and ultimately raised the standard of living. Social classes and distinctions shifted. The emergence of the territorial and later the national state altered man's relations with and view of political authority. The shattering of the religious unity of the Roman Catholic world in Europe marked the rise of a new pluralism. Military revolutions changed the nature of warfare. The books in this series emphasize the complexity and diversity of the human tapestry and include political, economic, social, intellectual, military, and cultural topics. Some of the authors focus on events in U.S. history such as the Salem Witchcraft Trials, the American Revolution, the abolitionist movement, and the Civil War. Others analyze European topics, such as the Reformation and Counter Reformation and the French Revolution. Still others bridge cultures and continents by examining the voyages of discovery, the Atlantic slave trade, and the Age of Imperialism. Some focus on intellectual questions that have shaped the modern world, such as Darwin's *Origin of Species* or on turning points such as the Age of Romanticism. Others examine defining economic, religious, or legal events or issues such as the building of the railroads, the Second Great Awakening, and abolitionism. Heroes (e.g., Lewis and Clark), scientists (e.g., Darwin), military leaders (e.g., Napoleon), poets (e.g., Byron), stride across its pages. Many of these events were seminal in that they marked profound changes or turning points. The Scientific Revolution, for example, changed the way individuals viewed themselves and their world.

The authors, acknowledged experts in their fields, synthesize key events, set developments within the larger historical context, and, most important, present a well-balanced, well-written account that integrates the most recent scholarship in the field.

The topics were chosen by an advisory board composed of historians, high school history teachers, and school librarians to support the curriculum and meet student research needs. The volumes are designed to serve as resources for student research and to provide clearly written interpretations of topics central to the secondary school and lower-level undergraduate history curriculum. Each author outlines a basic chronology to guide the reader through often confusing events and a historical overview to set those events within a narrative framework. Three to five topical chapters underscore critical aspects of the event. In the final chapter the author examines the impact and consequences of the event. Biographical sketches furnish background on the lives and contributions of the players who strut across this stage. Ten to fifteen primary documents ranging from letters to diary entries, song lyrics, proclamations, and posters, cast light on the event, provide material for student essays, and stimulate a critical engagement with the sources. Introductions identify the authors of the documents and the main issues. In some cases a glossary of selected terms is provided as a guide to the reader. Each work contains an annotated bibliography of recommended books, articles, CD-ROMs, Internet sites, videos, and films that set the materials within the historical debate.

These works will lead to a more sophisticated understanding of the events and debates that have shaped the modern world and will stimulate a more active engagement with the issues that still affect us. It has been a particularly enriching experience to work closely with such dedicated professionals. We have come to know and value even more highly the authors in this series and our editors at Greenwood, particularly Kevin Ohe. In many cases they have become more than colleagues; they have become friends. To them and to future historians we dedicate this series.

Linda S. Frey
University of Montana

Marsha L. Frey
Kansas State University

PREFACE

While the Napoleonic era comprises only a decade and a half of European history (1799–1815), the changes that the era brought to France and Europe were monumental. Napoleon brought order out of the chaos of the French Revolution and preserved revolutionary equality of opportunity. His troops took revolutionary ideas and the Napoleonic tenets of governmental organization across Europe. He was enamored with detail and had a prodigious memory for people, events, and projects. He dissected everything—from his relations with women, to the design of imperial monuments, soup kitchens and submarines, to casualty counts on the battlefield. His picture was proudly displayed on the walls of peasant homes, and he could rely on a majority of the survivors of Europe's most horrifying campaigns to fight with him again. He sent armies across the length and breadth of Europe, and he once said that he would not notice a million deaths. He was obsessed with taming Great Britain in order to create a greater France to control Europe. He was a visionary, a pragmatist, a cynical opportunist, and certainly a man of contradictions. But, he was also the man for whom the era was named.

Although the bicentennial of Napoleon's birth has passed, the first decade of the twenty-first century will commemorate his coronation on December 2, 1804; the creation of the *Grande Armée;* the inauguration of the *Légion d'Honneur;* his victory at Austerlitz; his reorganization of France; and the promulgation of his law codes. And then there will be June 18, 2015, the anniversary of Waterloo. Each year a wealth of books on the Napoleonic era arrives in bookstores throughout the world. The volumes may be picture-filled coffee table books, analytical studies, period memoirs in the original language or in translation, intriguingly titled explorations of the era, biographies of contemporaries, or an addition to the number of military histories that continue to be published. It is not surprising to ask: another book on Napoleon? This volume in the Greenwood Guides to Historic Events 1500–1900, has a specific purpose. Built around the life and actions of Napoleon, it is also the study of the era and its impact on the people who lived through it, whether they were members of Napoleon's court society, foreigners, inventors, soldiers, workers who passed an afternoon under the red umbrellas of their local drinking establishments, or residents of the areas that the Napoleonic armies annexed or occupied. It provides an overview of the historical debates that surround Napoleon while still being a general text for anyone new to this period of history.

Chapter 1 sets the stage for the Napoleonic era with an overview of the life of Napoleon who was born on one island—Corsica—and died on another—St. Helena. From his origins on Corsica, it traces his Corsican nationalism, his baptism in revolutionary ideas, and his early military challenges and triumphs. In Chapter 2 one meets the First Consul, whose position was first achieved through a coup d'état and then finalized by popular vote. He used his prodigious energy to bring peace and then to conduct the most systematic and comprehensive organization that France had ever known. Chapters 3 and 4 trace the changes that took place in everyday life for Napoleon's notables, his bourgeoisie, and working class men and women. Napoleon's creation of the Grand Army, his military maxims, and the lives of his soldiers form the contents of Chapter 5, followed by a narrative and analysis of the Napoleonic wars in Chapter 6. Chapter 7 concludes with the Napoleonic legend—first, his extraordinary return from exile to lead the French again; and second, the legend after his death as represented by two hundred years of writings, debate, commentary, and popular culture.

The Age of Napoleon also includes a chronology of events, several illustrative maps and tables, period illustrations drawn from the collection at the *Bibliothèque nationale de France* in Paris, and primary source documents ranging from a condensed version of Napoleon's first published political essay, to selected letters, and memoirs of his contemporaries. The book concludes with biographies of key figures during the period, an annotated bibliography, and a general subject index.

ACKNOWLEDGMENTS

I owe a debt of gratitude to those individuals who allowed me the opportunity to write this book. First, my greatest thanks are owed to Linda Frey and Marsha Frey, the editors of this series, who believed that I would do justice to Napoleon beyond the battlefields and the widely known anecdotes. Second, I owe thanks to my colleagues in academe who assisted me in a wealth of ways: Gary Shapiro, Dean of Arts and Sciences at Central Michigan University who provided a grant to assist me in locating illustrations in Paris; Thomas Sosnowski at Kent State University who provided insight and helpful suggestions; and my students who always provide inspiration for my projects. I also offer my *remerciements* to the staff of the engravings section of the *Bibliothèque nationale* in Paris for leading me to the right catalogues and collections; to Sheila Clayton, Jeri Harm, and Jill Hosier, who have maintained just the right amount of encouragement in the midst of crises in the Dean's Office. I owe additional thanks to Florida Southern College for allowing me to begin my position a week and a half late, since I was still in Paris on research. I would be remiss not to acknowledge Ron and Pat Currie who lent me their house in Scotland for my last writing frenzy. Finally, I owe particular thanks to my husband who rarely has a vacation because of my vocation, and to Orson Beecher and Donald Horward, whose instruction in French history continues to inspire me. And, finally, I thank the supportive staff at Greenwood Press for their thoughtful and thorough assistance. As any author should rightfully acknowledge, the errors of fact or interpretation are mine alone.

CHRONOLOGY OF EVENTS

1768	
May 15	France acquires Corsica
1769	
August 15	Birth of Napoleon Bonaparte in Ajaccio, Corsica
1779	
January 1	Napoleon enrolls at Autun to learn French
April 23	Napoleon transfers to military school at Brienne
1785	
October 19	Napoleon completes the program of study at Brienne and is admitted to the Ecole militaire, the school of future generals in Paris
September	Napoleon commissioned as a second lieutenant in artillery at Valence, France
1789	
July 14	Fall of the Bastille in Paris signals the outbreak of the French Revolution
1791	
April 1	Napoleon promoted to first lieutenant
October 1	Constitution of 1791 creates a constitutional monarchy
1792	
April 20	Declaration of war against Austria

May 28	Napoleon arrives in Paris and is present for the assault on the Tuileries (June 20) and fall of the monarchy (August 10)
	Napoleon promoted to captain
September 21	French National Convention proclaims the First French Republic
1793	
August	Publication of Napoleon's *Supper in Beaucaire*
September	Napoleon commands the artillery against the English in and around Toulon
December 22	Napoleon promoted to brigadier general after the successful capture of Toulon
1794	
July	Fall of Robespierre and the end of the radical Jacobin Revolution; revolutionary month of Thermidor
August 9–24	Napoleon imprisoned as a supporter of Robespierre and the Jacobins
1795	
June 22	Napoleon appointed brigadier general in the Army of the West, but remains in Paris
August 20	Napoleon appointed to the *Bureau Topographique* of the French government
August 22	Constitution of 1795 voted into existence creating a new government called the Directory, 1795–1799
September 15	Napoleon's name is stricken from the officer list because of his refusal to accept a post in the Army of the West
October 5	Napoleon suppresses a major uprising against the constitution with the "Whiff of Grapeshot." This event is also called the 13th *Vendémiaire* from its date on the revolutionary calendar.
October 26	Napoleon assigned as commander of the Army of the Interior
1796	
March 2	Napoleon assigned as commander of the Army of Italy

March 9	Napoleon marries Joséphine de Beauharnais
March 26	Napoleon reaches his headquarters at Nice, opening the First Italian Campaign against the Austrians
May 10	Battle of Lodi (Italy)
November 15–17	Battle of Arcola (Italy)
1797	
May–July	Creation of the new Republic of Venice, Ligurian Republic, Cisalpine Republic
October 17	Treaty of Campo Formio signed, ending the First Italian Campaign
December 6	Napoleon assigned as commander of the Army of England
1798	
February 15	Creation of the Roman Republic
March 29	Creation of the Helvetic Republic
April	Napoleon assigned as general-in-chief of the Army of the Orient
July 1	Egyptian campaign begins with Napoleon's landing at Alexandria
July 21	Battle of the Pyramids
August 1	Battle of the Nile
December 29	Formation of the Second Coalition against France
1799	
March–May	Siege of Acre in the Egyptian Campaign
October 9	Napoleon returns to France from Egypt
November 9–10	Coup of 18 Brumaire brings Napoleon to power as First Consul
December 25	Constitution of 1799 (VIII) creates the Consulate
December	Amnesty granted in the Vendée
1800	
January 6	Bank of France created
February 17	Local governments reorganized
May 15–23	Napoleon crosses the Alps at the St. Bernard Pass in the Second Italian Campaign

June 14	Battle of Marengo
December 24	Unsuccessful assassination attempt against Napoleon (Infernal Machine)
1801	
February 9	Treaty of Lunéville signed between France and Austria
July 15	Concordat finalized with Pope Pius VII
September	French forces evacuated from Egypt
October	Peace assured with Russia and Portugal; commercial treaties finalized
1802	
March 25	Peace of Amiens concluded with Britain
April 8	Concordat of 1801 along with the Organic Articles promulgated in France
April 26	Emigrés granted amnesty to return to France
May 19	Legion of Honor created
May	Slavery reinstituted in the colonies; War in the Vendée ends
August 2	Consulate for Life approved by plebiscite (Constitution of X)
September	Insurrection begins in Saint Domingue
1803	
March–April	Holy Roman Empire reorganized
April 12	Creation of the *livret* for all workers
May 3	France sells Louisiana Territory to the United States
November 30	Saint Domingue declares independence from France
1804	
March 21	Napoleonic Code inaugurated
May 18	Constitution of XII creates the First French Empire
December 2	Napoleon crowned as Emperor of the French in the Cathedral of Nôtre Dame
1805	
January	Levy of 60,000 soldiers for the international war
May 26	Napoleon crowned King of Italy in Milan

August 9	Third Coalition formed against France
October 21	Defeat of the Franco-Spanish fleet at Trafalgar by Lord Nelson
December 2	French victory at the Battle of Austerlitz
December 26	Treaty of Pressburg signed with Austria
1806	
March–June	Creation of the satellite kingdoms: Naples, Holland, Berg
May	British invoke the Orders-in-Council blockading the Continent (Brest to the Elbe River)
July 12	Creation of the Confederation of the Rhine
July	Fourth Coalition mobilizes against France
August 6	Dissolution of the Holy Roman Empire
November 21	Napoleon inaugurates the Continental System with the Berlin Decrees
1807	
January	British expand the Orders-in-Council
June 14	Battle of Friedland
July 7–9	Treaties of Tilsit signed between France, Russia, and Prussia
	Creation of the Grand Duchy of Warsaw
November	First phase of the Peninsular War begins
	Portuguese royal family flees to Brazil; French armies enter Lisbon
December 17	Napoleon expands the Continental System with the Milan Decrees
1808	
March 17	Creation of the Imperial University
May 2	Dos de Mayo uprising in Madrid
July 7	Joseph Bonaparte proclaimed King of Spain
August 1	Joachim Murat proclaimed King of Naples
July–August	French armies evacuate Madrid
	French armies evacuate Portugal after Convention of Cintra

December 13	Napoleon enters Madrid victoriously
	British withdraw to Portugal
1809	
March	Second French invasion of Portugal
May 17	Papal States annexed to France
June 11	Pope Pius VII excommunicates Napoleon
July 6	French troops arrest the Pope
July 5–6	Battle of Wagram
October 14	Treaty of Schönbrunn with Austria
December 15	Napoleon divorces Joséphine by *Senatus consultum*
1810	
April 1	Napoleon marries Marie-Louise of Austria
July 9	Napoleon annexes Holland to France
December 13	Napoleon annexes the north German states to France
	Russia leaves the Continental System
1811	
March 20	Birth of the King of Rome (Napoleon II), Napoleon's son
March–April	French armies begin retreat through Spain
December	Massive conscription of 120,000 soldiers
1812	
June 24	Napoleon begins invasion of Russia
September 14	Napoleon occupies Moscow
October 19	French troops begin retreat from Moscow
October 23	Malet attempts coup in Paris
December 18	Napoleon reenters Paris
1813	
January–February	France renews conscription
June–August	Grand Alliance (Sixth Coalition) formed against Napoleon
October 16–19	Battle of Leipzig (Battle of the Nations)
	French armies retreat

1814

January	Allies invade France
March 31	Paris surrenders to the Allies
April 6	Napoleon abdicates first to his son and later unconditionally
May 4	Napoleon arrives in Elba as the Emperor of Elba
May 30	First Peace of Paris promulgated
November	Beginning of the Congress of Vienna

1815

February 25	The Flight of the Eagle—Napoleon leaves Elba
March 1	Napoleon lands on French soil
March 20	Napoleon reenters Paris instituting the Hundred Days
June 18	Battle of Waterloo
June 22	Second abdication of Napoleon
July	King Louis XVIII reenters Paris
	Napoleon surrenders to the British
October 16	General Bonaparte arrives at St. Helena
November 20	Second Treaty of Paris formalized

1821

May 5	Death of Napoleon at St. Helena

1832

July 22	Death of Napoleon's son, Napoléon François Charles Joseph (Duke of Reichstadt)

1840

	Return of Napoleon's remains to France
December 15	Napoleon interred at Les Invalides

CHAPTER 1

NAPOLEON BONAPARTE: AN OVERVIEW

The Fire of Heaven

"I am nailed to a rock to be gnawed by a vulture," wrote Napoleon on the island of St. Helena. He had been exiled there in 1815 after his final defeat at Waterloo and his surrender to the English. He was ill, and he scarcely resembled the dashing general who had once led his troops across the Alps into Italy and across the battlefields of Europe. On that rocky wart of an island in the South Atlantic where Napoleon had been forced to spend his remaining years, he was consumed by the memory of his power and was gnawed by the powerlessness that had become his fate. He was isolated from his admirers and most of his friends; he was kept under the watch of his English jailers, as he thought of them. His residence was less than a cottage by his standards and no more than a "gentleman's country seat" by the standards of the elite, elegant, and powerful people of Europe; nonetheless, Longwood House was where he finished his life. He had never willingly retired, and he had little to do at St. Helena except to reflect on his life, his accomplishments, and the manner in which he wished to be remembered. His prose poem continued, "Yes, I have stolen the fire of Heaven and made a gift of it to France."[1]

Between August 15, 1769, and May 5, 1821, the dates of Napoleon Bonaparte's birth and death, it would not be an exaggeration to say that the Western world was altered dramatically and permanently. His armies had spanned Europe from Portugal on the west to Russia on the east. His satellite kingdoms had stretched from Holland on the north to Italy on the south. He had once fancied a worldwide empire, and he had looked to the east: the Levant and the Orient. He had looked also to the west

and sent his troops to Saint Domingue (Haiti). He had visualized a political and economic community in Europe (albeit with French hegemony)—a common coinage, common laws, and unified diplomacy and
trade—long before the European Economic Community of post–World
War II Europe was created or the Treaty of Maastricht was ever contemplated.

When Napoleon looked back on that period of history with his
companions at St. Helena, he took pleasure in laying the groundwork for
its interpretation. He said, in his confident way, "Posterity will judge
only by the facts."[2] And facts for this period abound. Among the primary
sources of the Napoleonic era are 32 volumes of Napoleon's correspondence, 28 of which average 700 pages each and in total contain some
22,067 letters and documents. There are hundreds of volumes of decrees
and legislation that provide an official chronicle of the French government, and articles and essays from the contemporary press are available
as well. Cartons of other Napoleonic records fill archives throughout
France and Europe. Regardless of what Napoleon said—that the facts
would pronounce *all* judgments on his period—even he knew that *more*
than simple facts, dates, narratives, and names would be necessary to
create a portrait of the age and of himself.

Time and history's abiding fascination with the small, slightly dark-
complexioned Corsican have left a legacy that is sometimes compli-
mentary to the point of hagiography and sometimes thoroughly
damning, but the bibliography is massive. Commemorations of the
bicentennial of Napoleon's birth in 1969, for example, brought forward
hundreds of books and articles to join the 100,000 titles that had already
been catalogued by historian-bibliographer Friedrich M. Kircheisen by
1912. In that same year, the *Revue des études napoléoniennes* was inaugurated in France to serve as a sounding board for scholarly research.
Since then, the *Revue* has been joined by dozens of other journals and
reviews during the twentieth century. In the United States, groups like
the Consortium on Revolutionary Europe began meeting in 1972 to give
presentations and discuss current research on the revolutionary and
Napoleonic era. Annually, the Consortium publishes its *Proceedings and
Selected Papers*. In recent years, Internet sites have further expanded
Napoleonic scholarship. They include the Web site of the Napoleonic
Alliance that was established for scholars, interested parties, and students of the period, and the Dutch omnibus site (in English) called the

Napoleon Bonaparte Internet Guide. The site of the French Napoleonic Foundation (also in English translation) includes an internet magazine, illustrations, a library, and receives 20,000 hits a month.[3] Further sources can be found in the bibliography at the end of this volume.

What does all of this mean? Certainly there is no scarcity of interest in Napoleon even today, and judgments about history, even those that we believe to be firmly grounded in facts, bear different interpretations and conclusions. Facts do not speak for themselves. They are found in a variety of sources, for example, government documents, correspondence, memoirs and recollections, plans and maps, places and place names, ephemera and artifacts. They provide the basis for history and its visions and revisions. They allow us to consider this period again. So it is, from thousands of documents and later interpretations, that Napoleon has been described as a modern tyrant, a dictator like Hitler, a new Alexander the Great, a caesar, a romantic tempered by *Realpolitik,* an heir of the Revolution, the reincarnation of an eighteenth-century enlightened despot, a masterful opportunist, or a genius who blundered into glory.[4]

As historian Alan Schom reminded us in his recent book on Napoleon, "Being neutral about Napoleon has never been easy."[5] While Schom was speaking about Europeans who remain extremely divided about their interpretations of the Napoleonic era, the same could be said for most writers about the period. What Napoleonic historians have tried to do is to lay out the evidence for comparison, search the facts and sources for internal inconsistencies and biases, and then come to conclusions about the man who so dominated Europe. What we do know, when all is said and done, is that a period of nearly two decades of history was named the Age of Napoleon and the title remains the same today.

Very Little Time to Be a Child

Five years before Napoleon Bonaparte was born on the island of Corsica, the famous English essayist James Boswell traveled there. The year was 1764, and Boswell described the small island as "agreeable," not so far from the coasts of France and Italy, with a temperate climate and over 200,000 inhabitants, most of whom were illiterate and lived primitively by European standards. The people were "frank, open, lively, and bold, with a certain roughness of manner."[6] The island contained a variety of flora and fauna, good harbors and rolling hills, and most noticeably an incredible, passionate, powerful patriotism. Boswell's visit, which brought Corsica into the European vocabulary, came the same year that Carlo Buonaparte, Napoleon's future father, married Letizia Ramolina. At that time, the island was still under the legal control of the republic of Genoa. For a decade, however, the Corsicans had treated themselves as independent, but disputes with the Genoese had left a legacy of bloodshed.

In 1768, the Genoese gave up their hold on Corsica, selling it to the French. The French then dispatched a government official known as an *intendant* to oversee their new territory, but they were met with hostility equal to Corsican hostility to the Genoese. The French had no recourse but to send an additional 4,000 seasoned troops to deal strongly with the Corsican insurgents. The success of the French sent the battered but still belligerent leader of the Corsican patriots, Pasquale Paoli, fleeing to England with many of his supporters. Carlo Buonaparte, a Corsican patriot at heart, considered fleeing with his countrymen but chose to remain on the island to support his wife and first son. Carlo Buonaparte resolutely attached himself to the new government, both as a realist and as an opportunist. He was not so different from many other Corsicans. Carlo, who carried with him generations of noble lineage on the island, saw an advantage in serving the new French government, and he used his education and training in the law to secure a position as a royal assessor.

In the summer of 1769, Carlo and Letizia became the parents of Napoleone, whom Carlo called Nabulio.[7] He may have been named for a distant member of the family or the name may have been given to him because of his birth on August 15, the birth date of an obscure saint of the same name. In any case, Napoleon was the second surviving child of the couple and the second son to be born. His mother, who was among the most beautiful women of Corsica, was chestnut haired, with dark eyes, an aquiline nose, and an air of nobility. She had been 14 at the time of her marriage to Carlo and was still only 18 when Napoleon was born. She had been given little formal education and had been taught almost exclusively in her role as a mother, as was customary in late eighteenth-century social circles. Out of that environment, Letizia became a strong matriarch and a severe steward to her eight children while learning to manage family affairs in the absence of her husband, who was frequently away on business.[8]

"I was born when my country was dying," Napoleon wrote about Corsica. He painted a scene of "thirty thousand Frenchmen disgorged upon our shores . . . drowning the throne of Liberty in a sea of blood." It was a "spectacle that offended my infant eyes. My cradle was surrounded, from the very day of my birth by the cries of the dying, the groans of oppression, and the tears of despair."[9] Above all, Napoleon had learned to be a Corsican patriot, vehemently opposed to all things French. His writing was hyperbole, of course, but Napoleon had always been passionate about the things in which he believed and the causes that he embraced. He was irascible, quarrelsome, quick to pick on his older brother Joseph, and the only one of the Bonaparte siblings who was not nursed by his mother. When he later described his early years, he noted, "I feared nobody, beating one, scratching another; making myself redoubtable to all. It was my brother Joseph who most often had to suffer." Napoleon concluded with a certain pride, "He was slapped, bitten, scolded, and I had already complained against him before he had time to recover himself."[10] There is no doubt that Napoleon's Corsican experience influenced his personality and framed many of his views. There was always a certain clannishness about him, and his competitiveness was extraordinary.

By the time Napoleon was nine, his father had risen well within the Franco-Corsican hierarchy of the island. He had qualified for French nobility based on his Corsican claims to the aristocracy, and then Carlo obtained a royal scholarship for Napoleon, in whom he saw more promise for the military than Joseph. The scholarship, which had been designated as a royal scholarship for noble boys who could document their poverty and literacy, first sent Napoleon to Autun to learn French and then to boarding school to complete his education, with the hopes that he might later qualify to enter the prestigious Ecole Militaire in Paris. After three months of language instruction in 1779 to make him marginally fluent, Napoleon moved to Brienne where he stayed for five and a half years, only seeing his mother and father once. The regimen was harsh, but Napoleon thrived on his studies. While he was ridiculed for the way he spoke French (as though he had "straw in his nose," a play on the way he pronounced his own name) and his inveterate Corsican patriotism, Napoleon concentrated on his work. Five and a half years later, not yet 15 years of age, he went off to Paris to learn the art of war.

If there were influences on Napoleon that came from these early years of his life, they would include his isolation from others, partially imposed by those around him and partially imposed by himself, and his interest in mathematics and history, almost to the exclusion of everything else. He also exhibited feelings of responsibility toward his family since the death of his father, continued contempt for the French oppressors of his island even though his studies were the result of their largesse, a lack of interest in religion bordering on agnosticism, and a marked seriousness of temperament. Napoleon's graduation certificate from Brienne catalogued those years: "Constitution and health, excellent; character, obedient, amenable, honest, grateful; conduct, perfectly regular; he has throughout distinguished himself by his steady work in mathematics. He knows his history and geography pretty well. Fencing and dancing very poor."[11] Napoleon had no particular interest in social graces, as his later behavior would attest. His handwriting was cramped and hard to decipher; his mastery of French, his second language, left much to be desired. But he was quick to learn those things that interested him and what he wanted most was admission to the school of France's finest officers.

In October 1784, Napoleon entered the Ecole Militaire in Paris, where scarcely a year later he graduated and was commissioned as a second lieutenant of artillery stationed at Valence, France. Much has been made of his rank of 42nd in a class of 58, but he had passed through France's leading military school in one year rather than two or three, and he had been the first Corsican to do so, working in a language and a society that he had known for less than seven years. It was now 1785, and Napoleon Bonaparte was 16 years old.

For the next seven and a half years, Napoleon lived a double life. In one life, he continued his serious military experience, as he fulfilled his responsibilities and read more history and literature. In the other, he roamed Paris, returned to his roots in Corsica, organized patriot groups, and found himself immersed in the writings of Rousseau in which he found renewed passion. Likewise, he was fascinated by England and catalogued all of her possessions, analyzed Frederick II of Prussia (Frederick the Great), looked to the Orient for inspiration, and wrote both fiction and military tracts. Twice before the Revolution he asked for and received leave from his commission in the French army to return to Corsica. Four more times after 1789 he went as well, one of them as a lieutenant colonel in the Corsican Volunteers, still hopeful that he could assist his countrymen in expelling the French occupation. Ultimately his partnership with Paoli, whom Napoleon once held up as the savior of Corsica, proved to be doomed as was the liberation of Corsica from France. His family was forced to flee from Corsica; Napoleon renegotiated his military career, which he had almost lost because of his protracted absences (29 months in all); and he committed firmly to France as his homeland. Gone were the impassioned words that he had said about his island and his denunciation of the "French chains" that had enveloped it. "In the eyes of God," he had written describing what France had been doing to Corsica, "the worst crime is to tyrannize over men."[12] That era of his life was over; he resolved to move on.

They Have Seen Nothing Yet

When the French Revolution began in 1789, Napoleon was initially more concerned about what was going on in Corsica than what was occurring in France. Shortly, however, neither he nor anyone else could ignore the events in and around Paris that moved France closer to constitutional monarchy and then to republicanism in a short three and a half years. The Old Regime, as the period predating the Revolution came to be called, was over. Napoleon had been born a citizen of France, and as such, he would be designated as an active citizen by the government, giving him all of the rights provided by the new French order.[13] For success, he no longer needed the aristocratic coat of arms that his father had worked so hard to guarantee. All he needed was to take advantage of the opportunities that were opening before him.

During the decade between 1789 and 1799 when Napoleon assumed the mantle of government, his rise was neither linear nor meteoric. During the first four years of that decade, Napoleon's double life continued. Alternating between Corsica and France for extended periods of time, by the summer of 1792, Napoleon learned that he had lost his regular commission in the French army. French politics were growing increasingly divisive, King Louis XVI was charading as a constitutionalist while intriguing against his detractors, and the French declared war against Austria in April of that year. The French economy continued

to decline, bread remained scarce, and the army officer corps was sorely
lacking qualified personnel. In spite of Napoleon's mixed allegiances, his
commission was returned to him, and Napoleon was promoted to captain.

It is not possible to place Napoleon in early French revolutionary
events because of his disinterest in French affairs, his preoccupation with
his family, and his obsession with Corsica. Napoleon had, in fact, missed
all of the early events of the French Revolution including the calling of
the Estates-General in 1788, one of the most severe winters in eighteenth-
century French history that damaged an already seriously impaired economy, and the fall of the Bastille. A newly established National Constituent
Assembly had abolished the vestiges of feudalism and aristocratic privilege in the late summer of 1789 and had begun work on a written constitution, the first in French history. The Declaration of the Rights of Man
had been decreed, although it went unratified by the king for months.
The Revolution was speeding forward as leaders like the abbé Emmanuel-
Joseph Sieyès; Antoine Barnave; Charles Maurice, prince de Talleyrand;
Honoré-Gabriel Riquetti, comte de Mirabeau; and Marie Joseph Yves
Gilbert du Motier, marquis de Lafayette, brought forward their recommendations for a liberal, constitutional regime to replace absolutism in
France. As would become true, Mirabeau had once remarked that the
question was not how to propel a revolution; it was how to hold it back
once it had achieved momentum. Further, revolutionaries had unceremoniously dismantled the Catholic Church and its formerly inviolate
lands while they ceremoniously celebrated the new order, later adopting
a revolutionary anthem, reveling in their fraternal consciousness, and
establishing a new scheme of revolutionary festivals. Citizenship had
taken on real meaning in the new order. Political clubs and associations
were widespread and numerous, and they quickly established themselves
as serious partisan contenders in national and local politics.

When Napoleon arrived in Paris on May 28, 1792, the Revolution
was already moving toward its more radical phase. He had nothing to
do with the events that had transformed France from a kingdom to a
nation and that had transformed Louis XVI from "Louis, by the grace of
God, King of France and Navarre," to "Louis, by the grace of God and
the Constitution of the State, King of the French." The change from King
of France to King of the French was enormous. Subjects had become citizens; the kingdom had become the state. But it should be remembered

that "Napoleon," as historian J. M. Thompson wrote, had not "made the revolution." Napoleon was only a member of "the generation that inherited it."[14]

Spring of 1792 was in many ways pivotal to the French Revolution and, in a very different way, pivotal to Napoleon. The declaration of war, the levy of troops for the international contest, and the continuing civil disarray in France sparked continued partisanship and unrest in the capital. The international war was not going well, yet the king refused to bring troops to Paris for training. Government ministers were replaced, and the Legislative Assembly became more active. It is not surprising that the streets became more active as well. On June 20, 1792, a mixed assemblage of thousands of working class Parisians and local leaders marched to the Assembly and then to the Tuileries Palace, where the royal family had been residing in Paris since they were forced to leave Versailles in the fall of 1789. Napoleon was there, and he chronicled the events to his brother two days later. The mob that overcame the National Guard "mounted cannon against the King's apartments," broke down the entry gates, and dismantled interior doors. The demonstrators were "armed with pikes, hatchets, swords, muskets, spits and pointed stakes." They were excessive, overwrought, and out of control.[15] Napoleon could not countenance the actions of a mob; they could in no way be justified under the guarantees of the Constitution of 1791. But by this time, Napoleon had also ceased to be a supporter of the ineffective king. Inside the Tuileries, away from Napoleon's gaze, the king had smiled benignly to the rabble that had assaulted his palace, raised a pewter cup filled with wine to toast the nation, and placed a red cap of liberty on his head. The crowd had disbanded, but the summer of 1792 was far from over. See Document 1: *Napoleon's Letter to His Brother Joseph, June 22, 1792* in Primary Source Documents at the end of this book.

By August 10, neither a toast to the nation nor a benign smile could save Louis XVI's constitutional position. In a carefully planned assault on the Tuileries beginning with the sounding of the tocsin at midnight the night before, thousands of armed demonstrators laid siege to the palace. The king, not wishing to cause harm, ordered his guards to lay down their weapons, and he and the royal family fled to the Legislative Assembly where they took refuge. As a result, the Tuileries became a scene of bloodshed and carnage as hundreds of the Swiss Guards, the traditional palace detachment, were killed and dismembered in the courtyard. Across the street from the assault, Napoleon watched the events unfold. He had heard the bells sounding the assault and made his way through the swirling mob. Accosted by members of that crowd, he had been forced to cry *vive la nation* (long live the nation) beneath a bloody head mounted on a pike. Ultimately the courtyard that he saw was littered with bodies greater in number than on a battlefield. Bodies of the fallen troops were stripped; according to some sources, women in the mob clipped off the private parts of dead guardsmen "and stuffed them in [the dead soldiers'] gaping mouths."[16] In yet another of his letters to his brother Joseph, Napoleon rued the ineffectiveness of the king. If only he had mounted his horse, Napoleon wrote, "victory would have been his."[17]

There were to be no more chances for the king, who was removed from office and placed under guard. In the fall of 1793, the government of France declared itself the First French Republic, and four months later the former king was executed. From King of France to King of the French, Louis XVI became simply Citizen Louis Capet who went to the guillotine for his crimes against the people and the nation.

By summer of 1793, the entire Bonaparte family was forced to change its way of life, as Napoleon tied his future to the Republic, the powerful Committee of Public Safety, and to Maximilien Robespierre, its most visible member. What ultimately brought about Napoleon's first significant command was Napoleon's allegiance to the principles of the Jacobins and his support from fellow Corsican and government representative, Christophe Saliceti. It was Saliceti who recruited Napoleon for an artillery command, its objective to expel the British navy from the French Mediterranean port city of Toulon. As Napoleon began his successful preparations for forcing the British out of Toulon, he also completed *Le Souper de Beaucaire: Dialogue entre un Militaire de l'armée de Carteaux, un Marseillais, un Nîmois et un Fabricant de Montpellier, sur les évènements qui sont arrivés dans le ci-devant Comtat à l'arivée des Marseillais* (translated in shortened form as *Supper in Beaucaire*). This was his first published work, although he had already completed his *Corsican Letters* and various writings on military affairs and other topics, and had once entered a competition sponsored by the Academy of Lyon.[18] *Supper in Beaucaire*, however, was different from his earlier works. It was an imaginary conversation between a soldier in Carteaux's army in the south of France (a not particularly veiled image of himself), two conservative defenders of Marseilles' decision to resist the Jacobins, a manufacturer from Montpellier, and a man from Nîmes. But more importantly, it laid out Napoleon's support for the Jacobin causes that included order and a centralized state authority as well as his belief in military prowess, particularly the efficiency of the artillery and the strength of the troops. As the men dined and debated in the small town of Beaucaire, the soldier took more and more control of the arguments, and by the end of the evening the men from Marseilles were left with the bill for the champagne they had consumed during their evening. Napoleon also took a very practical position in the pamphlet: to support the political leadership that would ultimately be victorious. He had written earlier, "If one must belong to a party, it must be that which triumphs; it is better to be the eater than the eaten."[19] An edited version of *Supper in Beaucaire* is included as Document 2.

The British roust from the port of Toulon could not have been more important for Napoleon. Putting together the pieces of a plan that had not been enacted earlier under a less skilled commander, Napoleon mastered the heights around the port so that the siege could take place. The British had little recourse except to withdraw their fleet. In the process of the assault, Napoleon was wounded by a British bayonet, one of only two injuries he received in his career of nearly two decades in harm's way. Although Napoleon was not individually credited for the victory at Toulon, he was well rewarded. He was promoted from lieutenant colonel to brigadier general, and correspondence from the men who had served with him and who had seen him in action was consistently laudatory. He was, according to the Chevalier Du Teil "a most uncommon officer."[20]

In the meantime, Napoleon continued to work in the south of France under the watchful eye of Saliceti. Through his compatriot, he received the continued support of the Jacobins in Paris. He also participated in the *amalgame,* strengthening the armies of France by merging the new recruits and volunteers of 1793 with veterans. By the early spring of 1794, Maximilien Robespierre's bother Augustin had also noticed Napoleon. He wrote to his brother, "I add to the names of patriots whom I have mentioned to you citizen Bonaparte, an exceedingly meritorious general in command of the artillery."[21] The praise was short lived, as were the lives of Maximilien and Augustin Robespierre and hundreds of their compeers. Napoleon, named so visibly as a Jacobin patriot, was not immune from the proscription that followed the quick and bloody coup that unseated the Jacobin stronghold on the Committee of Public Safety in July 1794.

If Napoleon had been stationed closer to Paris, one does not know what his fate might have been. As it was, Napoleon was imprisoned in Fort Carré near Antibes as a Jacobin sympathizer and a threat to the new government. Again Saliceti came to his rescue, by obtaining Napoleon's release after only 10 days and then by sending him toward his destiny. Napoleon was transferred to Paris and assigned first to the topographic office of the Army and then to the Army of the West. The latter was an appointment over an infantry brigade serving in the Vendée. But the civil war that had been spawned in the west of France in 1791 by the confiscation of the lands of the Catholic Church and then by its reorganization had grown more bloody. Conscription to fill the armies of France in the international war was the new provocation. In the Vendée, it was brother against brother, family against family, and a traditional church against a revolution. Napoleon's appointment in the Vendée was not what he had in mind, and he refused it. He was well aware, and even remarked, that civil wars bring no military glory to their combatants. Saliceti and Paul Barras, who was also well placed in government circles, managed to keep Napoleon in Paris.

Fortune again smiled upon Napoleon as he found himself instrumental in averting the next constitutional crisis. On October 5, 1795, mobs assembled and began their march against the Convention (legislative body of France) that had presented a new constitution to France. While the constitution had been established legally, it contained provisions that some Parisians found particularly abhorrent. Simply, a codicil to the constitution preserved the power of those men who had unseated Robespierre and the Jacobins. The preservation of one group of revolutionaries over another, however, was not precisely the problem. Rather, the issue was that the economic crisis that beset France continued unabated and the international war raged on, in spite of the promises of those men who remained in power. Parisians asked why the new Constitution of 1795 was a more legitimate solution to the problems of France than a royalist restoration.

In the midst of this turmoil, Barras turned to the youthful brigadier general Napoleon Bonaparte to defend the new government (soon to be called the Directory). That is precisely what Napoleon did. Unafraid to use serious crowd control, Napoleon brought in forty cannons, arrayed them to aim down the narrow streets that led to the Convention, and filled the cannon barrels with nails, scrap iron, and chains. No commander had ever before taken such strong action against a revolutionary mob in Paris. What took place became known, half a century later, as the "Whiff of Grapeshot."[22] As the crowds marched on the Convention, they were mowed down in a bloodbath of shrapnel spewing from the mouths of the cannons. Napoleon saved the new government, and his efforts went exactly to plan. Casualties on his side were light, and he reported to his brother Joseph that "I haven't had a scratch."[23] His invincibility now became an aura.

Napoleon's Parisian adventure in 1795 brought him into the social circles of the capital, into the new society that was much less inhibited than it had been under Jacobin control in 1793–1794, and into the arms of Marie-Joséphine-Rose Tascher de La Pagerie [de Beauharnais]. Uncharacteristically foolish and giddy for this brief period of his life, Napoleon drank in the "luxury, enjoyment and the arts" that defined a reborn Paris where life was exceedingly agreeable. Napoleon wrote, "Anyhow, who could be a pessimist in this mental workshop, this whirlwind of activity?"[24] He frequented book stalls, took in public lectures, and enjoyed the sight of scantily clad, beautiful women who could be seen everywhere. In the salons of Paris, he courted the widow of an Old Regime aristocrat who had lost his life during the Terror. More important, perhaps, was Joséphine de Beauharnais's well-known former liaison with Barras, who had given Napoleon his opportunity for recognition in the "Whiff of Grapeshot" and who later supported Napoleon's appointment as commander of the Army of Italy. In December 1795, Napoleon was agog with Joséphine's charms: "I awake all filled with you. Your image, and the intoxicated pleasures of last night, allow my senses no rest."[25] Joséphine, who had been born in Martinique, was a quintessential hostess and a model of perfection in the arts of grace and charm. To the socially inept Napoleon, she must have appeared a goddess. See Document 3 for one of Napoleon's early letters to Joséphine. Also see the biographies at the conclusion of this book for more information on Joséphine.

On March 9, 1796, Napoleon married Joséphine, in spite of her two children by a previous marriage and in spite of the fact that she was six years his senior in age. In only two days he was on his way to Nice to take up the command that would make his name a household word and begin his progress toward the throne of France.

When Napoleon arrived to take command of the Army of Italy, the French government (the Directory) saw it only as a diversion from the more significant contest that pitted the main French armies against Austria, the only remaining continental power in the First Coalition against France. What neither the Directory nor the seasoned, veteran commanders in Italy could know was that Napoleon intended to change the rules of war. In the end, not only did Napoleon make Italy the main theatre of the war, his personal courage so won over his troops that the aura of his invincibility was renewed time and time again. He created his own war chest, supplied his men, and negotiated his own military and diplomatic settlements. By October 1797, the contest was over and the Treaty of Campo Formio was signed, ending the First Coalition. Only Britain remained in the contest against republican France.

Napoleon had managed to do what no other commander in the French military had achieved at that time. It was "a miracle of leadership," according to historian Owen Connelly.[26] What Napoleon had done was to show his commanders, most of whom were older and taller than he, that war required infinite information, strategic planning, excellent rapport with his men, and a cool deference to loss of life. He accepted no sloth or lack of preparation from his commanders; he was an *homme terrible* (a man who brought fear to their hearts and beings). André Massena, who later joined Napoleon's closest circle of friends and companions, first saw his new army commander as a small, unimpressive general who looked out of his depth. Napoleon was only 26 at the time and in command of one of France's five armies. Massena later admitted, however, that when Napoleon placed his general's hat on his head, he "seemed two feet taller."[27] Few later questioned Massena's analysis, especially when the campaign was dispatched with such efficiency and so many rewards for the French republic. See the biographies at the end of this book for more information on Massena.

In concluding this First Italian Campaign, as it came to be called, Napoleon had already begun a reorganization of Europe that would characterize his later empire. Napoleon shepherded into place the creation of the Ligurian Republic from Genoa and the construction of the Cisalpine Republic from parts of Austria, papal territories, and Venetia. It should be remembered that, at the beginning of the nineteenth century, modern Italy did not yet exist. The Italian peninsula was comprised of a number of independent states and principalities until the last half of that century when Italian unification was achieved. From what had existed, however, Napoleon moved boundaries, organized diplomatic conferences, and exchanged islands. In the process he spread the benefits of the Revolution as he saw them—the abolition of feudalism and the guild system and the implementation of civil liberties in the areas where French troops passed.

By 1797 only Britain remained an enemy of France, and Napoleon was again in Paris. He had been elected to the prestigious Institut de France; and he felt, for the first time, the jealousies of government officials and military leaders who suddenly realized how visible and potentially powerful he had become. This time, Napoleon's plans were in league with Foreign Minister Talleyrand's program that looked to the East for relief from the British. The point was to attack Britain through her back door—the British trade through Egypt and the Levant—rather than a direct assault across the Channel that had originally been proposed. Napoleon's Egyptian campaign was memorable for its sheer scale and its aims that were well beyond its military objectives.

On May 19, 1798, Napoleon began the Egyptian campaign to bring Britain to its knees and to create a stronghold for the French in the East. When all was said and done 43,000 men, approximately 300 ships of all sizes, several thousand horses, hundreds of artillery pieces, and a group of scientists and scholars to study the treasures of Egypt departed for the Orient. From their first encounter at Malta to protect the Mediterranean, to their Battle of the Pyramids, to their contest in Turkish lands to the north, Napoleon oversaw the operations. Furthermore, he oversaw a complete recreation of the governmental infrastructure in Egypt, including reshaping political boundaries, naming new governmental representatives, building needed hospitals and social care facilities, coining new currency, and trying to make headway in a medieval system of commerce, while respecting religion and local customs. What Napoleon could not guarantee, however, was the skill of his naval commander and the role of the Ottoman Empire in this contest. In both cases he misjudged. Almost upon arrival, his fleet was destroyed at Abukir Bay, and shortly he learned that Talleyrand's representative had failed in negotiations with the Turks. The French could no longer be guaranteed that the Ottoman Empire would not challenge the French inroads into Egypt.

Regardless, Napoleon declared that he had come with the blessings of the Sultan of Turkey and the Koran, and he promised his men permanent colonies and a share in the wealth of the Orient. Instead, plague and casualties devoured his troops by 1799; yet, Napoleon reported to the Directory, "We lack nothing here. We are bursting with strength, good health, and high spirits."[28]

What Napoleon awaited was an opportunity to change the course of French history, much more than the Egyptian campaign was intended to do. As he consolidated what he could, Napoleon also took care to create a legacy and to build his own version of the campaign. He formed the Institute of Egypt in Cairo, and its multivolume *Le Description de l'Egypte* became one of the lasting results of the campaign. The volumes that were published later included the most comprehensive set of plans and drawings of the monuments of Egypt that had ever been prepared or seen in Europe. Napoleon also mastered the art of propaganda. To the Sultan of Darfour and to the Divan of Cairo, Napoleon began his letters, "There is no other god but God, and Mahomet [Mohammed] is his prophet!"[29] He pledged ecumenism, but he responded in very practical ways: those who supported his occupation were granted their local customs and rights of worship, but those who did not support the French would bear the wrath of Napoleon's military. Napoleon set forward his rules from his headquarters in Cairo: "Instruct an officer in command of the place to decapitate all prisoners taken with arms in their hands. . . . [T]heir headless bodies are to be thrown in the river."[30]

The Egyptian campaign, as it turned out, was among the most brutal of the wars of the French republic and empire. As he took on the Turkish armies, who were supported by the British, the sieges became murderous. In one of the sieges, out of Napoleon's 13,000 men, more than one-third were killed in action, left crippled, or left as victims of disease. According to one of Napoleon's subordinates, Jean-Baptiste Kléber, "Bonaparte was the kind of general who needed a monthly income of ten thousand men."[31] As Napoleon turned back toward Cairo and Alexandria from the Turkish lands to the northeast, he learned that the victories of his glorious Italian campaign had been squandered: Naples and Austria were at war with France, along with Turkey and Russia. Almost unnoticed, Napoleon turned over his command, gathered a few of his closest military confidants, and sailed for France to establish himself again and to assure his fortune. What he had done, although his letters and army bulletins presented a story to the contrary, was turn "the Egyptian romance, which had begun in a blaze of glory [into] a conspirator's flight."[32] To the French, whose appetite had been whetted by stories of the Orient and narratives of the illustrious campaign, it mattered little that the French army was stranded and the objectives of the campaign were never to be achieved.

When Napoleon arrived on French shores again, France's borders were endangered by the armies of the new coalition, the Directory government was in disarray after the Conspiracy of Equals and two electoral coups in the previous three years, and the economy had not fully recovered from its malaise. Napoleon, on the other hand, had returned from his glories in Egypt; there was something exotic about him. Furthermore, he was still bathed in his success from Italy nearly three years earlier. Napoleon's timing was impeccable. There was no question that the Directory government needed to be replaced; the question was by what type of new government and by whom. Almost at once Napoleon found himself involved with conspirators who included his former benefactor Barras, his younger brother Lucien, and one of the earliest revolutionaries and constitutionalists, Sieyès. In what came to be called the coup of 18–19 Brumaire (because of its date in November according to the revolutionary calendar), Napoleon and his co-conspirators took over and dissolved the Directory. Napoleon began the "cynical business of politics."[33] He constructed a new constitution—the fourth since the Revolution had begun—to create the Consulate of France. In a series of shrewd maneuvers, Napoleon, who had been enlisted in the conspiracy primarily to provide the military power for the coup moved himself into the position of First Consul. The French had seen nothing yet. Returning to the field, Napoleon ended the coalition against France on the continent, made successful overtures to Britain for peace, and by 1801 had begun his plan to remake France. He later noted that he had brought order out of chaos; he had solidified the best of the Revolution.[34] "We have finished the romance of the Revolution"; Napoleon told his Council of State in 1800, "history must now begin."[35] From then until 1815, it was Napoleon who was puppet master, controlling the strings of history.

Work Is My Element

From the coup and constitution that brought Napoleon to power until his first abdication, Napoleon was tireless in remaking France and Europe. During those years, both France and Europe were irrevocably changed. Those changes fall into the following categories: Napoleon's search for political stability, his work toward France's economic recovery, the creation of a court society befitting the French, a massive reorganization of the French government including an overhaul of the infrastructure of the state, constitutional reform and a commitment to religious toleration, support for the arts and industry, and an uncompromising commitment to the family—whether it was the larger family of France or the family of each citizen of the fatherland.

When Napoleon negotiated the first peace that France had known since 1792, he took great pleasure in reorganizing the French state. "It is the epoch of my life," he said, "in which I have shown the most ability."[36] Efficiency was important to the First Consul, but so were stability, civil accord, and a sound infrastructure. At the turn of the nineteenth century, the civil war in the Vendée and elsewhere in France continued and the economy showed improvement sporadically only after 1795; regardless of all of the ideological statements of the French during the Revolution, the rights of citizenship had not been systematically defined, education remained somewhat illusory, society was viewed as coarse and vulgar, and so much needed to be accomplished.

In the years between 1801 and 1814, Napoleon's metamorphoses took him from First Consul to Life Consul to Emperor of the French. In each case, a constitution defined Napoleon's growing powers, and a popular vote (a countrywide plebiscite) confirmed the constitutional authority that he was assuming. Napoleon's conception of government, as it was transformed in the three constitutions that he designed, was neither a republic nor a constitutional monarchy, both of which the French had tried during the Revolution. Nor did it attempt to combine the two political ideologies; rather, Napoleon prided himself that his constitutions were popular in origin but that in practice, France was a centralized, fundamentally absolutist state. Under his authority as chief of state, one of Napoleon's earliest decisions was to encourage a blending of the nobles who had fled during the Revolution with those Frenchmen who had become the new governing class. Careers, he said, should be open to talent and merit. The Old Regime's reliance on aristocratic bloodlines, venality, and privilege was to be erased from republican and imperial France. While the transition was not immediate, Napoleon welcomed back aristocrats whose services he could use, established his own award for talent and merit through the Legion of Honor (that still exists today as one of France's highest honors), organized a civil service devoid of partisan politics, and created a new aristocracy. The society that he fashioned mimicked in some ways the old dynasties of Europe, but he was prepared to compete on equal standing with them. His coronation harkened back to Charlemagne, and he felt perfectly comfortable in making marriage alliances with the ruling families of Europe for his brothers and himself. He was a patron of the arts, public works, and education; although he practiced censorship and was decidedly anti-intellectual when French and foreign intellectuals criticized him. He centralized police authority throughout France, and brigandage and local rivalries were subdued. He created new economic institutions to stabilize the French economy and championed a system of favored status and protective tariffs, not only to expand French industry but to usurp British trade domination.

Napoleon also turned to the laws that governed France and to the religious disputes that had unraveled order particularly in the west of France. By 1801, through his actions and the diplomacy of his brother Joseph, he had made a Concordat (an agreement) with the Roman Catholic Church. After a decade, the civil war was finally quieted, and Napoleon had reached a revolutionary settlement with the Church that remained until 1905. He had, through his actions, proclaimed religious toleration that later, in various forms, also included Lutherans, Calvinists, and Jews. As far as the laws of France were concerned, Napoleon achieved what no French leader had ever managed. He created the first comprehensive codification of French civil law, called the *Code Napoléon*. Undaunted by the magnitude of his endeavors, he oversaw the creation of six additional codes: a criminal code, a code of criminal instruction, a code of civil procedure, a rural code, a commercial code, and a penal code.

Finally, he worked toward a Grand Design for Europe—perhaps a federation of nationalities or a greater France (much larger than even Louis XIV had dreamed). It is here that the greatest disagreement among historians may be found. Even Napoleon's own words are not definitive.

Table 1.1

Family of Napoleon Bonaparte

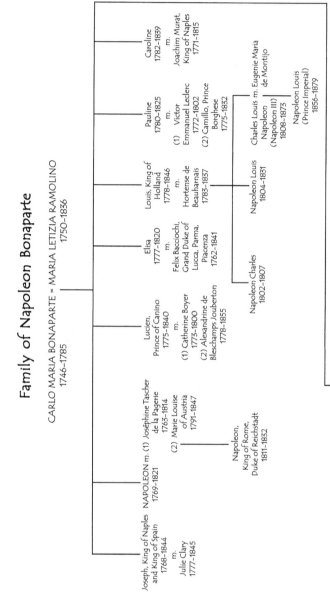

On the one hand, he claimed to Arch Chancellor Jean-Jacques Cambacérès, "I am not a fire-eater. Nobody loves peace more than I do. . . ." On the other hand, he also said, "War justifies everything."[37] From 1804 on, Napoleon continually challenged his neighbors through diplomacy, the threat of war, and war itself. If the revolutionaries had constantly spoken of "exporting the French Revolution," it was really Napoleon and his armies who spread revolutionary ideas that he had tamed and organized. His enemies knew that on the battlefield he was without peer, and when he commanded his troops in person, his mantle of invincibility remained strong (until the latter years of the Empire). Indeed, very few individual commanders ever challenged him.

While detractors of Napoleon challenged many of the words that he wrote and uttered, few would question his analysis of himself. He wrote: "work is my element." He had been "born and built for work."[38] His colleagues and companions knew that he scarcely slept, that he led a regimented life that they were required to follow, and that he *nearly* always mastered a situation. He had retrieved the crown of France from the gutter, he once said. He picked it up, placed it on his head, and left a legacy that dominated European diplomacy throughout the nineteenth century and only recently has found parallel in European affairs. See Document 4 for "Napoleon's Legacy as Viewed from St. Helena."

Notes

1. Napoleon, quoted in *The Mind of Napoleon: A Selection from His Written and Spoken Words, Edited and Translated by J. Christopher Herold* (New York: Columbia University Press, 1955), 281. The description of Longwood House is from Charles Darwin, quoted in J. M. Thompson, *Napoleon Bonaparte* (Phoenix Mill, U.K.: Sutton Publishing Ltd., 2001), 392.

2. Quoted in Owen Connelly, *The Epoch of Napoleon* (Malabar, Fla.: Robert E. Krieger, 1972), 2.

3. See the annotated bibliography of Napoleonic Web sites and their Internet addresses at the end of this volume.

4. See Frank A. Kafker and James M. Laux, *Napoleon and His Times: Selected Interpretations* (Malabar, Fla.: Krieger Publishing Company, 1989); as well as David Nicholls, *Napoleon: A Biographical Companion* (Santa Barbara, Calif.: ABC-Clio, 1999); David Lloyd Dowd, *Napoleon: Was He the Heir of the Revolution* (Hinsdale, Ill.: Dryden Press, 1957); and Pieter Geyl, *Napoleon: For and Against* (New Haven, Conn.: Yale University Press, 1963).

5. Alan Schom, *Napoleon Bonaparte* (New York: HarperCollins, 1997), xviii.

6. James Boswell, *Account of Corsica* (1768), quoted in J. M. Thompson, *Napoleon Bonaparte,* 2.

7. Napoleon was christened Napoleone Buonaparte, and he used the Corsican spelling of his name until the First Italian Campaign in 1796 when he first signed his dispatches as Bonaparte. While some historians use Napoleon's surname Bonaparte until his coronation as emperor in 1804, I have chosen to simplify and use Napoleon throughout this book. Although Napoleon is spelled in French with an accent (Napoléon), I have chosen to follow standard spelling in English and not include the accent.

8. Harold Parker, "The Roots of Personality," in Kafker and Laux, *Napoleon and His Times,* 4.

9. Napoleon to General Paoli, June 12, 1789, quoted in *Napoleon's Letters: Selected, Translated and Edited by J. M. Thompson* (London: Prion, 1998), 4. (Hereafter cited as *Napoleon's Letters.*)

10. Napoleon, quoted in Harold Parker, "The Roots of Personality," in Kafker and Laux, *Napoleon and His Times,* 3.

11. Thompson, *Napoleon Bonaparte,* 8.

12. Schom, *Napoleon Bonaparte,* 11.

13. Under the Constitution of 1791, French citizens were either designated as *active* citizens or *passive* citizens. The first category included all native-born males who were at least 25 years of age and who paid a certain amount of taxes (meaning that they owned some property). Passive citizens did not meet the criteria (e.g., males without property, servants, insane, felons, women). They were provided the protections of the law, even though they had no right to participate in making the law.

14. Thompson, *Napoleon Bonaparte,* 15.

15. Napoleon to Joseph, June 22, 1792, in *Napoleon's Letters,* 11–12.

16. Simon Schama, *Citizens: A Chronicle of the French Revolution* (New York: Knopf, 1989), 615.

17. Connelly, *Epoch of Napoleon,* 10.

18. See *Napoleon Wrote Fiction,* trans. Christopher Frayling (Salisbury, U.K.: The Compton Press, Ltd., 1972). Napoleon's essay, which did not win the award from the Academy of Lyon, was on the topic of "What Sentiments and What Truths should be inculcated in Men for their Happiness?"

19. Introduction to *Supper in Beaucaire, Napoleon Wrote Fiction,* 118.

20. Thompson, *Napoleon Bonaparte,* 38.

21. Ibid., 41.

22. The name "Whiff of Grapeshot" was coined by Thomas Carlyle in his *The French Revolution: A History* (1837).

23. Napoleon to Joseph, October 6, 1795, quoted in *Napoleon's Letters,* 16.

24. Napoleon to Joseph, July 12, 1795, quoted in ibid., 14–15.

25. Napoleon to Joséphine de Beauharnais, December 1795, quoted in ibid., 16.

26. Connelly, *Epoch of Napoleon*, 18.

27. Thompson, *Napoleon Bonaparte*, 62.

28. Napoleon to the Directors (1799), quoted in J. Christopher Herold, *The Age of Napoleon* (Boston: Houghton Mifflin Company, 1987), 71.

29. Napoleon to the Sultan of Darfour, June 30, 1799, and Napoleon to the Divan of Cairo, July 21, 1799, quoted in *Napoleon's Letters*, 51–52.

30. Napoleon to General Berthier, October 23, 1798, quoted in *Napoleon's Letters*, 50.

31. Herold, *Age of Napoleon*, 73.

32. H. A. L. Fisher, *Napoleon* (Oxford, U.K.: Oxford University Press, 1967), 39.

33. "An Introduction to the Age of Napoleon," *Napoleon: International Journal of the French Revolution and Age of Napoleon* (Fall 2000), 42.

34. Conversation (1816), quoted in *Mind of Napoleon*, 272.

35. Connelly, *Epoch of Napoleon*, 36.

36. Napoleon to Claire-Elisabeth, comtesse de Rémusat, quoted in Fisher, *Napoleon*, 42.

37. Napoleon to Cambacérès (1813), and Napoleon to Alexandre Berthier (1808), quoted in *Mind of Napoleon*, 206, 208.

38. "Some Maxims of Napoleon," in Fisher, *Napoleon*, 148.

CHAPTER 2

THE STRUCTURE OF NAPOLEONIC FRANCE

The Merchant of Hope

The time was nearly midnight on November 10, 1799. Just southwest of Paris at Saint-Cloud, Napoleon and two of his countrymen prepared to take an oath to "the Republic one and indivisible, the representative system, the division of powers, liberty, equality, security and property." That night, by a decree of the Legislative Body, a new French government was created. Three consuls, who were named by the outgoing legislators, headed the provisional government. Two 25-member commissions, serving as the legislative branch, were charged with preparing changes to the constitution, framing a civil code, and dealing with "urgent matters of police, legislation, and finance." In cases of extreme urgency, for example, "for the ratification of peace or [to deal with] serious public danger," they could convene in special session.[1]

On first reading, the Brumaire Decree[2] (as the decree of November 10, 1799 has been called), seems straightforward, very legitimate, and of no particular consequence. A new government replaced the old; the Consulate replaced the Directory. At the helm of the government was a three-person consulate, instead of a five-member Directory. Two commissions replaced the former bicameral legislature. The change, however, was not straightforward, nor was it legitimate. Furthermore, the consequences were enormous. In truth, the change that brought Napoleon into a position of political power had been cloaked in conspiracy. It was the result of a military-supported coup d'état.

Only a day earlier on November 9, 1799, the conspirators who created the Consulate had initiated their plan to overthrow the Directory.

They planned to place themselves in power, stabilize the government of France, and consolidate the best of the Revolution for their countrymen. Among the conspirators were Emmanuel-Joseph Sieyès, the well-known constitutionalist and revolutionary; Roger Ducos, a member of the government that was being overthrown; Lucien Bonaparte, a staunch republican and president of the Council of Five Hundred; Charles-Maurice de Talleyrand-Périgord, a former aristocrat and a former and soon-to-be Minister of Foreign Affairs; Joseph Fouché, a former terrorist and Minister of Police; and Napoleon himself. For more information on Talleyrand and Fouché, see the biographies at the end of this book.

The plan was reasonably simple, but it was based on a careful chronology. First, placards would be posted throughout Paris warning of an alleged radical threat to the government, and rumors would be circulated to add credence to the story. Second, once the threat of potential insurrection was planted, the Council of Elders would be encouraged to leave Paris for Saint-Cloud, a former royal property that continued to belong to the state. Saint-Cloud, however, was outside the constitutional radius and therefore unlikely to rise in revolt against any challenge to the government. Third, Napoleon, the widely known military hero, would be given command of the troops of Paris, ostensibly to maintain order but, in fact, to guarantee the resignation of less willing government members. Fourth, the Directors would resign, either by force or as adherents of the coup; and fifth, the Legislative Body (the Council of Five Hundred and the Council of Elders) would create a provisional government formalizing the events. The steps to the plot were clear, and those who were aware of it appeared supportive.

The first day of the coup went almost precisely as planned. The Councils agreed to move to Saint-Cloud, and Napoleon was appointed commander of the troops in and around Paris. The latter act was unconstitutional, but no one challenged Napoleon's appointment. A decree formalizing the changes was issued immediately. The government was, according to the decree, taking action to "curb the factions" that might unsettle the government and the economy. "Be calm," the decree concluded. "Common safety and common prosperity" will be assured.[3]

Late on the afternoon of the second day of the coup, the plot began to unravel; and the responsibility can be placed, at least partially, on Napoleon's own actions. Leaving his troops outside, Napoleon entered the meeting hall to join members of the Council of Elders who were in deliberation. Not surprisingly, they demanded to know what was *really* taking place. After all, a uniformed military commander in their presence was nothing less than a threat to their civilian authority. Napoleon's speech did not reassure them, and members of the Council found the young general "incoherent," his words troubling. "Yesterday," Napoleon informed them, "I was staying quietly in Paris, when I was summoned by you to provide military support for the transference of your session to Saint-Cloud. Now I am attacked as a second Caesar or Cromwell."[4] They already had been informed that no Jacobin insurrection had broken out in Paris. In essence, there had been no valid reason to move the assemblies to their new location. Instead, the five directors were no longer at the head of the government—four had resigned and one was under police protection. There were murmurings about the events, but the Council of Elders knew that their course had been set for them. The conspirators, including Napoleon, had already begun to dismantle the Directory, and their task was to confirm its dissolution. Napoleon left them with little room for debate: "I am not an intriguer: you know me well enough for that. . . . But if anyone calls for my outlawry, then the thunderbolt of war shall crush him to the earth. Remember that I march hand in hand with the god of fortune and the god of war."[5]

From the Council of Elders, Napoleon went to the Council of Five Hundred to encourage them to take similar action. Accompanied by four uniformed, armed grenadiers from the Legislative Guard, Napoleon entered the chamber. The meeting hall was cold, and members of the Five Hundred were weary from waiting to know what had transpired. Tempers were on edge, and the initial hostility of seeing troops in their governmental chamber quickly made the atmosphere of the room turn from cold to volatile. Members of the Council pushed into the aisles, scuffled with the guardsmen, pressed and manhandled Napoleon, and screamed and shouted, "Down with the dictator!" and "Outlaw him!" It was a fracas by any account.[6] Pandemonium reigned, and even Lucien Bonaparte, president of the assembly, could not bring order. Napoleon, who either fainted or was stunned, was carried from the room. Guard action was required, and Lucien, who feared that all of their plans would be destroyed, left the room to bring in guardsmen from outside. He had assured the troops that Napoleon was in danger and that only Napoleon could restore order to France. In a dramatic, almost theatrical moment, Lucien mounted his horse and drew his sword. Wielding it, he threatened to run his brother through if Napoleon's republican motives were not as pure as theirs. Theatrics triumphed.

Orders to the guard were dispatched; they were to clear out the dissidents as quickly as possible. Members of the Council of Five Hundred, who were in the process of debating a motion to outlaw Napoleon (i.e., to take away his civil rights and protections), spilled from the hall and leaped out of the large first-floor windows as the guard swarmed in. According to accounts of the event, they "ran, tripping over their toga-like robes of office and clutching their plumed hats" as they raced through the gardens, behind the shrubs and trees, and into the fields of Saint-Cloud.[7] To an observer, it looked like a bad comedy. To those who fled, it was clear that the government had been overthrown.

Later as Napoleon described the events that had transpired, his published account was interestingly quite different. "I presented myself at the Council of Five Hundred," he reported, "alone, unarmed, my head uncovered, just as the Elders had received and applauded me; I came to remind the majority of its wishes, and to assure it of its power." He then continued, "The stilettos . . . were instantly raised against their liberator; twenty assassins threw themselves upon me and aimed at my breast."[8] The guardsmen, who remained at the door in his version, rushed in to save him and to extricate him from the crush of hostile and murderous deputies. Only after he left the room did additional troops enter to rescue Lucien from the brawl. Disloyal dissidents fled, and the loyal members of the government remained. According to Napoleon's story, he had liberated France from its dangerously ineffective and vice-ridden government. He was a liberator, not a conspirator.

That evening, those who remained at Saint-Cloud formally dissolved the Directory and named Napoleon, Ducos, and Sieyès as the provisional consuls. By December 13, 1799, only a month later, a new constitution had been written and accepted. The Constitution of the Year VIII, as it was called, was the fourth constitution of the French Revolution in less than a decade. In many ways, it should also be considered the first constitution of the Napoleonic period, and it will be treated here in that manner.[9] In its 95 articles, Napoleon set the tone for the document. According to Napoleon's vision, the government would not be republican, but it should appear to be so; it would bring order to France through greater centralization, but it should appear to be broad based. Firmly and adamantly he imprinted his ideas on the document. See Document 5: *Napoleon Bonaparte's Letter to Talleyrand on Constitution Making* at the end of this book.

The constitution, as it was issued in final form, retreated from revolutionary republicanism. It was, in fact, one step on the way to empire; yet it received the largest popular vote of any of the revolutionary constitutions that had preceded it. The French were tired of the Directory, unclear about its principles, weary of the international war that had been going on since 1792, and ready for economic recovery. All they demanded was that the principles of the Revolution be safeguarded in some manner. As they perceived it, the new constitution could be no worse than the last. Perhaps it would even be better. When it was presented to French voters, after already becoming effective on December 25, 1799, there was no backlash. No demonstrations took place. Neither a bang nor a whimper escaped from the masses of the French.

The Revolution, Napoleon announced, was over. "Frenchmen!" he proclaimed, "A constitution is presented to you. It terminates the uncertainties which the provisional government introduced into external relations, into the internal and military situation of the Republic." He further instructed, "The constitution is founded on the true principles of representative government, on the sacred rights of property, equality and liberty. . . . Citizens, the Revolution is established upon the principles which began it: It is ended."[10] When the votes were counted, Napoleon's mandate was clear: 3,011,007 votes for the new constitution and 1,526 against.[11] Order finally seemed assured, confidence was returning, and even the Paris exchange was showing strength again. Through much of his earlier life, Napoleon had mused about government and governing. Now his time had come. He had noted, "One can govern people only by showing them the future; a head of state is a merchant of hope."[12] A merchant of hope had arrived for France.

The Short and Obscure Constitutions of France

The Constitution of the Year VIII (1799), which ushered in the Consulate, was not based on any other historic or contemporary model. While it contained provisions for the executive, judicial, and legislative functions of government, it was neither parliamentary nor republican. In fact, it was a creative hybrid. Napoleon had taken great care to design a government that would be far less susceptible to the results of direct elections, partisan groups, and personalities than former constitutions had been. He had also taken care to preserve the revolutionary language of popular sovereignty, while in reality transmitting authority to himself as First Consul.

In creating the constitution, Napoleon followed advice that "Constitutions should be short and obscure," and the Constitution of the Year VIII was certainly representative of that maxim.[13] It was the shortest constitution that the French had known up to that time, and Napoleon contrived it so that substantive change was obscured by revolutionary appearances. There was a certain Machiavellian tinge to it. The constitution, for example, began with an explicit recognition of France's revolutionary past. "The French Republic is one and indivisible," it stated. The language was identical to the first paragraph of the revolutionary Constitution of the Year I (1793) in which popular sovereignty had defined the government. Then, carefully buried within the reasonably brief document was the language that defined where authority lay: "the decision of the First Consul shall suffice."[14] In theory, sovereignty was guaranteed to the citizens of France as a legacy of the Revolution, yet in reality, sovereignty had been entrusted to the First Consul.

Title I of the constitution provided a definition of citizenship in revolutionary terms: all males 21 years of age who had been born in France and who currently resided there were counted as citizens. The constitution also contained some common disclaimers—persons who had become naturalized citizens of another country could not retain their rights to citizenship, nor could felons. The rights of citizenship were suspended when a Frenchman became a wage-earning domestic servant. While this latter provision may sound strange to modern ears, it was commonly believed that servants, whose loyalty lay with their masters, would be unable to exercise their vote independently. In essence, a master could stuff the ballot box by demanding his servants' loyalty.

Voting, as governed by Title I, became a curious system of lists, providing for direct election only at the local level but having the appearance of democratic elections throughout the process. In each town, township, or city electoral district, citizens listed the names of persons best qualified to administer public affairs. Those citizens who were listed most frequently were selected for the final list, and from that list, public functionaries were selected. The list could contain no more than one-tenth of the names of qualified citizens of the particular voting district. Citizens on the first list would then designate one-tenth of their membership for a departmental list. Members of the departmental list would select one-tenth of their membership to be sent forward for selection at the national level. As specified in the constitution, the first elections were not scheduled to take place until 1800, so in practice, nearly all government officials were initially selected by Napoleon and his advisors. While the constitution did not set qualifications for each of the electoral lists, enabling legislation spelled out increasing property requirements for membership on each of the lists. In the end, only one man in 1,000 might be designated for a national post. In the prerevolutionary Old Regime, however, that statistic would have been far lower.

On paper, the legislative power of the Constitution of the Year VIII was shared, but, in practice, the First Consul also controlled it. According to policy, the government (i.e., the First Consul with the assistance of his Council of State) drafted legislation that was then sent to the Tribunate, a body of 100 members who were at least 25 years of age, where drafts of the laws were discussed and recommendations were made for their adoption or rejection. The drafts of proposed legislation were then forwarded to the Legislative Body, composed of 300 members who were at least 30 years of age. The Legislative Body voted on the proposed legislation, but they did not debate the proposals. So-called orators sent from the Tribunate provided the pros and cons of the draft legislation. Then, the First Consul promulgated the law. While 400 of the most respected citizens were included in the process, in the final analysis, legislation began and ended with the First Consul.

Elsewhere in the Constitution, an 80-member body called the Conservative Senate was created. Membership was confined to French males, at least 40 years of age who met the qualifications for the national list. In spite of its name, the Conservative Senate was not a legislative body. It made judgments about the constitutionality of legislative and governmental acts in order to *conserve* the constitution; and, on the recommendation of the First Consul, it amended the constitution (as *senatus consulta*). The document also named the first two Senators. They were Sieyès and Ducos, both of whom had expected to be seated on the consular platform with Napoleon. Other members of the Senate were appointed from candidates submitted by the Legislative Body, the Tribunate, and the First Consul.

As far as the Second and Third Consuls were concerned, Napoleon made his own choices, sidestepping Sieyès and Ducos, who had been co-conspirators in the events of Brumaire. They were Jean Jacques Cambacérès, a well-respected jurist and legal expert who had voted for the death of the king, and Charles François Lebrun, a former official of the Old Regime who had royalist tendencies. The opposites did not stop there; where Cambacérès was a rotund gourmet, Lebrun was thin and nondescript. A better balance would have been hard to find to avoid criticism from either the political left or the political right. Their positions, however, were fundamentally advisory. As specified, the First Consul had the following powers: to promulgate the laws; to appoint and dismiss members of the Council of State, ministers, ambassadors, army and navy officers, local administrators, and commissioners of the courts; and to appoint all criminal and civil judges.[15] In legislation and staffing, almost everything crossed Napoleon's desk. Through the Council of State, which was constructed by an executive ordinance in late December, Napoleon monitored nearly every function of government, most often imprinting his opinion upon it. When the three consuls disagreed, the First Consul's decision sufficed.

Furthermore, the constitution included specifics about the French judicial system, economic matters, and threats to the government. Even though the Constitution of the Year VIII had retreated from the Revolution, the document still contained some significant revolutionary principles: the protection of property, inviolability of domicile, protection from arbitrary arrest and detention, the individual right to petition the government, and support for the arts and sciences. What was missing, though, was a declaration of rights, accountability of officials, the structure of the ministries that would assist the government, and a representative method for amending this new constitution.

Only twice more did Napoleon engage in constitution writing. When the government wished to reward him for his military efforts on behalf of France, he recommended extending his term, in fact, to make him First Consul for life. As the constitution was rewritten in 1802, other changes included creating electoral colleges to replace departmental and national lists, increasing the size of the Senate, and reducing the size of the Tribunate from 100 members to 50 while also restricting its powers of debate. In the case of electoral colleges, Napoleon created a system whereby notables, or men of property, would completely dominate political offices. Shortly, direct election became purely fictional. By increasing the size of the Senate with 40 additional members whom he could handpick, Napoleon assured himself that constitutional changes would be appropriately supportive of his future recommendations. In restructuring the Tribunate, he removed his most vocal opponents and minimized its opportunity for criticism. The plebiscite that was called to confirm the constitutional change provided another mandate for Napoleon as Life Consul: 3,568,000 votes in favor of the change and only 8,374 in opposition.[16]

The constitutional changes were dramatic, but so were Napoleon's accomplishments in the previous two years. He had negotiated peace in Europe, quieted the civil war in France, and brought economic prosperity. He had also been the object of an assassination attempt, a widely publicized event that he used to support his recommendations for a Life Consulate.[17] Two *senatus consulta* in August 1802 confirmed the changes that came to be known as the Constitution of the Year X (Constitution of 1802), although they were really amendments to the earlier constitution. One of the more vocal opponents to the change was Napoleon's own brother Lucien, whose theatrics on November 10, 1799 had saved the coup. Lucien had, in fact, always been a staunch republican, and in response to Napoleon's new constitution he published a pamphlet titled *Parallels among Caesar, Cromwell, Monk, and Bonaparte*.[18] The title said it all, but the contents were equally inflammatory. Lucien was summarily sent off to exile in Madrid. In general, most other opposition was limited and without serious threat to the new government.

Regardless of his popularity, Napoleon refused to let public opinion find its own voice or be swayed by critics. On one level, he believed that people should be governed "as the majority wish to be governed," but on another level, he believed that he had the right to tell French citizens what their wishes were.[19] He had created a system for public opinion in the best interest of France, and he relayed it in a later comment: "The entire secret in governing is knowing when you should take off the lion's coat in order to put on the fox's."[20] When it came to public opinion and propaganda, which he believed were inseparable, he always played the fox. He turned to his Minister of Police Joseph Fouché to monitor words, actions, and people. Fouché censored any kind of printed or written matter including newspapers, magazines, journals, theatrical productions, and illustrations. He also had the right to inter-

fere with private correspondence. One of Napoleon's more annoying critics counseled her friends: "[Fouché is] always in everybody's shoes."[21]
Already in 1800, he and his men had shut down 60 of the 73 political
journals in Paris on grounds of libel rather than censorship.[22] Later he
added national security to his list of excuses. In the end, no more than
four political papers continued to be printed in Paris; each department
could have only one. To carry out the massive chore of monitoring public opinion, a legion of informants was employed. In a set of instructions
to Citizen Ripault, who was Napoleon's personal librarian and, in practice, one of his ubiquitous snitches, Napoleon demanded that Ripault
monitor "institutes, literary meetings, sermons, new educational establishments, or fashionable trials [court hearings], that might be of interest from a political or moral point of view." On the list were also "bills,
posters, [and] advertisements."[23] Whether it was his brother's pamphlet,
street corner smut, an assassination attempt, or an international conspiracy, the response was swift and firm.

By 1804, war had broken out again in Europe and another plot to
kidnap or kill Napoleon had been discovered.[24] Timing was perfect for
his third constitution. By a *senatus consultum* in May 1804, Napoleon's
life consulate was fashioned into the French Empire, and Napoleon
became Napoleon I, Emperor of the French. This time, in a short but not
particularly obscure constitution, Napoleon's salary was increased dramatically, a line of succession was spelled out in the document, and his
power to appoint Senators was no longer limited. A plebiscite confirmed
the change to a hereditary imperial house: 3,572,329 in favor of the new
constitution and 2,579 in opposition. The Constitution of the Year XII
(Constitution of 1804) stated in simple terms that the *republic* of France
had been entrusted to an *emperor.* To a political scientist, what Napoleon
had created was an impossibility in theory or actuality. A republic and
an empire could not coexist in the same space. Napoleon, however, did
not feel that he needed to explain or justify what he had done. France
had returned, for all intents and purposes, to a hereditary monarchy. But
in no way did its foundation rest on the monarchy that had been dissolved in the heat of the Revolution. His imperial system was firmly constitutional, and French citizens had ratified the change. In December,
Napoleon was crowned in a lavish ceremony at Notre Dame. Again, he
made sure that he was not compared to Louis XVI, the former king of

France, or any of Louis's direct line. He went back even farther to the glories of an earlier empire to set the stage; he was the "successor to Charlemagne."[25] With the Constitution of the Year XII and his coronation, Napoleon had ended his constitutional experiment, just as four years earlier he announced that the Revolution was over.

The Mystery of the Social Order

> "*Question:* What should one think of those who fail in their duties
>   to the Emperor?
> "*Answer:* According to the Apostle Paul, they . . . [will] make them-
>   selves deserving of eternal damnation."[26]

The year was 1806, and the words could be heard anywhere in France. They came from the mouths of French children who were reciting the Emperor's new catechism. From their voices also came an important imperial message. The French people owed "love, respect, obedience, loyalty, military service and taxes" to Emperor Napoleon I.[27] They were rendering unto Caesar those things that were Caesar's.

Relations with the Catholic Church had not always been so cordial as they appeared in 1806. The Revolution had left a bloody and conflicting legacy concerning religion. Religious toleration in its broadest sense, however, had not been the issue. In fact, toleration, although imperfect, had been granted two years prior to the beginning of the Revolution, and throughout the revolutionary years, French men and women found neither their adherence to Protestantism nor their experiments with Theophilanthropism or other cults restricted by the government. The fate of the Catholic Church, however, was something quite different. Historically it had been allied both spiritually and politically with the monarchy; so, as revolutionaries dismantled the monarchy, they also dismantled the Catholic Church. First, the wealth of the Church was attacked, and then religious orders were dissolved. In 1790, Church lands were confiscated and nationalized by the Civil Constitution of the Clergy in an effort to forestall the bankruptcy of France. In the process, priests were required to take an oath supporting the revolutionary change. If they refused, they were classed as nonjuring clergy, unable to practice their vocation. If they took the oath, they were paid by the state but the pope excommunicated them for their conflicting allegiance.

French citizens were caught in the middle of a dispute that appeared to pit the Revolution against salvation; they could remain loyal to nonjuring clergy and become counterrevolutionaries or they could place their loyalty in the constitutional clergy, whose sacraments were invalid. Pockets of armed conflict broke out, and by 1793, entire regions of France were in revolt. In 1795, the Directory government declared the full separation of church and state in France. In this political climate, the Catholic Church no longer had any standing with the government. The Church had been disestablished, and salaries of the clergy ceased to be paid. The civil war raged on and issues of the conflict merged: protection of Catholic religious practice, support for nonjuring priests, resistance to taxation and conscription, and support for a return of the monarchy. Casualties in the conflict were enormous—estimated at between 180,000 and 300,000—as the civil war set brother against brother and French troops against their own people. Napoleon had, in fact, only missed military service in this civil war in the western departments (the region called the Vendée) because of powerful friends in Paris. The conflict had sapped the strength of France for the entire revolutionary decade. Something had to be done.

The civil war in the Vendée, however, was only one of the problems that Napoleon had to solve as he became head of the French government. The broader issue was domestic order, and there were no simple solutions to that problem. Rather, domestic order was a puzzle, and the pieces of the puzzle did not yet fit. As Napoleon worked through the solution, he had a number of issues to resolve. First, he needed to relax the laws concerning exiles and émigrés (those who had been forced to leave France or who had fled from France during the Revolution). In doing so, he hoped to bring back wealthy and talented men who could support his government and to lessen the chances of unrest sponsored by malcontents outside of France. Second, he intended to provide amnesty for those who had been caught in the civil war. Then, he could formally begin his negotiations with the Catholic Church to resolve revolutionary differences. To restore order would conceivably require other negotiations, and Napoleon was willing to take them on. By 1808, all of the pieces of the puzzle had finally been put in place.

Napoleon began gradually, explaining what he was doing at each stage of his plan for domestic order so that he would not generate severe criticism or outright hostility. In the process of inviting expatriates to return, he eliminated the revolutionary lists of émigrés that had proscribed them. Furthermore, he reminded émigrés that the new French government was not a partisan creation; it included a former terrorist (Fouché) and a member of the prerevolutionary nobility (Talleyrand), along with hundreds of men who were chosen for their merit, not for their coats of arms. The few exceptions to Napoleon's leniency were the royal family and their most intractable supporters. In areas of civil war, Napoleon took a different tack. It was not leniency but firmness that he projected. His proclamation of amnesty to rebels in western France allowed them ten days to lay down their weapons. If they rejected amnesty, they would be rounded up and executed. When he sent additional troops into the area, he instructed them: "it would serve as a salutary example to burn down two or three large communes chosen among those whose conduct is worst."[28] It took less than a month to restore general peace. By March 1800, Napoleon had made the first two pieces of his puzzle fit: émigrés were returning to France, bringing their wealth and talents with them, and the decade-long civil war was over.

Continuing his secret negotiations with the papacy, Napoleon moved forward with the third piece of his puzzle. Napoleon wanted an agreement with the pope to end the schism that the Civil Constitution of the Clergy had created. Napoleon was not a practicing Catholic, but he recognized that the majority of French men and women had remained Catholic throughout the revolutionary years. When it came to peasants, the figure was closer to 85 percent. What mattered to Napoleon was that the French government be based on moral order, and the restoration of religious practice seemed to have the most promise to insure that end. In order to preserve the principles of the Revolution while, at the same time, successfully negotiating with the Pope Pius VII, Napoleon refused to waiver on two principles: first, the irrevocability of the sale of church lands after 1789; and second, the required resignation of all French bishops, coinciding with Napoleon's right to appoint new bishops. In return, the pope retained the right to invest bishops with their spiritual power and the symbols of their office. When all of the negotiations were over, Napoleon had achieved his aims. The Catholic Church was restored to France as the church of the *majority* of the French, rather than as the church of France. Implicitly, the agreement also affirmed religious toleration and the French government's secular right to register all births, marriages and deaths. The pope was guaranteed his Papal States in Italy, and the French confirmed that they would pay clerical salaries because the landed wealth of the church would not be restored.

In the time between the conclusion of the Concordat in July 1801 and its publication on Easter Sunday in 1802, Napoleon also added a set of Organic Articles that spelled out the day-to-day practices of the Catholic Church in France. Included were provisions concerning the publication of papal letters (acts) in France, specifics on the content of seminary instruction, and requirements for a civil ceremony prior to performing the sacrament of marriage. Even the dates of religious holidays had to be state approved. What Napoleon had achieved was no less than a diplomatic miracle. He had preserved religious freedom in France while reconciling with the pope. While his detractors fumed about the restoration of the Catholic Church in France, he had repaired massive tears in the fabric of society. To Napoleon, that was the point of it all. "They will say that I am a papist; I am nothing at all; in Egypt I was a Mohammedan; here I will be a Catholic, for the good of the people."[29] Napoleon had shrewdly rendered to God what was God's, without giving more to the pope than he wished. Yet, in the end, Napoleon had created a rift with the pope that he could never mend. To some members of French society, the Concordat was instead a Discordat. To others, it was clear that Napoleon had rejected the formal separation of church and state that the Revolution had begun. Only time would tell what the settlement really meant.

"For me, religion isn't the mystery of incarnation; it is the mystery of the social order," Napoleon had also remarked.[30] In that spirit, Napoleon reconfirmed religious toleration for French Protestants. With Calvinists and Lutherans, he concluded agreements framed on the Catholic model, organizing each church at both the national and local levels and defining its relationship to the state. The French government paid the salaries of Protestant pastors just as it did for Catholic priests. To Napoleon, the treatment of French churches had to be parallel, and he took care not to give preference to any established church. Atheists alone were excluded from Napoleon's largesse.

By 1806, there was only one religious group of French men and women with whom Napoleon had not dealt. They were the Jews of France who had been emancipated by the revolutionaries in 1790–1791, but who had not experienced any of the benefits of religious toleration. "Dispersed and persecuted," wrote Napoleon, "the Jews have been subjected either to punitive taxation, or to enforced abjuration of their faith. . . ." Napoleon intended to end both of those practices, but he also expected the Jews to become French in the process. It was a reciprocal relationship that Napoleon had in mind, one that would lead to the assimilation of the Jewish population into the French state. Where the Jews had been forced into specific occupations, including usurious money lending, Napoleon expected them to "revive useful arts and professions."[31] Where they had been hounded into particular regions, he intended to erase those boundaries. Other changes would be made as well, and Napoleon instructed his Minister of the Interior to bring together the leaders of the Jewish community to begin that work. Later he convened the Great Sanhedrin to make final recommendations to the Jews and to the French state.

The instructions, not surprisingly, came directly from Napoleon. Among the types of questions that required answers were the following: "Is it lawful for Jews to marry more than one wife?"; "Is divorce permitted by the Jewish religion?"; "Can a Jewess marry a Christian, or a Christian woman a Jew?" He inquired whether or not Jews regarded Frenchmen as their brothers, and if French-born Jews saw France as their fatherland. Were any professions prohibited to Jews under Jewish law? The most pointed questions dealt with money lending and commercial activities: "Does the law forbid Jews to practice usury in dealing with their brethren?" and "Does it forbid or does it allow them to practice usury in dealing with strangers?"[32] Some of the questions and answers were humanitarian; others were purely political. On the political side of the ledger were those questions, for example, concerning marriage and commerce. Because polygamy was rumored still to take place within the Jewish community, as part of the settlement with the Jews, Napoleon intended for the Jews to abjure such a practice in writing and end the rumor once and for all. In the case of divorce, he wanted to discourage the dissolution of marriage within the Jewish community just as he had done with non-Jews. As far as intermarriage was concerned, Napoleon instructed the Great Sanhedrin to support marriages between Jews and non-Jews because he believed that tensions would be lessened as their communities became related. On the question of usury, Napoleon was insistent: only in places where Jews were still subject to "vexatious treatment" could their religious law tolerate "illicit gains." France had ceased its discrimination, so usury would not be allowed within its borders. On the humanitarian side of the ledger, Napoleon insisted that equal treatment be provided to all citizens of France. Citizens were citizens, according to Napoleon, regardless of their race or religion. With equal treatment, he believed that Jews also had an equal responsibility to pay their dues to the French government and to its armies.

To finalize relations between Jews and the French state, Napoleon issued an imperial decree in 1808. It confirmed his commitment to humane and equitable treatment so that the Jews of France would "find Jerusalem" within his empire.[33] Consistories were established as governing bodies for communities of Jews, usury was restricted, and Jews were encouraged to attach themselves firmly to France and French customs. In the end, through intermarriage, education, inducements, and incentives, Napoleon wanted to see an end to the separate and distinct Jewish community that existed in France. He believed that Jewish religious practice could and should continue, but he wanted intermarriage and co-mingling of Jews and non-Jews to complete the work of the Great Sanhedrin and the French decrees that followed it. Ultimately he prophesied that "Jewish blood will cease to have any distinctive characteristic," and France would become purely French.[34]

Although Jews in Alsace and in other areas of France did not intermarry in large numbers or merge quickly into mainstream French culture, their agreement with Napoleon provided equal opportunity and, as such, a wider scope of activity. For the most part, they considered him an enlightened administrator as they paid their taxes and sent their sons to serve in French armies. To later historians, however, Napoleon's relations with the Jews have undergone different interpretations. On the one hand, Napoleon has been held up as the emblem of toleration in an intolerant age. On the other hand, he has been viewed as a man of his times whose bias against the Jews led him to attempt to eliminate their identity as Jews through intermarriage. Napoleon would have found both interpretations troubling. To him, religious toleration was a revolutionary principle that he espoused, not for its solution to religious problems, but for its solution to social turmoil. He was committed to social order, and the edict of 1808 represented that commitment.

Like a Hawk to Food

Among the most lasting of Napoleon's accomplishments was the Civil Code (better known as the Napoleonic Code or *Code Napoléon*) that was promulgated on March 14, 1804 and reissued with minor changes under an imperial imprimatur on September 3, 1807. It was a meticulous compendium of law, based in principle on revolutionary precepts, but also borrowing from Roman law and French custom. The idea of a codification of French law, however, was not new. In fact, proposals for a uniform French code dated back centuries, and revolutionaries had already created five draft proposals. Napoleon's contribution was that the Code actually came into being. Although it was formulated by a hand-picked committee of legal experts, Napoleon actually presided at 55 of the 106 meetings where each of the principles was discussed, debated, and approved.[35] His imprint on the document is clear, both in the penciled, marginal notes that he left and in his ideas that are imbedded in the document, although much of the credit for the Code must also be given to Second Consul Cambacérès who supervised the work.

In its final form the Civil Code was composed of approximately 120,000 words, and pocket editions became widely available. The Code was divided into major headings called books and then subdivided into chapters, titles and paragraphs for easy reference. The three major books dealt with persons, types of goods and property, and the acquisition of property. Interestingly, neither case law nor precedent provided the primary foundation for the provisions. Roman law, instead, provided a partial model. Structure, uniformity, and order were what mattered. The Code also protected significant elements of the Revolution in its provisions: individual freedom, equality before the law, civil rights, the abolition of privileges based on bloodlines and social class, inheritance rights, contractual law, religious toleration, and the inviolability of property.

In its sections on property, the legacy of the Revolution is particularly evident. But, where revolutionary law was frequently cursory, the Code was explicit. An entire section, in fact, provided meticulous definitions of the types of goods and property (moveable goods and fixed goods) that were covered under civil law. Fixed goods, for example, included real estate, windmills, permanent buildings, animals, and equipment used in cultivating a farm (because the farm would be unworkable without them), planted but unharvested grain, perennial

flora, permanently affixed glass, and even statuary if placed in a permanent niche that had been designed for it. In the case of a furnished residence being sold, the list of goods that could not be removed was also
spelled out: rugs, beds, seating, clocks, tables, decorative items, porce-
lains, and paintings. Elsewhere, moveable goods were defined when an
unfurnished structure was being sold, and other kinds of wealth were
listed: currency, precious metals and stones, books, medals, scientific
instruments, horses and carriages, and wines, among others.[36] While the
lists and definitions were extensive, the point being made was simple.
The law should be explicit about property because "the right to hold
property is the right to enjoy and dispose of things in the most absolute
manner, so long as the use is not prohibited by laws or regulations."[37]
French citizens had the right to property, to its wealth, and to its protection; the Revolution had granted them that right, and Napoleon permanently protected it.

The most distinctive part of the Civil Code, however, was its devi-
ation from revolutionary principles where women and children were
concerned. Although women had been granted certain civil liberties
under French revolutionary law, Napoleon found the system personally
uncomfortable, disruptive, and in opposition to the social order that he
was trying to create. His own Corsican upbringing placed the father visibly in control, and the vision that he had for France was a strict, conservative family model. Just as he was head of state, the father would be
head of the family. The provisions of the Civil Code came as no surprise
to French men and women. Napoleon's comments had been widely circulated: "I don't like masculine women any more than effeminate men,"
he was reported as saying in 1803. He had also conveyed his feelings
about women engaging in public activities: "I don't like women to mix
in politics."[38] Much later echoing his earlier statements, he described his
problems with women: "Women receive too much consideration in
France. They should not be regarded as the equals of men; they are, in
fact, mere machines to make children."[39]

On issues of marriage, divorce, and children, Napoleon established
a simple pattern: women and children were subordinate to men under
the law. A woman could have no other residence than her husband's; his
authority was required in nearly all of her dealings including the control of her dowry; and divorce was made nearly impossible unless her
husband brought his mistress to live under their roof or he was insane

or a felon. In a marriage, a husband had an obligation to provide for his wife, but he also controlled her person, her goods and the children of their marriage. According to the Code, "the husband owes protection to his wife, the wife obedience to her husband."[40] Napoleon was adamant about women's roles in the French family and in the French state, and in one of the deliberations, he was reported to have said, "the husband must possess the absolute power and right to say to his wife: 'Madam, you shall not go out, you shall not go to the theatre, you shall not receive such and such a person; for the children you will bear shall be mine.' "[41] When it came to the control of children, age limits were explicitly set for marriage (exceptions could only be made by Napoleon), and parents could stop the marriage of a male under the age of 25 or a female under the age of 21. In the case of a dispute, the father's decisions were binding. When miscreant children were the problem, fathers could discipline them with one month's imprisonment if they were not yet 16 years of age and six months imprisonment for each misdeed until they reached the age of majority.

In all aspects of personal and family life, the Napoleonic Code was intrusive, as it attempted to sweep away what Napoleon believed was the laxity of the Revolution. Because one marriage in every five ended in divorce, he would make divorce much more difficult. Because children had been given too many freedoms, their families would rein them in and have the right to discipline them more strenuously. Because adoption had become too irregular and illegitimacy too prevalent, regulations would be put in place to protect families against immorality and licentiousness that led to abortion, infanticide, and abandoned children.

In the final analysis, the Civil Code represented both the revolutionary decade and the Napoleonic era. As one historian described it, "The Code was the Revolution made law, supported by the full authority of social conservatism."[42] Its provisions were carried across Europe as Napoleonic armies expanded the boundaries of France. Its guarantee of property rights remains a cornerstone of republican government, and its restrictions on women were so long lived that they were not repealed until the middle of the twentieth century. What Napoleon had accomplished in the Civil Code, however, was only part of the restructuring of France that he envisioned. In the end, his regime fathered six additional codes: the Code of Civil Procedure (1806), the Commercial Code (1807), the Criminal Code and Code of Criminal Procedure (1808), the

Penal Code (1810), and a Rural Code that was never promulgated.[43] He was obsessed with order, and he intended France to reflect his orderliness. There would be nothing obscure about that. As one historian concluded, "he picked up law, as the hawk food."[44] He probed, he questioned, and he consulted the depths of his own prejudices. The Old Regime was gone; and Napoleon's choice was to preserve the elements of the Revolution that he thought were appropriate and efficient for the new regime. At the same time, no one would forget that he was Napoleon I, Emperor of the French.

Notes

1. "The Brumaire Decree," November 10, 1799 (19 Brumaire, Year VIII) quoted in John Hall Stewart, *A Documentary Survey of the French Revolution* (New York: The Macmillan Company, 1951), 762.

2. The coup that brought Napoleon to power took place on November 9–10, 1799. The French, however, had already adopted a revolutionary calendar that gave the dates as 18–19 Brumaire, Year VIII, so contemporaries called the overthrow of the Directory "18 Brumaire," and historians have continued to do so.

3. "Decree Transferring the Legislative Body to Saint-Cloud," November 9, 1799 (18 Brumaire, Year VIII), quoted in Stewart, *Documentary Survey,* 760.

4. *Journal militaire,* as quoted in J. M. Thompson, *Napoleon Bonaparte* (Phoenix Mill, U.K.: Sutton, 2001), 141–42.

5. Ibid.

6. Owen Connelly, *The French Revolution and Napoleonic Era* (Chicago: Holt, Rinehart, and Winston, Inc., 1991), 200. See also J. Christopher Herold, *The Age of Napoleon* (Boston: Houghton Mifflin Company, 1987), 80, and Thompson, *Napoleon Bonaparte,* 142.

7. Connelly, French Revolution and Napoleonic Era, 2000.

8. "Bonaparte's Statement upon Becoming Consul," November 10, 1799 (19 Brumaire, Year VIII), quoted in Stewart, *Documentary Survey,* 764.

9. Ibid., 767–68.

10. "Proclamation of the Consuls to the French People," December 15, 1799 (24 Frimaire, Year VIII), quoted in ibid., 780.

11. Herold, *Age of Napoleon,* 126.

12. Lucian Regenbogen, *Napoléon a dit: aphorismes, citations et opinions* (Paris: Les Belles Lettres, 1996), 15.

13. Jacques Godechot, "Constitutions," in the *Historical Dictionary of Napoleonic France, 1799–1815,* ed. Owen Connelly (Westport, Conn.: Greenwood Press, 1985), 129.

14. "The Constitution of the Year VIII," December 13, 1799 (22 Frimaire, Year VIII), as quoted in Stewart, *Documentary Survey,* 773.

15. Ibid., 773.

16. "Constitutions," *Historical Dictionary of Napoleonic France,* 129.

17. The assassination attempt, called the Plot on the Rue Nicaise or the Infernal Machine, occurred on Christmas eve, December 24, 1800 as Napoleon, Joséphine and their entourages crossed Paris to attend a performance of Haydn's oratorio "The Creation" at the opera. Assassins, who had filled a water cart with explosives, pushed the disguised "bomb" into the procession of carriages. The Emperor's carriage took a slightly different route, their timing was off, and they missed Napoleon, but there were significant numbers of casualties nonetheless. The assassination attempt proved to be an excellent opportunity to rid France of Jacobin troublemakers who were immediately rounded up and deported to the colonies. When evidence revealed that royalists had actually engineered the plot, the Minister of Police purged them, sending some to firing squads and some to prison. Propaganda from the office of the First Consul reported that assassins would be less likely to make attempts on someone who was more visibly a head of state, like other monarchs in Europe. The life consulate would provide him that protection.

18. Thompson, *Napoleon Bonaparte,* 191.

19. Napoleon (1800) quoted in Regenbogen, *Napoléon a dit,* 16.

20. Napoleon (1802) quoted in ibid.

21. Germaine de Staël, quoted in Herold, *Age of Napoleon,* 159.

22. Thompson, *Napoleon Bonaparte,* 200.

23. Napoleon to Citizen Ripault, July 23, 1801, quoted in *Napoleon's Letters: Selected, Translated and Edited by J. M. Thompson* (London: Prion, 1998), 71.

24. What has been called the Cadoudal Plot had been monitored by Fouché for almost a year before the police swept down upon the conspirators. The plot was complex, international, and extremely dangerous. Allegedly royalists who had fled to London were to join with the republicans in France to overthrow Napoleon and to place Louis XVI's brother on the throne as Louis XVIII. Key players included Georges Cadoudal, who had been a commander in the French civil war, and General Pichegru, who was also in residence in England. Implicated in the plot were Moreau, a French general in good standing, who was perceived as the leader of the republican faction, and an unnamed relative of the former king. When the Minister of Police took action, the conspirators were arrested one by one. Pichegru was found strangled in his cell, Moreau was imprisoned and exiled, Cadoudal was tried and executed, and the unnamed Bourbon prince was identified as the Duc d'Enghien, a distant relation of Louis XVI who lived just across the French border in Baden. There was no evidence to support charges against the duke, but Napoleon pressed on with his court martial. Troops quickly crossed the border in violation of international law and took him prisoner by surprise. The court martial was brief, and the charges were never specified. He was executed within the same day. This attempt on Napoleon became a new propaganda ploy in 1804, but it did not pass public scrutiny. Napoleon had misjudged the French with his contrived execution of the Duc d'Enghien; but with war at hand, they bent to his will and

supported his designs on an imperial crown. The point he drove home, after refusing to admit the immorality of executing the duke, was that a hereditary empire would outlast even his death. The point was hard to refute.

25. Napoleon, quoted in Regenbogen, *Napoléon a dit,* 46.

26. Herold, *Age of Napoleon,* 165–66.

27. Thompson, *Napoleon Bonaparte,* 254. The full text of the catechism is included on 254–55 of Thompson's work.

28. Napoleon to General Hédouville (1800), quoted in *The Mind of Napoleon: A Selection from His Written and Spoken Words, Edited and Translated by J. Christopher Herold* (New York: Columbia University Press, 1955), 172.

29. Napoleon (June 1801), quoted in François Furet, *Revolutionary France, 1770–1880* (Oxford: Basil Blackwell, 1992), 226.

30. Napoleon, quoted in Regenbogen, *Napoléon a dit,* 68.

31. Napoleon to the Minister of the Interior (August 23, 1806), quoted in *Mind of Napoleon,* 112.

32. Napoleon to M. de Champagny, August 23, 1806, quoted in *Napoleon's Letters,* 135–37.

33. Ibid., 137.

34. Napoleon to the Minister of the Interior (November 29, 1806), quoted in, *Mind of Napoleon,* 115.

35. Thompson, *Napoleon Bonaparte,* 180. Connelly gives the figure as 57 of 102 meetings. See Connelly, *French Revolution and Napoleonic Era,* 202.

36. *Code Napoléon du 3 September 1807* (Leiden: B. Blankenberg, 1888), 95–101. A full text of the Code in English can be found at <www.napoleon series.org>.

37. Ibid., 100.

38. Herold, *Mind of Napoleon,* 14.

39. Ibid.

40. *Code Napoléon,* 213.

41. Napoleon, quoted in Herold, *Age of Napoleon,* 149.

42. Roger Dufraisse, *Napoleon* (New York: McGraw-Hill, Inc., 1992), 73.

43. "Constitutions," *Historical Dictionary of Napoleonic France,* 295–96.

44. H. A. L. Fisher, *Napoleon,* (Oxford, U.K.: Oxford University Press, 1967), 54.

CHAPTER 3

NAPOLEONIC SOCIETY: THE NEW REGIME

Impossible Is Not a French Word

Gentlemen tied their cravats more carefully, and women's necklines inched upwards. Members of French society stopped calling each other citizen and citizeness, replacing their revolutionary greetings with courtesies such as monsieur and madame. Scaffolding was raised in Paris to build commemorations of French accomplishments and victories, and museums were stocked with the treasures of Europe. Nothing was impossible as Napoleon fashioned a new, more orderly regime. To do so, not only did he need to be the political arbiter of Europe, he needed to be the arbiter of fashion, taste, ceremony, education, and literature. If he needed to create a new aristocracy, he would do so. If he needed to provide new rewards for the French, he would dazzle them. He could, with the stroke of his pen, safeguard and expand carriage service; construct canals to encourage trade and provide water for Paris; appoint a Latin professor for the Collège de France; list the 10 most talented painters, sculptors, composers, and architects in France; and oversee the festivals that glorified his authority.[1] "Impossible is not a French word," he said, and his efforts supported that assertion.[2]

Napoleon had dealt with the legal codes of France, ended turmoil in the Vendée, stabilized relations with the papacy, and reinforced religious toleration. In doing so, he had also founded his new regime on certain principles. There would be a new aristocracy based on talent and merit, a new educational system in support of public service, a restoration of Paris as the center of Europe, widespread public approval for his work, and a place for himself in the pantheon of the powerful.

By 1804, Napoleon had survived two serious plots, overseen three constitutions, and negotiated peace in Europe. He was not just a household name—he was Emperor of the French. On December 2, 1804, he stood in Nôtre Dame cathedral before French citizens, members of his family, guests from throughout Europe, and his ministers and government bureaucrats. In their presence, he lifted the crown of France to his head. He had found it "in the gutter," he once said.[3] He had picked it up—through his victories and accomplishments and through the prosperity that he had brought to France—and now it was his turn to place it on his head. The coronation was a "theatrical triumph," wrote one historian, as Napoleon blended Roman imperial pageantry with the purported memory of Charlemagne's power and splendor.[4] Charlemagne's sword had been retrieved from Aix-la-Chapelle, and the pope had traveled to Paris to bless the event and to show, by his presence, that he acknowledged the new French Empire. No expense had been spared. According to government tallies, the entire cost was over 8.5 million francs.[5]

Only a day before the imperial ceremony, Napoleon had spoken to the Senate: "I mount the throne to which I have been called by the *unanimous* voice of the Senate, people, and the army."[6] He exaggerated somewhat; but, in fact, the mandate that created the Empire was very impressive.

When the coronation ceremony began in the heart of Paris, Napoleon was dressed in a crimson velvet cape over a white embroidered satin tunic. His cape was adorned with white feathers and diamonds, and he wore white silk stockings and ceremonial slippers of white velvet and gold. His garments cost 99,000 francs, but Empress Joséphine's robes were even more expensive. Her train was a massive creation, and two of Napoleon's sisters were required to carry it as she moved toward the altar. She was draped in velvet, Russian ermine, taffeta, and satin. A choir of 400 voices sang Luigi Paisiello's *Mass* and *Te Deum*, and street corner peddlers, who had obtained advance permission, hawked drinks and hors d'oeuvres to the observers.[7] Fireworks dotted the Paris sky, a coronation balloon was sent across the Alps to Italy, and Napoleon commissioned his court painter Jacques-Louis David to create a massive canvas of the event.[8] What Napoleon had achieved was a coronation fit for any monarch in Europe. But he did not intend to be a monarch according to the model set by the Old Regime. "To be a king is to inherit old ideas and a genealogy," he remarked. "I don't want to descend from anyone or depend on anyone. The title of Emperor is greater; it is a bit inexplicable [for France], but it creates a wonderful illusion."[9] Along with his victories and his reorganization of France, the Corsican soldier had created a formidable presence both in France and in Europe. See Document 6 at the end of this book for a description of Napoleon by his private secretary (*Description of Napoleon by his Private Secretary Méneval*).

A Balloon No Longer Drifting in Air

The splendid coronation ceremony that Napoleon had choreographed was only one element of his new France. Even before the coronation, he had already begun to put other elements of his new regime into place. Initially he welcomed back the émigrés who had been proscribed and threatened by the Revolution. Then in 1802, he created a new recognition to reward those men whose abilities and accomplishments set them apart from the rest of French citizens. After the coronation, he continued his work by designing a new nobility to be based on merit *and* antiquity.

According to Napoleon, among the most significant of his civil and military acts was the creation of the Legion of Honor. The award, he stated, was to be conferred only on those men "who, by their knowledge, talents, and virtues, have contributed to establish and defend the principles of the Republic."[10] They would be his elite, bound together by honor and devotion to the fatherland. According to Napoleon, they were a true family of France. Whether in civilian or military employ, they would be an example of public service at its best.[11]

In spite of Napoleon's well-stated intentions, even his strongest supporters found the proposal somewhat difficult to accept. One of the hallmarks of the Revolution had been the principle of equality, and less than 13 years had passed since titles, awards, and sinecures associated with the absolutist monarchy had been swept aside. The memory of those ill-gotten privileges was still fresh in many minds, and no one knew yet what Napoleon was doing with his new system of privileges. So, when Napoleon took his proposal to the Council of State, outright hostility greeted him. After lengthy discussions, the proposal for the Legion of Honor passed by a slim margin of four votes in the Council of State (14–10). When the proposal passed the Tribunate, more than a third opposed the recognition (50–38), and in the Legislative Body, the vote was equally mixed: 166 to 110.[12] Furthermore, the law was twice as long as the Constitution of the Year VIII (1799). Napoleon had made it clear that he wanted all of the provisions setting up his hierarchy of military and civilian rewards to be indisputable. There was nothing short or obscure about the new recognition. Fifteen different levels of distinction were defined from the *grands dignités* of the Empire to the *grands officiers* and lesser dignitaries. Appointment to the Legion of Honor was for life and carried a stipend. In some cases, substantial estates were also granted to the recipients. The distinction, as Napoleon had designed it, clearly recognized ability, talent, and merit; in reality, it also conferred significant wealth.

Even after its promulgation by the government, the Legion of Honor was still regarded with some distaste and concern. The climate for the Legion of Honor, however, became more welcoming after Napoleon distributed the first medals; and later Frenchmen came to covet the ribbons and medals. In July of 1804, as Napoleon personally handed out the first decorations, André-François Miot (later the Count de Melito) was in attendance. "It was gratifying," he wrote, "to see services so diverse, merit and talent so different, rewarded with the same honors."[13] A common soldier could stand next to his general; a schoolteacher next to an internationally known savant. Napoleon, in fact, had been correct in his judgment about the men who surrounded him. Anyone of ability could be tapped for the recognition; the Legion of Honor represented equality of opportunity. During that first ceremony at Les Invalides in Paris, Napoleon led recipients in a spirited oath. "Honor! Fatherland! Napoleon!" shouted the Grand Chancellor, demanding their loyalty and their labors for the good of France. Then Napoleon questioned: "Do you pledge it?" According to reports, "an immense affirmative cry" swelled from the assembly. A few months later, Napoleon traveled to the military camp at Boulogne on the English Channel where he continued his distribution of the Legion of Honor to soldiers in the field. There, when the awards were granted, a hundred thousand voices pledged their loyalty.[14]

The medals that Napoleon passed out were white enameled stars hanging from a red ribbon. Later he incorporated a green laurel wreath and crown into the design. The design was new. In fact, there was nothing about the decoration that harkened back to prerevolutionary France. Furthermore, the men who received the distinction were very different from Old Regime notables. They included musician Etienne Méhul, engineer Gaspard Monge, artist Jacques-Louis David, astronomer Pierre-Simon Laplace, writer Jacques-Henri Bernardin de Saint-Pierre, alongside esteemed generals in the service of France. For the first time in French history, civilians were recognized in the same manner as military recipients. In total during the First Empire, 33,000 to 35,000 men wore the red ribbon and white cross of the Legion of Honor and experienced its benefits both for themselves and their families. The Legion of Honor, in fact, became a model recognition for later republican states.

The Legion of Honor was only the beginning of Napoleon's reorganization of French society. In May 1804, the Emperor established an imperial court, resplendent with titles, livery, and pomp. Later that year, he selected the symbols that would define his new regime. They included the eagle and the bee. The bee, for its industry, replaced the Bourbon *fleur de lys* on imperial tapestries and garments, and the eagle became the outward symbol of the power of the Empire. The rooster (*le coq*) that had been identified for centuries with France was swept aside. To Napoleon the choice was simple: "The rooster has no force; it cannot be the image of an empire such as France. One must choose among the eagle, the elephant and the lion." Then he chose the eagle: "the bird that carries a thunderbolt and never turns from the sun."[15]

After the empire was established, he increased the rewards of the Legion of Honor to include education for the daughters of France's most able citizens. Then in March of 1808, he completed the establishment of his new nobility with titles and additional rewards for Frenchmen of talent and merit. Members of the Legion of Honor were designated as *chevaliers*, or knights, and their ranks became hereditary. Napoleon further expanded his aristocracy with the appointments of princes and dukes, titles formerly reserved for imperial family members. Other dignitaries such as government officials, councilors of state, bishops, and mayors became senators, counts, and barons. The final tally came to 31 dukes, 451 counts, 1,500 barons, and 1,474 chevaliers.[16] Along with the additional estates, stipends, and pensions that were attached to noble ranks, Napoleon also liberally granted purely honorific peerage to his military commanders. Their titles became a virtual map of Europe. André Massena, for example, became the duc de Rivoli (Italy) and the prince d'Essling (Germany). Andoche Junot became the duc d'Abrantès (Portugal); Michel Ney became the prince de Muscovy (Russia).

Everything about the new aristocracy had been carefully planned, including who would be ennobled first. "It was not without design that I bestowed the first title I gave on Marshal Lefebvre," Napoleon explained later.[17] François-Joseph Lefebvre was an interesting choice. He was rough, earthy, and coarse, and he had joined the royal *Gardes françaises* as a private in 1773. Parisians remembered him best for his service as a sergeant of the Guard, long before he had fought in France's revolutionary wars and had been promoted through the ranks. Furthermore, his wife was outrageous. A washerwoman in the employ of the armies, she could offend almost anyone by her poor manners, and she was renowned for her drinking and swearing. Napoleon's chief point, however, was that Lefebvre was a fine soldier and commander. Good bloodlines, refined language, an elegant spouse, and old money did not matter in an appointment to Napoleonic nobility. Lefebvre, in spite of his dirty boots, lack of education, and colorful wife, was an asset to the French armies and to the fatherland. As such, he became the duc de Danzig.[18]

In the following years, Napoleon also took care not to overlook prerevolutionary nobles who had returned to France. They, too, could earn the praise of France for their contributions to the fatherland. As an observer of people, Napoleon had determined that men were best led by rewards, whether they were trinkets or baubles, as he sometimes called the medals that he distributed, or hundreds of thousands of francs in property and pensions.[19] So, he expanded the Legion of Honor and nobility; and, in the process, he worked toward merging his new Napoleonic nobility with old nobles so that further distinctions would cease. When he looked back on what he had done, he was pleased with his success. Yet, he had not had enough time to invest his nobility with antiquity so that their European counterparts would have held them in esteem. Historian Jean Tulard described the legacy in this manner: "[It was] an extraordinary mixture of refinement and bad taste—of old traditions and military manners."[20] Among his accomplishments, Napoleon's nobility carried a mixed message.

Regardless of what others thought, Napoleon's guiding principle was his firm and fervent belief that every state needed some form of nobility. An aristocracy brought stability to the state; it brought order and security. Citizens would know who their leaders were and respect them for their accomplishments. He had taken equality of opportunity to its logical conclusion. During his exile on St. Helena, Napoleon further explained what he had intended with the creation of his new nobility. "A state without an aristocracy," he said, "is like a balloon drifting in the air." Without an elite group of men on whom he could count, the balloon would neither land nor take off. Air currents, when least expected, would bounce it about, and it would never find a direction. Using a more common metaphor, he also said: "Without [an aristocracy], the State is a rudderless ship."[21] He had brought order out of chaos, and he intended to maintain a firm hand on the ship of state.

A Dynasty Is Born

Along with the direction that Napoleon's aristocracy provided to the government, Napoleon also intended for his new society to make Paris a showcase for France and particularly for Europe. Everything had to be designed toward that end. Regardless of the fact that his regime was new, there was no room for criticism. When critics scoffed at his court, he simply attacked them and banished them. When they cast aspersions on his aristocracy, he countered with equally scathing remarks. Then he worked harder to assure that appropriate notice was taken. From his efforts, *le style Empire* (the imperial style) was born in fashion, interior decoration, art, architecture, and even coinage.

In women's fashion, the Emperor championed styles reminiscent of antiquity—of empires of the past. He encouraged the use of decorative, heavier fabrics to replace the revealing garments that had formerly been fashionable. His taste included raised waistlines and higher necklines. Furthermore, in one of his widely quoted remarks, Napoleon made clear his position on the translucent décolletage that had been the rage of revolutionary and consular society. Surveying the partially exposed chest of one of his female guests, he paused, then looked her straight in the eye, and remarked, "I assume you are still breastfeeding your child." She was speechless, but the point had been made that low-cut, revealing garments were no longer appropriate. When he wanted others to recognize his authority and to wear longer sleeves, he commented to another guest: "my how red your elbows are."[22] He also demanded that his family purchase only those fabrics that were produced in France, and his government passed laws restricting the importation of foreign goods.[23] Military elements even found their way into women's attire. For the most part, however, Napoleon expected ornate formality in dress; and women of the bourgeoisie and new aristocracy conformed to his expectations. Everyone wanted to know where Empress Joséphine found her garments, where her hair was coiffed, and from where her jewels came. *Au Grand Turc* became the rage for silk scarves. Her perfumer was *A la Cloche d'Argent,* and only the best lace from Chantilly and Brussels would do.[24] For whatever reason, watches became a mania as well, whether they were worn around the neck on elaborate jeweled collars or as finger rings.[25]

Fashion and style, however, were not purely the domain of women during the Empire. Men also looked to the Emperor and his officials for guidance. The simple rule was that men's fashions should be complementary to women's attire. As women's garments became more decorative, men at the court found themselves in embroidered coats and colorful costumes more in keeping with the Old Regime than the Empire. But Napoleon had a second desire in supporting elegance: the French silk industry and embroidery needed support. Soon the ballrooms of fashionable society saw grisly grenadiers dressed in embroidered silk and a former regicide in a full suit of gold fabric.[26] Napoleon, on the other hand, chose to set himself apart as Emperor. Typically he wore an unornamented riding habit, along with his greatcoat if the temperature so required. It was not just frugality that governed his decisions; he preferred to be distinctive. Even his simple attire was carefully purchased. In one requisition, he demanded four military frock coats, two hunting coats, one civilian coat, dozens of undergarments, and four dozen shirts, breeches, waistcoats, and vests. Added to the order were hats, colognes, two dozen silk stockings, and twenty-four pairs of shoes that were to last in total two years. The cost was not extravagant, but it was 16,000 francs.[27]

Interior space also felt the influence of Napoleon. As early as the First Italian Campaign in 1796–1797, Napoleon began bringing the treasures of Europe back to France. The Government Commission for the Research of Artistic and Scientific Objects in Conquered Countries appropriated canvases, sculptures, and manuscripts to add to the collections of the new national museum housed in the former palace of the Louvre.[28] In Egypt, Napoleon commissioned Vivant Denon and scores of artists, engineers, cartographers, surveyors, and interpreters to catalog the treasures of the Nile. Frequently under a hail of bullets, they followed the armies and completed their work in Upper and Lower Egypt. One of Napoleon's engineers, in fact, discovered the Rosetta Stone that ultimately unlocked the mysteries of ancient Egypt. Napoleon was also a patron of the French arts, and he frequently bought or commissioned artwork that would either glorify the Empire or represent it. In 1805, for example, he purchased Antoine-Jean Gros's huge canvas titled *The Plague at Jaffa*, which was based on a controversial event in his Egyptian campaign. Smaller artistic purchases that were described in the same memorandum included landscapes, a scene at a village fair, and a sketch of the signing of the Concordat in 1801.[29]

Not surprisingly, decorative arts and architecture also took on the flavor of Napoleon. Artists and engineers were fascinated by Napoleon's exploits in Italy and Egypt, and neoclassicism quickly became the most desirable style. Popularized by Charles Percier and Pierre Fontaine, the imperial style was financed splendidly by Napoleon. Architecture was, in fact, a tool of politics; and among Napoleon's first imperial visions were four triumphal arches to represent the victories at Marengo and Austerlitz, his concordat with the pope, and peace. Only two of the triumphal arches were completed. There were also to be fountains erected at the Place de la Révolution, where the guillotine had once stood, and the Place de la Bastille, where a gigantic bronze elephant was to be situated.[30] Within a decade, the Arc du Carrousel, Arc de Triomphe, Vendôme column, Madeleine (Temple de la Gloire), and Palais des Archives had been commissioned. Public buildings like the university were under contract, and slaughterhouses and fountains were built and rebuilt. Four bridges were constructed across the Seine River, as well as the Odéon theatre, 12 marketplaces, and an expanded site for Père Lachaise cemetery.[31] The rue de Rivoli was completely redesigned with a classical arcade spanning blocks and blocks of identical façades.

Order, symmetry, and harmony were architectural mandates. But Napoleon's projects also had to have an air of grandeur and the monumental. Prior to his coronation, for example, he ordered the demolition of a topsy-turvy collection of houses and shops that faced and surrounded the cathedral of Nôtre Dame. His aim was to create a splendid, open space. Blocks of similar nondescript buildings were cleared from around the Louvre and Tuileries, and he planned to build a colossal palace as his royal residence after the birth of his son in 1811. The latter residence, to be called the Palais du Roi de Rome in honor of his own son, was planned for the western suburbs of Paris on the heights of Chaillot. Only the foundations of the palace were built because of the downturn in Napoleon's personal fortune and the fortunes of France, but he had planned for it to dwarf even Versailles.[32]

Even coinage, whether commemorative or official, came under Napoleon's personal oversight. In 1802, his bust was placed on metallic currency. His look was austere, stern, Roman, and republican. Although Napoleon had been heralded by cries of "Long Live the Emperor" when he assumed his position as Emperor of the French in 1804, he did not remove the words "République française" from French coinage until three years later. At that time his image took on a more imperial persona; the laurel wreath on his head was reminiscent of Caesar.[33] Beyond the official coinage of the Empire, Napoleon also inaugurated a set of historic medallions, designed competitively by members of the prestigious Institut de France, and called the *Histoire métallique de Napoléon le Grand* [*The Commemorative History of Napoleon the Great in Medallions*]. The first of the designs showed Napoleon on his return from Egypt. France, represented by an allegorical female figure, welcomed Napoleon back from his campaign. Later the national mint continued production of a significant number of commemorative coins.[34] The collection of medallions, so carefully overseen by the Emperor, represented yet another example of neoclassicism and Napoleon's interest in his living legend.

As Napoleon moved further into his creation of an Empire modeled on antiquity, he also saw himself as the creator of a dynasty. Although he had been granted the right to adopt an heir and his stepson Eugène de Beauharnais brought him a great deal of pride, he still wanted his own son to inherit the Empire. While the Empress Joséphine had announced several times that she was pregnant, as the Empire aged, so did the Empress with no results. When Napoleon fathered one child by a mistress of his and was expecting another, he determined that Joséphine was sterile, and he began negotiations for their divorce and his remarriage. The issue was politics, as everyone knew, not his affection for her. To spare her knowledge of the events as they unfolded, he kept his plans within his closest circle of associates. On October 20, Joséphine arrived at Fontainebleau to discover that the door connecting their chambers had been permanently sealed. A month later, Napoleon informed Joséphine that their Deed of Separation would be finalized by a *senatus consultum* no later than December 15, 1809, in order to proceed with his plans for remarriage.

Throughout the months of January and February 1810, Napoleon then negotiated for a new bride from either of the royal houses of Austria or Russia; and later that spring, Napoleon married Marie Louise von Hapsburg, archduchess of Austria. She was the daughter of Francis I of Austria, 20 years younger than the Emperor, and she had twice fled from the French armies as they laid assault to her homeland. In his marriage, Napoleon followed quintessential royal style. He had made an arranged political alliance, and he had sealed the arrangement with proxy nuptials before Marie Louise even set foot on French soil. He likened his marriage to Marie Louise to his victory at Austerlitz. Both, he said, had been superbly planned and executed. Twelve buffets were set up to feed the throngs who reveled in the new marriage. The menu included 4,800 pâtés; 1,200 tongues of beef; 1,040 legs of lamb (or horsemeat); 1,000 shoulder roasts; 240 turkeys; 360 capons; 360 chickens; 3,000 sausages; and "fountains of wine."[35] The stock market climbed, and police reports confirmed "the old dynasty and the new share pride . . . about the Emperor's marriage."[36] Even more importantly, within a year Napoleon had achieved what he wanted. His son, whom he called the King of Rome, was born. "He has my chest, my mouth, my eyes," Napoleon proudly reported to the former Empress Joséphine. Then he added, "I hope that he will fulfill his destiny."[37] A salute of 101 guns was fired for the heir to the throne (there would have been 21 guns for a daughter), and the newspapers reported that Marie Louise was in excellent health. Celebrations took place throughout the city, and Marie-Madeleine Blanchard, a noted aeronaut, lifted off from the Ecole Militaire in her hot air balloon to announce the child's birth to the environs of Paris and the surrounding countryside.[38] Order was assured; the dynasty was complete.

I Have Always Loved Analysis

Away from the celebrations, the new regime also set a very serious tone. In 1808, for example, Napoleon sent a memorandum to his personal librarian. He wanted a portable library of 1,000 volumes, printed in small type, with no margins "so as not to waste space," and loosely bound so that the books would lay flat while he read them on campaign. He estimated that the collection would include 40 volumes on religion,

40 epics, 60 volumes of poetry, 100 novels, and 60 volumes of history, with the remainder being historical memoirs. Education was personally important to Napoleon, and he specifically included in the collection works on nonwestern religions, the geography of the Middle East and Far East, and detailed histories of France. Having been strongly influenced by Rousseau as a young man, he included Rousseau's *Confessions* and *La Nouvelle Héloise,* but he specifically excluded other essays that he considered "useless treatises."[39] Education, he believed, should be useful to one's position. As Emperor of the French, he knew that he could not afford to lack the knowledge that he needed. When it came to women, he believed that religion suited them best. For men who would serve the fatherland as civilian and military leaders, an education based on the classics, histories, and practical training was particularly appropriate. He even felt that he must educate members of his own family. To his stepson Eugène, he sent a lengthy epistle on becoming Viceroy of Italy. Learn Italian, he counseled, and avoid talking too much. Learn one's limitations and use silence to unnerve opponents and to maintain control. To his younger brother Jérôme, who had joined the navy and whose skills he often found lacking, he wrote sanguinely telling him not to lose his watch and to keep his compass dry.[40] Furthermore, he never stopped educating himself. "I have always loved analysis," he said. "Why? and How? are useful questions one cannot too frequently ask oneself."[41] According to a contemporary, his mind was never at rest.[42]

From the time of Napoleon's coup in November 1799, he had been interested in reforming French education. His plans became clear by 1801 when he wrote to the Minister of the Interior with very specific advice for closing the *écoles centrales* (secondary schools) that had been created by the revolutionaries. In Napoleon's plan to replace them, boys younger than 12 years of age would take four courses of instruction. He wrote, "In the first class [course of instruction] they should learn reading, writing, arithmetic, and the elements of grammar; in the second, spelling and the principles of Latin." In the third class, they would concentrate on higher mathematics and "those parts of education which cannot be done in a year, drawing, dancing, and the use of arms." Finally, they needed training in memory skills, natural history, geography, ancient history, languages, and "patriotic and moral ideals."[43] After the age of 12, they would be divided into two groups: those who would go into the military and those who would pursue civilian careers. In each case, curricula were specified, uniforms were required, and drills and physical training were mandated. Napoleon further regulated the number of scholarships per school along with the size and contents of each library.[44]

State-supported boarding schools were soon complemented by *lycées* and *écoles secondaires* that expanded educational opportunities for worthy young men. By 1805, 39 *lycées* and 1,083 secondary schools existed in France, many providing free education for the sons of Napoleon's officers.[45] The expansion of educational opportunities, however, also meant that the quality of education had to improve, and Napoleon focused on the idea of a Teaching Order. Adapted from a Jesuit model, Napoleon envisaged a system where men would enter the teaching profession as bachelors and devote themselves to their careers and to their students until they were wealthy and well situated enough to marry. By then, they would have been promoted through the professorial ranks to receive the same esteem as public officials. Napoleon's teaching corps would not be so different from his Legion of Honor. These men would form a "body of teachers with fixed principles" that would serve as models for others.[46]

By 1806, Napoleon had finalized his plans for a comprehensive state system of instruction that included all educational institutions except local primary schools. In 1808 the plan was implemented, creating what was called the Imperial University, whose function was to oversee public education throughout the Empire. In spite of its name, it was, in practice, a nationwide board of education with extraordinary powers. There was something almost medieval about the regulations: teachers had to report where they were going on vacation; they could not visit Paris without permission; they had to take oaths of obedience to their administrators; the curriculum was prescribed by the central authority; and there was no tolerance for innovation. The aim was to produce good civil servants; and in the process, the state would know precisely what French students were learning. In 1809, to measure students' achievements, the baccalaureate examination was instituted as a nationwide graduation requirement. This nationally administered examination, which exists today, became an admissions requirement for all French institutions of higher education.

Just as revolutionaries had dismantled much of the primary and secondary school system in France, they had also demolished the pre-

revolutionary university system. In its place, they had created special-
ized schools, called *les grandes écoles,* in fields like law, medicine, phar-
macy, public works, and teacher education. Napoleon retained these
institutions and established the military academy of Saint-Cyr, based at
least partially on the model of the Ecole Militaire. Beyond these institutions, Napoleon saw little reason for expanding higher education further. He simply did not believe that it was necessary. "It follows," he said,
"that a school for advanced study is not an educational establishment,
in the ordinary sense, but an establishment devoted to the instruction
of men destined for some particular science or learned profession."[47]

To Napoleon, the *grandes écoles* were training schools or institutions of advanced professional education. When the Minister of the Interior, for example, asked Napoleon to consider establishing an institution
for advanced studies in literature, Napoleon found the request to be ill
founded. After all, Napoleon asserted, great writers were born with their
genius; they did not learn it. Therefore, advanced studies in literature,
composition, or grammar were irrelevant. On the other hand, history
and geography were sciences, suitable for advanced study in the
Napoleonic plan, so he recommended that the *Collège de France* be considered for such a role. "Something is surely lacking in a great state," he
concluded, "if a young student cannot get competent advice on the subject he wishes to study, and is obliged to grope his way, wasting months
or years in fruitless reading, whilst he searches for the information he
really needs."[48] The comment from Napoleon was, of course, autobio-
graphical. He had spent years teaching himself history and geography,
and he resented the fact that no one had helped him in his quest.

Women's education in the Napoleonic era was another issue
entirely. Since girls were not reared to become public servants, government officials, professors, doctors, lawyers, engineers, soldiers, or commanders, their education did not fall under the purview of the Imperial
University. Nonetheless, Napoleon's influence on women's education
was profound. First and foremost, he believed that the best education for
girls was not found in the schools; it was found in the training "a mother
gives her daughters."[49] Yet, Napoleon realized that not all girls and
young women could be guaranteed a mother's education. As a pragmatist, he laid plans for a girls' school at Ecouen where orphans and daughters of members of the Legion of Honor would receive training to
"become wives suitable for poor and humble homes." Unlike the secu-

lar general education that was a hallmark of Napoleon's plan for male instruction, the education of girls and women would be primarily religious and practical. Their days would be regimented around prayers, mass, and catechism. Their curriculum would then include writing, arithmetic and elementary French (spelling), a small amount of history and geography, and household economy. "Care must be taken not to let them see any Latin," since it was not suitable for their minds, and they should learn physics only to "prevent gross ignorance and silly superstition." They should not engage in exercises of the mind that might lead to reasoning, Napoleon continued, because their brains were weak and their ideas unstable. "What we ask of education," the Emperor noted, "is not that girls should think, but that they should believe."[50]

Much of the year, Napoleon insisted, should be devoted to manual labor. At Ecouen, girls and young women should know how to sew, embroider, and clean. They should be able to calculate prices, practice economy, and run the household, even if it included a small farm. Because students at Ecouen would be drawn from the poorer classes, Napoleon did not want them to experience luxury. They were required to wear long-sleeved uniforms "as health and modesty require," and their meals would be simple: soup, boiled beef, and a small entrée. While they would not be expected to cook, Napoleon expected them to learn the art of baking. He also allowed dancing, as "is necessary for the health of the pupils," and vocal music. For all intents and purposes, Ecouen was to be run like a convent.[51] To make the system work, Napoleon appointed Jeanne-Louise-Henriette Campan as the superintendent. She had served Marie Antoinette as a lady-in-waiting, but she had also a personal understanding of useful education for the less fortunate. As it turned out, the model at Ecouen was translated into other institutions of women's education throughout the nineteenth century.

Also important over time was Napoleon's interest in care for the ill. In the case of women, the Minister of the Interior drew up a national plan for midwifery education shortly after he received Napoleon's designs for a girls' school. In the memorandum on Ecouen, the Emperor had stressed that women ought to have "some idea of medicine and pharmacology," and in 1808 his recommendation was transformed into the national normal school of midwifery in Paris, called *La Maternité*, along with departmental institutions patterned after the Parisian model. Like other Napoleonic institutions, the curriculum was prescribed.

Future midwives should be fully competent in the practice of birthing babies, vaccinations, therapeutic bleeding, and the use of medicinal plants. Textbooks and instrument kits were standardized, and female mannequins were designed for instructional use. In all, some 1,500 graduates of these midwifery schools practiced in Napoleonic France.[52]

Other aspects of medicine were regulated as well. Building on the medical schools that had been created in 1794, Napoleon insisted that medicine be clinical and practical. While doctors of medicine and surgery were trained at the university level in one of the *grandes écoles,* Napoleon established a second tier of health professionals (*les officiers de santé*) who apprenticed under a physician or who were instructed in a shorter program of medical education. In this manner, he made a strong commitment to public health at the local level. With these efforts, medical care became much more available within the boundaries of France. On the battlefield and in army encampments, however, medical care was less available than it had been previously. Between 1800 and 1802, the number of military medical personnel dropped by two-thirds. Napoleon claimed that he was responding to the temporary nature of war as he centralized and economized the profession, but Napoleon was also caught in an interesting dilemma. As a military commander, he wanted injured soldiers back on duty as soon as possible; as a head of state, he was expected to value human life and to have a permanent commitment to the well-being of his citizens, including the long-term care of soldiers. When his soldiers were on campaign or on retreat, the wounded were always a burden; and rather than establishing military hospitals along the way, many soldiers were simply abandoned. As far as Napoleon was concerned, military medicine was not an imperial priority. Nonetheless, independent of support from the government, army surgeons developed the tourniquet and ligation of blood vessels to manage injury-induced bleeding and created better surgical and bandaging techniques.[53]

Even as Napoleon believed that education was the pursuit of ideas and the dissemination of knowledge, he also had strong beliefs about which ideas should be shared. The case of literature is perhaps the most notable example. Not only was Napoleon hostile to studies in literature, he was hostile to contemporary French writers. Compared to the authors of antiquity, he found them sorely lacking. French writers were, he said, for the most part "a load of metaphysical windbags" who produced very little literature of note.[54]

Fundamentally Napoleon's position on literature was that nothing in it should tarnish either his reputation or the reputation of France. He read nearly everything, and what he did not personally review passed under the scrutiny of government censors and the police. His insistence went so far as to restrict the use of allusions to historical events and allegorical references if he believed that they could be viewed in critical ways. In one notable case, Racine's *Athalie* was purged of the following line: "The blood of our kings cries out, but it is not heard." Allegedly, Napoleon argued, the public might be drawn to think unfavorably of the execution of the Duc d'Enghien. In another case, Napoleon asked François Rayouard, a playwright whose works he customarily admired, to reconsider the topic of his play. Napoleon wanted a tragedy in which "a savior of the nation" would mount to the throne.[55]

Meeting places and salons of some of the better-known French writers, philosophers, and scientists also came under scrutiny. The *idéologues*, as he named them, had taken republican principles and positivism too far. What was troubling to Napoleon was their materialism, their belief in human perfectibility, and their failure to include him in their debates. They "talk, talk, talk," Napoleon had ranted about them, as they continually tried to meddle in politics. In fact, even though he had initially enjoyed good debates with members of his Council of State, times had changed. He relegated men like the Abbé Sieyès, physician Pierre Cabanis, and others who had survived the Revolution to some distance from himself. They were never outward opponents, but Napoleon never felt that he could completely trust them. He could also never silence them because they did nothing worthy of full-scale censorship. When asked about his testy relationship with men who were recognized writers and critics—some of whom had been his earlier political colleagues—Napoleon brushed them off. "They have a craze for interfering with my policies," he said. "These poor scholars don't understand themselves."[56]

Another less defined group of writers included, among others, Germaine de Staël-Holstein and Benjamin Constant. While Napoleon allowed the *idéologues* their peccadilloes, he played no games with outright detractors and virulent critics, and Mme de Staël fit both categories.

Initially she had been enamored by Napoleon's organizational skills and his support of toleration and constitutionalism. Yet, she also believed in human perfectibility and was a constant critic of Napoleon's practices. By 1803, her circle of friends, acerbic tongue, feminist and anglophile writings (in the novel *Delphine*), and alleged ties to anti-Napoleon conspirators brought down his wrath. She was exiled from Paris and then escorted across the French frontier. While outside of France she continued to write, again facing Napoleon's anger when he read her manuscript on Germany. "Your latest work is not French," his minister of police wrote to her, and Napoleon confiscated the manuscript and had it destroyed.[57] Her colleague and lover Benjamin Constant had an equally stormy relationship with the governments of consular and imperial France. As a liberal, he could not countenance the Empire. Constant was forced to become a political exile by the man whom he called "Attila" and "Genghis Khan." Regardless of where he was, he continued to send his message forward: liberty had to be protected from despotism.[58] France, he argued, had to be protected from Napoleon. For further information on Mme de Staël, see the biographies at the end of this book.

Napoleon's response to his critics was consistent with his politics. He told them that he refused to govern by theories, platitudes, or speculation. Instead he would govern by "the experience of centuries." The history of France had shown him that Frenchmen would embrace monarchy and aristocracy again so long as the principles of the Revolution were not effaced. They would accept new structures and solutions so long as they could feel proud and prosperous again. Napoleon was, after all, a pragmatist. "Politics is only good sense," he remarked, "applied to great things."[59]

Notes

1. J. M. Thompson, *Napoleon Bonaparte* (Phoenix Mill, U.K.: Sutton, 2001), 195.

2. Alan Schom, *Napoleon Bonaparte* (New York: HarperCollins, 1997), 297.

3. "Why Did Napoleon Become Emperor?" *Napoleon: International Journal of the French Revolution and Age of Napoleon*, 17 (Fall 2000): 45.

4. J. Christopher Herold, *The Age of Napoleon* (Boston: Houghton Mifflin Company, 1987), 163.

5. Schom, *Napoleon Bonaparte,* 351. According to Schom, the cost was 8,527,973 francs in 1804. Using sources posted by the Economic History Series (http://eh.net) for conversion of the cost, the value would have been approximately $102 million in 2001 American dollars.

6. *Correspondance de Napoléon,* no. 7021, quoted in Schom, *Napoleon Bonaparte,* 345.

7. Ibid., 346ff.

8. The 19′ × 30′ painting that now hangs at Versailles was not completed until 1807, and Napoleon encouraged David to take liberties with the treatment of the events. Napoleon, who saw almost everything in terms of public relations, had his mother placed in the center of the painting, although she had not attended the ceremony. His sisters, who allegedly had been disruptive as they carried Joséphine's train, were portrayed as standing idly behind the empress in her moment of glory. The pope was given a particularly commanding presence just behind Napoleon. For further information on David's painting, consult David Lloyd Dowd, *Pageant-Master of the Republic: Jacques Louis David and the French Revolution* (Lincoln: University of Nebraska Press, 1948).

9. Lucian Regenbogen, *Napoléon a dit: aphorisms, citations et opinions* (Paris: Les Belles Lettres, 1996), 121

10. Title II of the Law of 29 Floréal, year X, quoted in "La Légion d'Honneur," in *Dictionnaire Napoléon,* ed. Jean Tulard (Paris: Librairie Arthème Fayard, 1987), 1055.

11. Ibid.

12. Robert B. Holtman, *The Napoleonic Revolution* (Baton Rouge: Louisiana State University Press, 1967), 197.

13. *Memoirs of Count Miot de Melito,* 353, quoted in George Gordon Andrews, *Napoleon in Review* (New York: Alfred A. Knopf, 1939), 216.

14. "La Légion d'Honneur," in *Dictionnaire Napoléon,* 1058.

15. Regenbogen, *Napoléon a dit,* 123.

16. "La Légion d'Honneur," in *Dictionnaire Napoléon,* 1059. See also "La Cour Impériale," in *Dictionnaire Napoléon,* 544–45.

17. *Napoleon on Napoleon: an Autobiography of the Emperor,* ed. Somerset de Chair (London: Cassell, 1992), 197.

18. "Lefebvre," in *Dictionnaire Napoléon,*1051.

19. Jean Robiquet, *La vie quotidienne au temps de Napoléon* (Paris: Librairie Hachette, 1942), 66.

20. Jean Tulard, *La vie quotidienne des Français sous Napoléon* (Paris: Hachette, 1978), 272.

21. *The Mind of Napoleon: A Selection from His Written and Spoken Words, Edited and Translated by J. Christopher Herold* (New York: Columbia University Press, 1955), 97

22. Louis Antoine Fauvelet de Bourienne, *Memoirs of Napoleon Bonaparte* (New York: Charles Scribner's Sons, 1891), 324.

23. Napoleon to Princess Elisa, February 22, 1806, in *Napoleon's Letters: Selected, Translated and Edited by J. M. Thompson* (London: Prion, 1998), 121.

24. Melanie Byrd, "Women's Fashion during the Empire," in *Napoleon: International Journal of the French Revolution and Age of Napoleon* 17 (Fall 2000): 52; Melanie Byrd, "Clothing Fashion, Women's" in *Historical Dictionary of Napoleonic France, 1799–1815*, ed. Owen Connelly (Westport, Conn.: Greenwood Press, 1985) 117–19; and "Costume" in *Dictionnaire Napoléon*, 536.

25. Walter Markov, *Grand Empire: Virtue and Vice in the Napoleonic Era* (New York: Hippocrene Books, 1990), 205.

26. Robiquet, *Vie quotidienne*, 161.

27. Napoleon to General Duroc, Grand Marshal of the Palace, August 19, 1811, quoted in *Napoleon's Letters*, 255–57.

28. "Louvre," in *Historical Dictionary of Napoleonic France*, 310–13. In 1803, Napoleon renamed the national museum the Musée Napoléon and appointed Vivant Denon as his director-general of museums.

29. Napoleon to M. Estève, Keeper of the Privy Purse, January 9, 1805, quoted in *Napoleon's Letters*, 92.

30. Guerrini, Maurice, *Napoleon and Paris: Thirty Years of History* (London: Cassell, 1970), Appendix II: "Buildings undertaken in Paris during the Consulate and Empire. Principal Buildings begun, restored or completed."

31. Markov, *Grand Empire*, 197. See also "Architecture" in *Historical Dictionary of Napoleonic France*, 18–20.

32. Guerrini, *Napoleon and Paris*, 225.

33. "Symbolism and Style," *Historical Dictionary of Napoleonic France*, 461.

34. "Médailles historiques," *Dictionnaire Napoléon*, 1154–55.

35. Robiquet, *Vie quotidienne*, 241.

36. Guerrini, *Napoleon and Paris*, 225.

37. Napoleon to Joséphine, March 22, 1811, quoted in *Napoleon's Letters*, 249.

38. Guerrini, *Napoleon and Paris*, 239.

39. Napoleon to Barbier, July 17, 1808, quoted in *Napoleon's Letters*, 193–94.

40. Napoleon to Eugène, June 5, 1805, and Napoleon to Jérôme, August 16, 1801, quoted in ibid., 104 and 71.

41. "Some Maxims of Napoleon," in H. A. L. Fisher, *Napoleon* (Oxford, U.K.: Oxford University Press, 1967), 147.

42. François Furet, *Revolutionary France, 1770–1880* (Oxford: Basil Blackwell, 1992), 222.

43. Napoleon to Chaptal, Minister for Home Affairs, June 11, 1801, quoted in *Napoleon's Letters*, 68–70. See also Godechot, "Institutions," in Frank A. Kafker and James M. Laux, *Napoleon and His Times: Selected Interpretations* (Malabar, Fla.: Krieger Publishing Company, 1989), 293.

44. Ibid.

45. Thompson, *Napoleon Bonaparte*, 205.

46. Note on a Teaching Order, February 16, 1805, quoted in *Napoleon's Letters*, 95.

47. "Remarks on a Scheme for Establishing a Faculty of Literature and History at the Collège de France," April 19, 1807, quoted in *Napoleon's Letters*, 156.

48. Ibid., 160.

49. "Note," May 15, 1807, quoted in Thompson, *Napoleon's Letters*, 170.

50. Ibid., 168.

51. Ibid., 169–71.

52. "Women, Education of," *Historical Dictionary of Napoleonic France*, 511.

53. Dora B. Weiner, "Medicine," *Napoleon and His Times*, 258–64.

54. Markov, *Grand Empire*, 119.

55. Thompson, *Napoleon Bonaparte*, 202.

56. "Conversation, 1803," quoted in *Mind of Napoleon*, 69.

57. Savary to Mme de Staël (October 5, 1810) quoted in Markov, *Grand Empire*, 118.

58. "Constant, Benjamin," *Historical Dictionary of Napoleonic France*, 128.

59. Regenbogen, *Napoléon a dit*, 17.

CHAPTER 4

DAILY LIFE IN NAPOLEONIC FRANCE

Under Red Umbrellas and Along the Footpaths of France

Although the Napoleonic era is most often equated with military campaigns and the re-creation of Europe as the Emperor envisioned it, Napoleonic France was also found in villages, behind stone walls and hedgerows, in marketplaces, in the festivals of the new order, and among the citizens whom the Revolution had created. As historian Jean Robiquet notes, sometimes larger and better-known events hide smaller ones from us. It is easy to "neglect what took place in the houses along the rue Saint-Denis, under the red umbrellas of the Parisian markets, or beneath elm trees in the provinces." There were, after all, 30,000,000 French men and women who were part of Napoleonic France—from peasants to tenant farmers, from the urban working classes to shop keepers and craftsmen, from the emerging bourgeoisie to new nobles. Their stories provide an additional image of Napoleonic France away from the battlefields and corridors of power. Historian Robiquet further suggests, these are the "details that merit our attention because collectively they make up history." In fact, they make "history more human."[1]

When Napoleon became First Consul in 1799, France was still fundamentally a peasant state. Eighty-five percent of its inhabitants lived in the countryside, and agriculture was at the base of the French economy. Most people traveled little, unless they happened to be drafted into the Napoleonic armies. Their lives followed the rhythm of the seasons and the clock tower that intoned the beginning and the waning of each day.[2] While it appeared that little change had occurred in the country-

side, in fact, feudalism had been thoroughly eradicated and more property was available for purchase. As part of the revolutionary restructuring of the French state, municipal and departmental governments were
created, and the sale of offices (*venality*) was ended. Privileges based on
bloodlines and titles were also struck from French law. Yet, it was widely
known that the newly elected officials easily and quickly fell to
favoritism, bribery, and corruption. Under the new order it appeared that
revolutionary functionaries had simply replaced royal officials as the
new thieves and brigands of France.

As Napoleon moved to his seat of power in the Consulate, he was
painfully aware of the quagmire in which he found municipal affairs. In
1799, he wrote to his brother Lucien: "Mayors, assessors or municipal
councilors have stolen the by-road, stolen the foot-path, stolen the tim-
ber, robbed the church, and filched the property of the commune."[3]
There was, in his opinion, little that they had not stolen in their positions of authority. Napoleon was no doubt exaggerating the extent of the
corruption that he saw, but the problem was real. It was a new kind of
brigandage, according to the First Consul, and it had to be stopped.

As rural France struggled with its problems, urban areas were also
not exempt from revolutionary changes. In fact, the dislocation of the
Revolution and the international wars that accompanied it had affected
cities even more fiercely. While towns of 5,000 inhabitants were the
norm for France, significant population centers existed at the time of the
Revolution and Napoleonic era: Paris housed over a half million in population; Lyons over 100,000; Marseilles, Bordeaux, and Rouen between
85,000 and 100,000; Lille and Strasbourg over 50,000; and Amiens and
Caen over 30,000.[4] Unemployment was rampant, and in places where
the French economy was based on exported luxury goods like lace, fabrics, and cutlery, warehouses stood empty and the vast majority of man-
ufacturing workshops had been closed. According to one source, the
port city of Bordeaux on the Atlantic was so economically devastated
that the city treasurer could not even pay to fill city street lamps with oil.
The Napoleonic period was long before electricity, and the only means
of street lighting was oil. Without oil, cities were dangerous wastelands
after dark. In the case of Bordeaux, which was darkened by both lack of
use and nightfall, it had become no more than a "ship cemetery."[5]

Paris had its own problems. Fast money was made—and lost as
quickly—in gambling; loose women were everywhere; and walls,

houses, bridges, and streets were in disrepair. Bullet holes could still be seen in the façade of the Tuileries palace, and the effects of vandalism were evident throughout the city. There were no sidewalks, shallow ditches ran through the center of the streets in the absence of a sewer system, and garbage collected everywhere. Charnel houses, where the bodies of the dead were stacked in lieu of burial, were located in the center of the city near slaughterhouses and tanneries where the gutters ran red with blood and foamed with chemicals. From the outskirts of Paris, cows were periodically herded through the narrow streets to commercial butcheries. As small herds navigated the streets and lanes, they endangered pedestrians and carriage traffic. If those problems were not enough, the stench was horrific. And, it was also commonplace. Only a good rainstorm could provide some amount of sanitation and relief from the noxious odors, since municipal ordinances were, for the most part, ineffective.[6] House numbering looked more random than planned; and, according to one visitor to Paris, mail service was almost totally lacking. "I could with a good wind," Redhead Yorke reported, "send a letter to Jamaica faster than a letter would arrive from the provinces."[7]

Napoleon's work awaited him. As he framed the Constitution of the Year VIII (1799), he also understood that he could not push too quickly to change the language, the institutions, or the meaning of the Revolution. It had been only a decade since the French experiment with constitutionalism had begun and only seven years since the French had adopted republicanism. What Napoleon seemed to know intuitively was that his authority came from his military victories. His long-term popularity, however, could be assured only by his strength as an organizer, administrator, and manager of the French state. In such a capacity, he has been pictured both as a drill sergeant and a schoolmaster, the latter probably with a piece of cane in his hand to rap the knuckles of his less willing students. It is unlikely that he would have challenged either image.[8] What he intended to do was to bring order out of chaos, and immediately he set to work to do so.

As he stood at center stage in France in the fall and winter of 1799–1800, Napoleon Bonaparte looked unassuming. He was, after all, a republican general who had taken on a new role to stabilize a fragile government (the Directory) and an equally fragile economy that he found upon his return from the Egyptian campaign. Physically he was in his prime, rising early each morning to work without distractions or to meet with his councils or diplomatic corps. It was rumored that he dictated from 50 to 100 letters and proclamations a day when he was fully engaged in civilian and military endeavors. On those days, "he would wear out several secretaries trying to keep up with him."[9] He frequently ate only two meals a day, avoided etiquette and ceremony unless a state occasion was scheduled, and looked really quite ordinary. He liked old hats, according to one writer, and rarely changed the style of his clothing regardless of fashion. Although he bore a title comparable to *princeps* (given by the Roman Senate to Augustus) and was, for all intents and purposes, head of state, Napoleon limited his quarters in the Tuileries to a bedroom, bathroom, study, dining room, conference room (audience chamber), and a large antechamber. Only later did he renovate a state residence at Saint-Cloud and establish his court at the former royal palace at Fontainebleau. Initially, there was little pretension on his part. His staff remained small: 10 senior attendants (including a librarian and chef) and 15 subordinates. What Napoleon did was work tirelessly and make decisions.[10] "Strong coffee, and plenty, awakens me," he noted about his work habits. "It gives me unusual force, a pain that is not without pleasure."[11]

As an administrator, Napoleon first sought to avoid unnecessary antagonisms and to seek out those who could assist him. Although the coup that had brought him to power had not gone precisely as planned, the majority of the French had welcomed him as a peacemaker, both domestically and internationally. In his proclamation to the French people, he had furthered that image: "To make the Republic loved by its own citizens, respected abroad, and feared by its enemies—such are the duties we have assumed in accepting the First Consulship. Its citizens will love it if the laws and the authoritative acts of Government are always marked by the spirit of order, justice and moderation."[12] People flocked to serve Napoleon. Whether it was because they believed in the program that he was fashioning or because the lure of his power attracted them, Napoleon quickly had a willing and growing staff to support him.

In his first six months as First Consul, the pace Napoleon set for domestic affairs was prodigious, but his decisions always reflected the Revolution from which he had come. The words *République française* (French republic), for example, remained on the coinage, even though a much less republican Consulate had replaced the government of the

Directory. Other revolutionary iconography remained as well. At the same time Napoleon set himself to conducting substantive change: completely restructuring both the national and local governments and adapting electoral policies, framing public opinion, establishing order through a new bureaucracy and system of policing, creating a peasant policy, restoring and centralizing banking, encouraging industry and agricultural innovation, and raising the lifestyle and material well-being of most French citizens. His successes were legion. "Everywhere in Europe," he remarked in 1800, "some chord is for me. There are people who respond to my laws, others to my victories—everywhere there is at least one chord. All that needs be done is touch it."[13]

New Names, New Times, and a New Administration

After 10 years of massive revolution from 1789 to 1799, new place names, new children's names, and even new holidays had been created. They were all unfamiliar under the prerevolutionary Old Regime. And then, Napoleon celebrated New Year's Day. Such an event was extraordinary and particularly meaningful to the French people.

New Year's Day had been abandoned since 1793 when a new calendar replaced the old. The new calendar had changed everything, including the length of the week (10 days) and even when the year began. De-Christianization purged France of saint's days, and the revolutionary republicans had eliminated the old names of months and weekdays that had previously lent order to French citizens' lives. But by 1800, it was widely known that workers and peasants had abandoned as much of the new calendar as they could, shunning the *decadi* (the 10th day of the 10-day week) as their day of rest, in spite of earlier government mandates, and reverting to Sundays. Along with other early Consular acts, Napoleon's official celebration of New Year's Day in 1800 served as an assurance that the Revolution was over. As quickly as the announcement was made, bakers and confectioners filled their windows with hastily created delicacies including, not surprisingly, "bonbons à la Bonaparte." Carriages lined the streets, and one visitor to Paris wrote that he had not seen anything in a long time quite as humorous as eight young gentlemen crammed into a carriage and then piling out along with their celebratory food and drink. Carnivals reopened, masked dances were scheduled again, and the streets were filled with activity.[14]

The pattern was set quickly; Paris became known for its pleasures. "The bonbons and the sweetmeats of the finest sort . . . were much better than those in Berlin," wrote a Prussian visitor in 1802. "The fact that Bonaparte's portrait was produced on everything goes without saying. . . ."[15]

Celebrations spread to the provinces as well, where peasants and agricultural workers equally awaited an end to revolution. Certainly there had been benefits brought by the Revolution, but many of the changes remained tenuous or incomplete. While the Revolution had provided religious toleration, it had also spawned a bloody and protracted civil war. Outside the boundaries of France, the international war that the king and Legislative Assembly had begun in 1791 still consumed young conscripts. The Revolution had provided lands for purchase, but guarantees that those lands would always be available seemed lacking. A perennial question was whether or not aristocrats would return to reclaim them, with or without the sanction of the government. Furthermore, the Revolution had reduced and reallocated taxes, yet no one knew how long the new system would be in place. Commerce and travel had opened up when Old Regime tolls were eliminated and standard weights, measures, and currency were put in place; but the transition had been fraught with problems: hoarding, inflation, and lack of confidence. Frankly, over four-fifths of the French population had yet to experience the long-term, positive results of a decade of revolution. Always a pragmatist, Napoleon slowly but surely began to transform their world.

Who were these people? According to Jean Tulard, who has written extensively on everyday life in France, the peasants were a diverse group, in many ways incapable of generalization. They were manual laborers, seasonal workers, cultivators and planters, domestics, servants, tenant farmers, owners of small plots of land, agrarian landlords, and absentee farm owners.[16] In spite of their differences and their different needs, Napoleon seemed to know how to reach them. First, he proposed to his brother Lucien, who also served as Minister for Home Affairs (also called Minister of the Interior), a complete restructuring of local government. While the Revolution had promoted the idea of individual liberty, Napoleon saw collective change as the way to prosperity. "If one is to regenerate a nation," he wrote, "it is much simpler to deal with its inhabitants a thousand at a time than to pursue the romantic ideal of individual welfare. Each local body in France represents 1,000 inhabitants. If you work for the prosperity of 36 thousand communities you

will be working for that of 36 million inhabitants."[17] Napoleon acknowledged in his memorandum that his proposal was similar in intent to
what France's well-loved King Henry IV (1589–1610) had put forward
two centuries earlier. King Henry IV was known to every school-aged
child in France for his pledge to put a chicken in every pot by rebuild-
ing France's economy after two decades of religious and political conflict. Napoleon saw Henry IV as an excellent model.

To put his plan into action, Napoleon demanded a survey of all of
the municipalities of France to determine which were solvent or nearly
so, which were profitable, and which were hopelessly in debt. The communes that were massively debt ridden would be stripped of their mayors, assessors, and councilors. Replacements would be sought, and
France's officials of the state—prefects and subprefects—would practice
strict oversight including frequent and meticulous audits. Within two
years, those mayors who had achieved profitability would be rewarded;
if communes had not achieved solvency within five years, they would be
put into receivership. By the Law of February 17, 1800, the new system
was in place.

Within the new system, Napoleon did not dramatically change the
French administrative order that had been set by the revolutionaries. As
established, departments were administrative units directly under the
national government. Departments were then subdivided into districts,
and districts into cantons and communes (municipalities). What
changed, however, was that formerly *elected* officials were replaced by
appointed prefects (departments), subprefects (districts) and mayors (for
cities over 5,000 in population). These appointments were, in fact, made
in Paris. In the case of smaller towns and communities, prefects at the
department level made the appointments. Napoleon was aware that
these changes in the method of staffing administrative posts might pro-
voke controversy; so, in order to avoid criticisms that he had abrogated
the principles of the Revolution, he reaffirmed its electoral policies. Voting privileges remained the right of all male citizens who met certain age
and residency requirements, but elections were no longer direct. At the
local level, voters established electoral lists from which appointments to
governmental posts would be made or from which other lists of eligible
officeholders would be drawn. Eligibility for one or more of the electoral
lists was based on property holding. For whatever reason, the change
from elected officials to electoral lists and appointed functionaries went

into effect almost without notice. Although the change could have appeared draconian or heavy-handed to French citizens, it began to restore order and with it, prosperity.

Among the primary concerns of Napoleon was order, and the prefects whom he appointed as his chief administrative officers were responsible for overseeing a well-managed state. As such, Napoleon judged his prefects on the comprehensiveness and promptness of their reports, the efficiency with which they handled conscription, and the state of public works, including roads, in their departments. They were expected to work with the subprefects, police, forestry agents, and justices of the peace systematically to stamp out crime, highway robbery, and brigandage and to show no leniency toward draft dodgers. His order was comprehensive, and his intent was to bring an end to the anarchy that he saw at the local level.

Even senators at the national level were enlisted in centralizing France and restoring order. In a note for the Secretary of State in 1805, Napoleon made no pretense about the importance of information to govern France. Senators were ordered to reside in their jurisdictions no less than three continuous months per year; "the ostensible object . . . will be to get to know the situation, character, condition and value of the property from which the income of your *senatorerie* is derived." The real object was "to supply [Napoleon] with trustworthy and positive information on any point which [might] interest the government." Reports were required once a week, without fail.[18] The contents of the reports were also specified: information about the behavior of public officials, comments about the clergy and their influence, estimates of the numbers of draft-dodgers, surveys of public education including specifics about "teachers of marked ability and . . . those who have done nothing to deserve public confidence," notes on agriculture including information on the rearing of horses, wool bearing animals and livestock, estimates of food supply and future harvests, evaluations of the condition of roads and other public works, and, most important, analyses of the state of public opinion.[19] In Paris, Napoleon employed even more stringent surveillance. There Joseph Fouché, as the French Minister of Police, oversaw a coterie of spies within the state and throughout Europe, ceaselessly perused reports from his police informants, began a massive crackdown on crime, and made sure that the press reflected Napoleon's positions correctly. To do so, in the first few months of the Consulate,

Fouché was entrusted with closing down 47 of France's newspapers and ferreting out conspirators against the new regime. His contemporaries described him as a quintessential policeman, devoid of feeling and obsessed with order. According to historian Alan Schom, "he rarely moved, apart from his long, bony hands, only his weasel eyes and alert ears following everyone and every conversation, noting everything, missing nothing."[20] He was a man to be feared, and everyone knew it.

Napoleon's administrative plan was also based on another of his principles—to reward talent and merit in visible ways. Although one of the chief revolutionary principles was equality, Napoleon made no apologies for creating a social order that contained distinctions. Those distinctions were based on something tangible—talent and merit—and the privileges that accompanied them were earned. Later, when Napoleon felt comfortable, he created new military and civilian awards and an aristocracy replete with coats of arms and titles. In 1800, however, the time was not yet ripe for a new aristocracy, but the trinkets that he distributed carried sufficient weight to do what he intended, whether he scheduled a medal ceremony, invited a mayor to Paris for an audience with the First Consul, or rewarded an inventor for his new patent. According to one story, the recipient of an early Napoleonic award was so awed by the presence of the First Consul as he received his recognition that he remarked, "Instead of giving me a medal, if he had asked to sleep with my wife, I would have been just fine with it."[21]

For peasants and agricultural workers, the greatest reward was the expansion of property holding. According to one historian, "The revolution turned the French peasants into free men on free land. However, this freedom did not simply drop into their laps."[22] In fact, the right to acquire land did not always translate into the ability to buy it until the Napoleonic period when banking and currency were stabilized and peasants had more resources. By the time Napoleon had completed two years as First Consul, one third of the auctioned, available lands was in the hands of peasants. By the end of his reign as Emperor, the tally was 60 percent, although most of the plots were of modest size or small. At the same time, a rural middle class, holding larger parcels of land, came into existence.[23]

Napoleon was fully aware that peasants were still the backbone of the economy as France entered the nineteenth century. In order to increase the prosperity of France and French citizens, agricultural productivity had to increase—not just in output but in quality as well. What mattered was the willingness and capacity of French farmers to innovate. Yet, even with the expansion of property holding, Napoleon did not witness the amount of agricultural innovation that he desired. While farmers were not bound to the medieval two-field system, leaving a field fallow each year, or the three-field system with crop rotation, nevertheless, such agricultural practices remained the norm. Sheep raising, wheat, and potatoes continued as common agricultural commodities.

By 1805, however, Napoleon was fed up with agricultural stagnation. Instead of working with the Imperial School of Agriculture to make change, he simply abolished it and designed his own plan for modernizing French agrarian practices. Just as he had done when he restructured the local administrative governments of France, he commissioned a survey. This time he surveyed agricultural production in the various departments of France. The results were encouraging in the northern departments of France, along the Channel, and in the Rhineland, but elsewhere there was substantial room for improvement. What Napoleon quickly recognized was that common manual laborers and owners of the smallest of parcels were too busy simply making a living to be concerned about improving their holdings and increasing their ability to produce more. He realized that he could not expect them to buy into his plan until they were more able to do so. Rather, the wealthier peasants and landowners were more likely to respond to governmental favor. In studying wealthier peasant landowners, Napoleon determined that financial incentives were not sufficient or plentiful enough to bring about the desired results. He noted: "People of this kind are not encouraged by grants or money, but by medals, and decorations, and eulogies addressed to them by or on behalf of the sovereign."[24] He then entrusted prefects and subprefects with the task of identifying prime candidates for medals and recognitions. Although Napoleon's decision seemed counterintuitive, time proved him correct.

In the same "Note on Agriculture," Napoleon also expanded the distribution of Merino sheep from Spain (especially rams), stallions, and foreign bulls. Furthermore, he counseled, "Good landlords should be encouraged to send their sons to study the methods in use in Departments where agriculture is flourishing."[25] To Napoleon, good models almost always served as the best teachers.

When by 1810–1811 French agriculture still did not fully supply national needs and France's embargo (under the Continental System) made supply of even the basic commodities a problem, Napoleon again interceded in agriculture. In this case, by Imperial Decree, he set aside 80,000 acres for sugar beet production and established six schools to teach the principles of cultivation. Tobacco farmers were instructed to abandon tobacco in favor of sugar beets; cattle farmers were counseled to use the waste products of sugar beets for cattle feed.[26] Beginning in 1813, the importation of English cane sugar was prohibited, but the production of sugar from beets and its profitability remained marginal. Peasant farmers refused to participate in the program and returned to wheat, if they had changed to beet production at all. Other projects that Napoleon endorsed included the production of pastel (blue dyes) and chicory. In the case of dye, Napoleon's prize had been 100,000 francs for its successful production. But profitability in the short term was again the downfall of this experiment. Napoleon's aim had been to have the French state become self-sufficient, rather than to be held hostage by colonial or foreign trade. By 1813, with France engaged in withdrawal from Spain and retreat from Russia, the French no longer had the luxury of experimentation.

Even though Napoleon could not fundamentally alter French agriculture, he had shown what needed to be done, and during the Empire, material life improved for the vast majority of peasants. Only the landless migrant workers were left behind by revolutionary and Napoleonic reforms. As had been true in the past, households were typically composed of multigenerational extended families, including servants. Houses were cramped, decorations and furnishings were limited, and a common room served as a space for eating, sleeping, domestic chores, conviviality, and celebrations. Privacy was only found in the curtained bed enclosure that provided a haven from the cold and prying eyes when couples engaged in intimacies. Yet, over the Napoleonic years, wealthier peasant families acquired armoires or wardrobes for their growing possessions, and some families added clocks, ornamental candlesticks, and porcelain services to their inventories. Even food was reasonably plentiful until 1810 when the harvest was mediocre at best. Until then, families could count on meat and fruit to augment their standard diet of bread, locally grown vegetables (particularly beans), and occasional meat from the hunt. Wine, frequently diluted with water, was the most common drink.[27]

Toward the end of his reign as Emperor, it was common knowledge that nearly every peasant household displayed a portrait of Napoleon on its cottage wall. Members of the peasant class considered him the People's Emperor, even when the Napoleonic wars were incessant and their sons and brothers continued to fight so long and so hard for him.

New Currency, New Incentives, and New Public Works

In spite of Napoleon's many and varied early efforts as First Consul, the economy did not turn around as quickly as he would have liked, and he found himself dealing with a shortfall in French revenues, lack of specie, continued unemployment, and inflation. He quickly shifted his focus from municipal affairs to banking and specifically to the treasury of France. While Napoleon always felt that he knew what he was doing on the battlefield and in politics, the First Consul recognized that his knowledge of fiscal matters was really quite limited. When in doubt, he always turned to men whose mastery of the subject he admired. In the case of French finances and fiscal policy, he turned to Minister of Finance Michel Gaudin; François-Nicholas Mollien, director of what was called the Sinking Fund; and François de Barbé-Marbois, director and later Minister of the Treasury. Together, their recommendations were instrumental in bringing France back from the brink of financial disaster. To centralize and stabilize banking, the Banque de France (Bank of France) was created in 1800. Its authority included setting interest rates for loans, being a repository for government funds, issuing securities, and serving private customers as well. The bank was founded with stock held both privately and by the government, and in 1803 it was granted the sole right to mint money. Initial deposits came from tolls, the national lottery, and the sale of securities. Once the Bank of France was established, additional permanent revenues came from direct taxes (property and income) as well as customs duties, taxes on luxury goods, liquors and tobacco, and business and commercial licenses.

Under Michel Gaudin's purview was the *Caisse d'amortissement*— a cash reserve to protect the government against France's national debt (i.e., the Sinking Fund). It alone, however, could not insure confidence about French solvency, so a significant portion of the French debt was repudiated or written off by the government. In 1801 by national law, the debt was reduced from 100 million francs to 37 million francs; and recently acquired territories and occupied lands were subjected to extraordinary taxes to bring immediate assets into the treasury. Additional measures designed to inspire confidence in the government included payment of pensions and interest on a regular schedule in specie (gold and silver) and the creation of an Office of Direct Taxation that took taxation out of the hands of local officials, both to eliminate corruption and to provide accurate accounts and audits.[28]

As far as currency was concerned, the French experience with anything other than precious metals had been tragic, so Napoleon moved swiftly to return to specie. Early in the eighteenth century, John Law's experiment with paper currency based on the value of French North American lands had left France in massive debt and Law in exile. Other attempts under the revolutionary governments to use paper currencies called *assignats* and *mandats territoriaux* had failed as well. The experiments had been fraught with overprinting, devaluation, inflation, and ultimately lack of confidence. In the case of the *assignats,* for example, their decline had been precipitous. Issued in 1791, they were worth only 3 percent of their value at issue by 1795. To picture a peasant or Parisian worker with his wheelbarrow heaped with *assignats* to buy a few loaves of bread would not have been far from the truth, except that he would have been unable to find a baker or merchant ready to accept a wheelbarrow filled with currency. What Napoleon endorsed by a law of March 28, 1803 was the establishment of the franc as the basic unit of currency, its value based on 5 grams of silver or the equivalent of .322 grams of gold. As the Banque de France issued bank notes, they were tied expressly to the value of treasury deposits of those precious metals. Interestingly, the gold and silver standard set in 1803 remained for 123 years as the basis of the franc.[29]

Even before Napoleon engineered his currency adjustments, he was able to announce a balanced budget of 500 million francs in 1801. Throughout the Napoleonic period, direct taxes remained equitable across the population, the franc maintained its value, the Banque de France remained solvent, and interest on the national debt was paid regularly. This is not to suggest, however, that the French did not feel the effects of financial crises during the Napoleonic period. In late summer and fall of 1805, France experienced a severe run on the Banque de France, commercial difficulties, and the failure of several private banks. Rumors exacerbated the problems, but Napoleon's victory at Austerlitz restored confidence. In 1806–1807 the economy again bottomed out, and the Banque responded with loans at 2 percent. In 1810–1811, at the height of the Continental System, Napoleon was forced to extract more wealth from conquered territories.[30] When he was questioned by merchants and government officials about his policies, he replied testily, "I am the only one in Europe with money today."[31] Regardless of the difficulties, which were almost exclusively tied to the resumption and continuation of war, Napoleon demanded strict adherence to the fiscal policy that only he could adapt. And, over all, the combination of a sound currency and stable banking system—along with steady direct taxes, indirect taxes as needed, and wealth extracted from conquered territories by the Napoleonic armies—proved effective.

Industrial growth was next on Napoleon's agenda. Woefully behind England in industrialization, Napoleon encouraged French innovation to make up the pace. Beginning in 1802, Napoleon sponsored trade fairs and industrial exhibitions, one of the largest taking place in 1806 when 1,400 exhibitors participated. When Napoleon saw ingenuity, he rewarded it, for example Joseph Marie Jacquard, who developed a power loom to produce and reproduce large patterns in textiles. François Richard, whose firm was later called Richard-Lenoir, became the "French cotton king" through his expansion of cotton production and development of blends of wool and cotton fibers. At the height of his success, over 12,000 laborers were engaged in spinning, weaving, and textile production.[32]

Since the Revolution had eliminated guilds, Napoleon envisioned governmental oversight assuring quality in industrial production. Quality control was important because Napoleon wanted to see French industry dominate the continent, fully supplying the state, conquered lands, and allies. In 1807, for example, writing to the Minister of the Interior, he enjoined the minister to contact local groups of workers to tell them "that the local factories are not doing their work in such a way as to maintain their reputation." What prompted his involvement in tapestry production at that moment was his displeasure with the rose and gold-trimmed green tapestries that they had produced for his residence at Saint Cloud. He was annoyed because the tapestries were already looking noticeably worn. "Foreigners [who might visit him]," he remarked, "are bound to form a very bad impression of the Lyon factories."[33] French goods needed to be competitive; it was an issue of national prosperity.

Napoleon's concern for industry was coupled with a drive for full employment. While France was at war throughout most of the Napoleonic period, conscription and employment in the military rarely accounted for more than 3 percent of the population and positions at all government levels for more than 5 percent. In order to track unemployment, Napoleon turned again to a centralized solution—the *livret d'ouvrier*—a worker's passport or identity card that laborers were required to present in order to work. So long as workers were employed, the employer kept the *livret* on file. Workers without *livrets* or permanent addresses could be arrested as vagabonds and vagrants and jailed. In such a labor environment, workers clamored for their *livrets* to avoid almost certain police action against them. Since the revolutionary Le Chapelier Law of 1791 continued to be enforced during the Napoleonic period, labor unrest was at a minimum, although illegal strikes certainly took place.[34] The Le Chapelier Law, which was based on the revolutionary principle of individual rights, precluded collective or unified action by associations of workers. As far as labor conditions were concerned, the workday averaged 10 hours, down from the longer days of the Old Regime and revolutionary eras. Nowhere in Europe, however, had health and safety issues been addressed, and child labor at early ages remained a constant in France. Not until much later in the century would further work conditions be addressed.

When the government noticed unemployment creeping up again, it engaged as many workers as possible in military supply. Cobblers were set to making shoes for the army, so long as the shoes were of good quality; hat makers' skills were enlisted to make shakos (military headwear); and other unemployed workers fabricated baggage carts.[35] When even those measures could not better the condition of the unemployed and disadvantaged, Napoleon called for the expansion of soup kitchens for the distribution of Rumford soup. Created by an American-born inventor-scientist, it was free to indigents and sold at low cost to others. According to reports, Rumford soup was a miracle broth requiring no flour in its preparation, and it was allegedly as nutritious as bread. While communes could, in all likelihood, manage their own distribution, Napoleon contracted out the building and maintenance of these agencies of social welfare in Paris. By 1812, in Paris alone 30,000 pounds of bread and 40,000 bowls of Rumford soup had fed the population. The work had been so successful that Napoleon reported, "We may fairly boast nowadays that not a single inhabitant of Paris suffers from lack of food."[36]

Through all of the changes, Napoleon kept his fingers firmly on the pulse of France. At one moment, he might be counseling his ministers to survey for new bridges across the Seine while instructing them to erect statues to famous men and figures of antiquity whom French citizens should note: Demosthenes, Alexander, Hannibal, Cicero, Washington, and Frederick the Great, among others. At another moment, he reminded his police to enforce the laws on posting anything on the walls of Paris or displaying anything counter to good morality. Among all of the activities, he also took interest in regulating gambling and creating a system for dealing with the ubiquitous prostitutes of the city. In their case, the French government began its system of registration and medical checkups to control the spread of sexually transmitted disease.[37] In one note, he excoriated a priest at Bourges for his "extremely bad sermon"; in another, he approved erecting a statue of Joan of Arc in Orléans as a symbol that "there is no miracle French genius cannot perform in face of a threat against national freedom."[38] Cemeteries and charnel houses with their open graves and decaying bodies were removed from the center of Paris. Where other public projects unearthed human bones, they were cleaned and removed to the Parisian catacombs where they were stacked neatly by bone type as the Romans had done. Ultimately the catacombs became "a source of wonder and amusement" for special imperial guests.[39] Reconstruction began on the city sewer system, although the present gravity-fed underground system was not completed until several decades later.

If peasant cottages in the countryside always displayed their portraits of Napoleon, there was no need for urban residents of Paris to do so. The city itself was a Napoleonic emblem—from public parks to public art and architecture. Daily life had been permanently altered, and ultimately many French citizens placed Napoleon alongside Charlemagne, Henry IV, and Louis XIV in the pantheon of great French leaders.

Yet, for all of the constructive changes that had taken place, it must always be remembered that common French men and women, particularly those who owned little or no property, remained the least touched by the Revolution and Napoleonic prosperity, as long as it lasted. Historians generally disagree on the reasons for Napoleon's continued popularity with the masses, but they can agree that there was a cult-like quality to his continued favor. A police report in 1808 intoned: "The multitude has work and is comfortable. It is content. It loves the Emperor."[40] For urban dwellers, there had been at least a 25 percent increase in salaries, although the increase had not affected all French men and women equally and costs had increased proportionally. Yet, there was a perception of greater material well-being. In the countryside, in spite of conscription into the Napoleonic armies, the peasants were "his warmest partisans." According to one of Napoleon's officials, what mattered most was that he had "reassured them against the return of tithes, feudal rights, the restitution of property to émigrés, and the oppression of the lords."[41] He had brought order to them, efficiently and simply. And, it should never be forgotten, he brought military glory, and he shared it with them.

Notes

1. Jean Robiquet, *La vie quotidienne au temps de Napoléon* (Paris: Librairie Hachette, 1942), 7.

2. Jean Tulard, *La vie quotidienne des Français sous Napoléon* (Paris: Hachette, 1978), 18.

3. Napoleon to Lucien Bonaparte, December 25, 1799, quoted in *Napoleon's Letters: Selected, Translated and Edited by J. M. Thompson* (London: Prion, 1998), 58.

4. Tulard, *La vie quotidienne*, 198.

5. Robiquet, *La vie quotidienne*, 14–15.

6. Ibid., 73–78. See also Nicholas Restif de la Bretonne, *Les nuits de Paris or the Nocturnal Spectator* (New York: Random House, 1964), Alain Corbin, *The Foul and the Fragrant: Odor and the French Social Imagination* (Cambridge, Mass.: Harvard University Press, 1986), and Donald Reid, *Paris Sewers and Sewermen: Realities and Representations* (Cambridge, Mass.: Harvard University Press, 1991).

7. Henri Redhead Yorke, *Paris et la France sous le Consulat* (Paris: Perrin, 1896), 302.

8. Owen Connelly, *The Epoch of Napoleon* (Malabar, Fla.: Robert E. Krieger, 1972), 169.

9. "Napoleon Governs an Empire," *Napoleon: International Journal of the French Revolution and Age of Napoleon* 17 (Fall 2000): 46.

10. François Furet, *Revolutionary France, 1770–1880* (Oxford: Basil Blackwell, 1992), 219. See also J. M. Thompson, *Napoleon Bonaparte* (Phoenix

Mill, U.K.: Sutton Publishing Ltd., 2001), 156, and J. Christopher Herold, *The Age of Napoleon* (Boston: Houghton Mifflin Company, 1987), 125.

11. "The Dawn of Gastronomy," *Napoleon: International Journal of the French Revolution and Age of Napoleon* 17 (Fall 2000): 50.

12. *Correspondance de Napoléon*, no. 4447, quoted in Thompson, *Napoleon Bonaparte*, 146.

13. *The Mind of Napoleon: A Selection from His Written and Spoken Words*, Edited and Translated by J. Christopher Herold (New York: Columbia University Press, 1955), 163.

14. Robiquet, *La vie quotidienne*, 26–29.

15. J. F. Reichardt, quoted in Walter Markov, *Grand Empire: Virtue and Vice in the Napoleonic Era* (New York: Hippocrene Books, 1990), 193.

16. Tulard, *La vie quotidienne*, 22–50.

17. Napoleon to Lucien Bonaparte, December 25, 1799, quoted in *Napoleon's Letters*, 57.

18. Note for the Secretary of State, March 28, 1805, quoted in *Napoleon's Letters*, 97.

19. Ibid., 98–99.

20. Alan Schom, *Napoleon Bonaparte* (New York: HarperCollins, 1997), 264.

21. Robiquet, *La vie quotidienne*, 37.

22. Markov, *Grand Empire*, 79.

23. Connelly, *Epoch of Napoleon*, 38.

24. Note on Agriculture, March 1, 1805, quoted in *Napoleon's Letters*, 96.

25. Ibid., 97.

26. Note for the Minister for Home Affairs, March 18, 1811, quoted in *Napoleon's Letters*, 248–49.

27. Tulard, *La vie quotidienne*, 55–57. See also Anne-Marie Nisbet and Victor-André Massena, *L'Empire à table* (Paris: Adam Biro, 1988), 149.

28. Connelly, *Epoch of Napoleon*, 42–43 and Roger Dufraisse, *Napoleon* (New York: McGraw-Hill, Inc., 1992), 54–57.

29. "Franc," in *Historical Dictionary of Napoleonic France, 1799–1815*, ed. Owen Connelly (Westport, Conn.: Greenwood Press, 1985), 191.

30. Schom, *Napoleon Bonaparte*, 395–96, 567.

31. Napoleon's Address to the Council of Commerce and Manufactures, (Spring 1810), quoted in Schom, *Napoleon Bonaparte*, 567.

32. Markov, *Grand Empire*, 91.

33. Note for M. Crétet, Minister of Home Affairs, September 2, 1807, quoted in *Napoleon's Letters*, 175.

34. Markov, *Grand Empire*, 92–95.

35. Napoleon to General LaCuée, May 2, 1811, quoted in *Napoleon's Letters*, 252.

36. Napoleon to the Ministerial Council, March 11, 1812, quoted in *Napoleon's Letters*, 265–66.

37. Linda Merians, ed. *The Secret Malady: Venereal Disease in Eighteenth-Century Britain and France* (Lexington: University of Kentucky Press, 1996). See also Jill Harsin, *Policing Prostitution in Nineteenth-Century Paris* (Princeton, N.J.: Princeton University Press, 1985).

38. Napoleon to Portalis (September 19, 1805), and Napoleon to Chaptal, February 9, 1803, quoted in *Napoleon's Letters,* 112, 79.

39. Reid, *Paris Sewers,* 16.

40. Police report of August 26, 1808, quoted by Raymonde Monnier, "An Example: the Parisian Wage Earner," in Frank A. Kafker and James M. Laux, *Napoleon and His Times: Selected Interpretations* (Malabar, Fla.: Krieger Publishing Company, 1989), 165.

41. Jean-Antoine Chaptal quoted by Jean Tulard, "A Survey of Peasants and City Workers," in ibid., 152.

CHAPTER 5

NAPOLEON AND THE FRENCH ARMIES

In War There Is Only One Favorable Moment

In 1803, Napoleon approved a resolution to erect a statue of Joan of Arc in Orléans. In part, the resolution stated: "There is no miracle French genius cannot perform. . . . The French nation has never known defeat."[1] Although Napoleon was commenting on Joan of Arc's career, he was never shy about his own military genius or his ability to remain undefeated. "Military genius is a gift from heaven," he later wrote; and the gift had been reserved for himself.[2] From Arcola in the First Italian Campaign in 1797 to his retreat from Russia in 1813, he consistently described himself as a man who took charge and as a man who was in control. He could instill a fanatical love for France in his troops and drive them forward at unheard of speeds. He was a master at seizing an opportunity, because he knew that there were no second chances on the battlefield. "In war," he remarked, "there is only one favorable moment. The greatest talent is to know it."[3]

Students of Napoleon quickly learn that battles, operations, and military campaigns tend to dominate writings on the period. Standard biographies of Napoleon, for example, often follow a traditional pattern of chapter titles: from Corsica to Toulon and Nice; to Italy and Egypt; then, after the Peace of Amiens, either a history viewed through campaigns or defined by his chief enemies (Austria, Prussia, Russia, Britain); and finally Leipzig, Waterloo, and his personally embattled exile on St. Helena.[4] Statistics of Napoleonic military history easily confirm the pattern. He fought over 60 battles in his 23 years of active service, and two million native-born men served in his armies from 1804 until 1815. He oversaw 32 drafts, and final casualties have been placed at over a million men, among them 15,000 officers.[5] His campaigns took French soldiers from Scandinavia in the north of Europe to Sicily in the south. His men went as far as Lisbon on the west and Moscow on the east. The world outside of Europe was also his domain; his men saw duty from the Caribbean basin all the way to Egypt and Syria on the Mediterranean Sea. India and the Far East provided an allure, although he was never able to follow through. Louisiana would not have been impossible except for the revolt in Saint Domingue (Haiti) that ended his designs in the New World.

During his time and later, Napoleon was described as the Corsican ogre, a man of blood, a modern Attila, Robespierre on horseback, and the prime instigator of Armageddon. But, he was also placed on the list of redoubtable leaders for his powerful personality, piercing gray eyes, hypnotic presence, iron determination, prodigious memory, and ability to analyze.[6] He had amazing energy and the ability to scramble his troops. He was a master of contingencies, responding to chance and turning it to his advantage.[7] As he practiced the art and science of war, he also studied it. In his youth, he had devoured writings on great military leaders of the past, and he continued to do so throughout his life. They included Gustavus Adolphus of Sweden, Marshal-General Turenne, Prince Eugene of Savoy, Frederick the Great of Prussia, Alexander the Great, Hannibal, and Caesar.[8] From them he distilled the essence of his strategy: "to keep [the] forces united; to leave no weak part unguarded; to seize with rapidity on important points."[9] Later he added additional tenets: "to be up and doing and to be firmly resolved to die a soldier's death."[10] In the final analysis, the great commanders of history had also known "how to master chance."[11] When he took to the field, he appeared unstoppable. He inspired fear, if not terror. In over two decades of battles, he was only wounded twice; and to his enemies and troops he appeared invincible. See Document 7 at the end of this book for a selection of observations on war that he shared with Las Cases during his exile.

Behind the legends that Napoleon built, there was also a man who was obsessed with detail. He likened his brain to a cabinet: "Different subjects and different affairs are arranged in my head as a cupboard. When I wish to interrupt one train of thought, I shut that drawer and open another. Do I wish to sleep? I simply close all the drawers and there I am—asleep."[12] Just as his brain was organized in a certain way, he systematically organized his military information. On campaign, for example, he commissioned portable boxes with easily accessible compartments that were designed to hold small cards. Information, regiment by regiment and battalion by battalion, was posted on each card, so that Napoleon would know at a glance the enemy's position, troop strength, and potential movements. In companion compartments, he could access his own intelligence data. Napoleon also designated one individual who was fluent in the language of the region to maintain the traveling card file.[13] Along with his correspondence and notes, his portable box was never out of his sight unless it was carefully secured.

It is easy to picture Napoleon as he sat at his camp table, note cards and documents laid out in front of him. There in the wealth of information, he mastered detail, made choices, and let nothing slip by. In one case, for example, he laid out false information to confuse the enemy. In another case, while plotting his enemy's troop maneuvers, he interrupted himself to order a new patriotic song and to commission inspiring plays for the French public and for performances in his casernes.[14] He knew that the morale of his country was as important as the morale of his soldiers. The drawers in the cupboard of his brain were easily opened; his card file was always available.

An Argument without End

Although Napoleon was master of Europe for a decade and a half, the title "Napoleon the Great" was never applied to him; and there are no simple answers to explain why. Napoleon was, without a doubt, both a great and controversial figure in his own time, and he remains so today. In fact, Pieter Geyl, who wrote a classic work called *Napoleon: For and Against* (1949), said it best: "History is indeed an argument without end."[15] In reviewing the writings of historians, Geyl knew that there were unanswered questions—polemics and controversies that had no easy answers. In the case of Napoleon's military legacy, the debate centers on two primary questions. First, what were Napoleon's contributions to warfare? Did he create a new method? Was there a formula for victory? Second, was Napoleon a man of peace? Did he ever intend to have peace? If he did strive for it, under what circumstances would he have negotiated it? To understand Napoleon as a commander who never became "Napoleon the Great," we cannot ignore these questions.

In attempting to answer the first question, perhaps we should restate it. Did Napoleon invent anything new in the theory or practice of war? Biographer H. A. L. Fisher has provided one of the more categorical answers to this question. He wrote simply, "He invented nothing."[16] Fisher's judgment may initially sound harsh to students of the Emperor, but other historians have at least partially agreed. As we answer the question, we should consider Napoleon's contributions to warfare in two aspects: the first relates to the theory of warfare and its use in planning and the second deals with equipment and operations on the field of battle. As far as theory and planning are concerned, historians who have relied on Napoleon's writings have found themselves lacking evidence. Napoleon did not help his case. "I never had a plan of operations," Napoleon was quoted as saying.[17] "Everything is common sense," he reported, "theory is nothing."[18] And it is true that no Napoleonic battle was a copy of another. If we believe Napoleon's words that he never had a plan of operations, it was because he had many possibilities. Napoleon's more likely meaning was that he never formulated so strict a plan that he was irrevocably bound to it. Rigidity had to be avoided; mobility had to be preserved. To Napoleon, responding to accident could make all of the difference in the world, so he planned for it "almost mathematically."[19] He laid out what he intended, placed himself in the opponent's position, and then recalculated everything—time and time again. For the most part, he also did not like to commit his plans to paper. It was better, he thought, to keep his commanders guessing until the battle was committed. In practice, the latter principle became one of his hallmarks: unity of command.

In operations, Napoleon borrowed extensively from proven military tactics; and, when evaluating equipment, he saw no reason to redesign what had previously proven its worth. For artillery, he followed the lead of Count J.-B. Vacquette de Gribeauval (1715–1789), who had designed field pieces for Louis XV and Louis XVI. Gribeauval had, in fact, standardized guns into three types (12-, 8-, and 4-pounders), complemented by howitzers and mortars. Furthermore, in recasting weapons, Gribeauval had been able to reduce their weight to increase their mobility. Additional improvements included inclination markers, better sighting, prepackaged shot, and better carriages. Along with Gribeauval's mechanical improvements, Napoleon had learned the lessons of the Chevalier Jean du Teil (1733–1820), whose book on the use of field artillery counseled the commander to begin battles with artillery fire followed by the deployment of infantry, and to amass his guns at critical moments. The advice was well taken. Although one might assume that Napoleon increased artillery strength because of his training, in fact, Napoleon kept the ratio of cannon to men approximately what it had been: three cannon per 1,000 men, although he had hoped to increase the ratio to four per 1,000 men.

Other influences on Napoleon included Jacques-Antoine-Hippolyte de Guibert's *Essai général de tactique* (*General Essay on Tactics*), Pierre Bourcet's writings on mountainous warfare, and Marshal Victor François de Broglie's use of the division as the standard unit of maneuver, although Napoleon later adopted the corps instead of the division. From Guibert, in particular, he learned that an army's speed was critical to its success. When needed, therefore, an army should reduce or abandon its army train and live off the land. He also perfected the *ordre mixte* for the attack—the use of both line and column.[20] From Frederick the Great, Napoleon learned guile and cunning, if he did not already know them, and the importance of a decisive outcome. He followed the Prussian king's advice on flanking maneuvers, and he made a point of preserving his line of operations almost at all cost. Lazare Carnot, the "Organizer of Victory" under the Jacobins and Directory, provided the system of supply, as well as foundries and factories to support the war effort.

What then was Napoleon's contribution to warfare? Very simply, he functioned effectively and he achieved victory, battle after battle, year after year. The rest, most historians would agree, lay in his genius for taking the lessons of the past, combining them with elements of the present, and maneuvering like no one else could have imagined.[21] According to historian Owen Connelly, "Napoleon's personal tactics defy analysis." While he used patterns set by French revolutionary armies, he then added something else. According to Connelly:

> His rule was "Engage and then see what develops." He normally held back a large part of his army until the pattern of enemy action became clear. Then his remarkable intuition came into play. Sensing the opponent's weak point, he would hurl overwhelming force

against that point at just the right time—artillery blasting, infantry rolling forward, and cavalry moving in for the *coup de grâce.* Never, however, did he leave himself without a reserve, at least the Old Guard—until Waterloo.[22]

Genius and intuition, however, are impossible to codify and equally impossible to teach. Perhaps if Napoleon had achieved a lasting peace, he might have become "Napoleon the Great," but he did not. Except for 14 months during the Consulate, Napoleon did not sustain peace. This brings us to the second major question that historians have raised when dealing with the military history of the Napoleonic era.

What was Napoleon's commitment to peace? Was he a man of peace, as he sometimes portrayed himself? Again, Napoleon provided little personal insight. His writings are inconsistent; his language is troubling at times. On the one hand, Napoleon told the King of England that he was a man of peace and that his most sincere desire was to assure a general peace in Europe. On the other hand, his *Army Bulletins* and pronouncements that were intended for a French audience reminded his countrymen that France was embattled and that Britain was to blame. The allies against France, he continually reported, had provoked him, had preyed upon him, and had caused the continuing contests. Peace could not be assured until France controlled that peace. In 1805, Napoleon had written to his brother Joseph on the topic: "You do not get peace by shouting 'Peace!' . . . Peace is a meaningless word; what we need is glorious peace." In 1813, he had further defined peace: "What I call peace is merely the disarmament of my enemies."[23] Later that year, in a note chastising his Minister of Police for some indiscreet and improper remarks, Napoleon reminded him firmly: "I don't make war my business in life. No one is fonder of peace than I am. But I regard the conclusion of peace as a serious undertaking; I want it to be lasting; and I must consider the situation of my Empire as a whole."[24]

From the battlefield, Napoleon also sent a mixed message. After viewing the battle of Eylau in March 1807, Napoleon described the carnage. There were ten thousand corpses and five thousand dead horses. The field was covered with abandoned cannon and carbines, expended shells and balls. Remnants of the battle lay haphazardly on the snow-covered plain. "A sight such as this should inspire rulers," he wrote in his *Army Bulletin,* "with the love of peace and the hatred of war." His less public persona, however, often belied his pacifism. Much later during the Empire in a personal note, Napoleon quoted a Roman emperor: "The corpse of an enemy always smells sweet."[25]

If one listens to Napoleon's own words, then the sweetest smelling corpse would have been an Englishman. To Napoleon, in fact, everything about peace revolved around Britain's lack of willingness to participate in it. He said that he had been forced to fight throughout the world trying to tame that "nation of shopkeepers," as he derisively called the English. Britain was always in the background, manipulating politics, dominating the seas, and at various times and in various theatres supplying the allies with men. Facts, he said, would support his contention that the blame was not his. In fact, he always noted, he had been the invader only twice—in campaigns against the English in Portugal and against Russia. "All my victories and all my conquests were won in self-defense," Napoleon wrote from his exile at St. Helena; and by then, he had convinced himself that what he said was true.[26]

Recent historians have looked both at peace as an aim of the French Empire and also at the time when Napoleon's achievements began to wane and peace was no longer attainable. Among them, David Chandler pinpointed 1806 as a defining year. After 1806, the campaigns of the Fourth Coalition showed less genius, he said, and Napoleon took the first perilous steps in creating the Continental System, aimed at breaking England. Alistair Horne chose a year later—1807—when Napoleon concluded the Treaties of Tilsit that granted him "unchallenged, and unchallengeable, dominion over the mainland of Europe."[27] During the previous two years, according to Horne, Napoleon had achieved victory at Austerlitz, had commanded a significant number of successful battles, and had begun his project to tame England. As late as 1812, according to Owen Connelly, Napoleon might have preserved his dynasty in Europe.[28] The expansion of the French Empire and military reverses, however, made that impossible. Napoleon would not stop, and the seeds of his ultimate defeat were sown. Although Napoleon always protested that he had no ambition, he also admitted that he might not recognize it. Ambition was simply part of his being, like "the blood that circulates in my veins, like the air that I breathe."[29] Power, he also said, was his mistress.

How serious was Napoleon about peace? Whether it was simply an occasional flirtation, whether he always set the conditions too high, or whether his actions placed the conditions outside of his control, Napoleon cannot be viewed as a man of peace. Peace could only have been possible if he had been willing to compromise and to set his sights lower.[30]

A Profession of Positions

When Napoleon organized the Grand Army (*Grande Armée*) that was to serve him until his exile, he applied to his task the same interest in detail that had characterized his reorganization of France and his previous military campaigns. "A good general, good cadres, good organization, good instruction, and good discipline can produce good troops, regardless of the cause they fight for," he wrote in his *Notes on the Art of War*.[31] A bit of fanaticism on the part of soldiers never hurt a cause, but victories could be assured only if all of the details were in place.[32]

The Grand Army, that became synonymous with Napoleon's victories throughout Europe from 1805 on, was created in Boulogne on the northern coast of France in 1803–1804. At that time, Napoleon looked across the Channel toward an invasion of England, but in the meanwhile peace on the continent provided him with the luxury of reorganizing the military. In 1803, the standing army of France was between 500,000 and 600,000 men, but Napoleon preferred to have a field army of approximately 200,000 soldiers when he began a campaign. The Grand Army was precisely that. Furthermore, it was a professional army of Frenchmen directly under the command of the Emperor himself.

The standing army, therefore, could contain several field armies, assigned in different areas if the need arose. Below the level of the army came the corps, typically 20,000 to 30,000 men, commanded by a marshal or a general-in-chief. The corps that Napoleon designed, in fact, may have been his greatest contribution to warfare, and they were certainly his most powerful weapons against the powers of Europe. To Napoleon, the effectiveness of the corps was a "general principle at war." He placed his full confidence in them: "A corps of 25,000 to 30,000 men can be isolated; well led, it can either fight, or avoid battle and maneuver according to circumstances without experiencing any misfortune, because it cannot be forced into battle and finally it should be able to fight for a long time. . . . War is a profession of positions, and 12,000 men are never engaged unless they choose to be. This is even more the

Table 5.1 Composition of the Grand Army, August 29, 1805

Unit	Composition	Commander*	Gross Strength
The Imperial Guard		Jean-Baptiste Bessières, Marshal of the Empire	7,000
1st Corps	2 divisions (3 regiments each or 9 battalions) 1 light cavalry division	Jean Bernadotte, Marshal of the Empire	17,000
2nd Corps	3 infantry divisions 1 light cavalry division	General Auguste Marmont	20,000
3rd Corps	3 infantry divisions 1 light cavalry division	Louis-Nicholas Davout, Marshal of the Empire	26,000
4th Corps	3 infantry divisions 1 light cavalry division	Nicholas Soult, Marshal of the Empire	40,000
5th Corps	3 infantry divisions 1 light cavalry division	Jean Lannes, Marshal of the Empire	18,000
6th Corps	3 infantry divisions 1 light cavalry division	Michel Ney, Marshal of the Empire	24,000
7th Corps	2 divisions (3 regiments or 9 battalions) as a reserve	Pierre Augereau, Marshal of the Empire	14,000
Reserve Corps	3 divisions (Bavarians, Württembergers, and Badeners)	Assembling and unassigned	26,000
Reserve Cavalry	*Cuirassiers* and *dragoons*	Joachim Murat, Marshal of France	22,000
Reserve Artillery		General E. A. C. Dommartin	5,000

Total strength was 219,000 men; effective strength was 210,500 men and 396 guns. All of the corps commanders who are listed as marshals had been named to the marshalcy in 1804, prior to the creation of the Grand Army. Only Dommartin and Marmont did not carry that title. Marmont was named as marshal of France in 1809.

Adapted from Chandler, *Campaigns of Napoleon*, 1103, and Napoleon's *Correspondence*, XI: 141–44, no. 9137.

case with 30,000 men, especially when these 30,000 are followed by other troops."[33] Table 5.1 shows the composition of the Grand Army in 1805, particularly the corps.

Each corps was, by definition, a miniature army that was semiautonomous. If needed, a corps could scatter and easily reassemble. It typically consisted of two or more infantry divisions, a brigade of light cavalry, six to eight companies of artillery, sometimes a company of engineers, and a limited army train that might include supplies, medical personnel, equipment, teamsters to handle the horses, and other support personnel or camp followers. Napoleon believed, however, that a corps should not have an extensive army train, and his men were expected to live off the land where feasible. In an age of potatoes and turnips, one historian noted, living off the land might mean precisely that, as well as pilfering or purchasing goods from locals.[34]

Napoleon's army, just like those before, was heavily based on its infantry, and each infantry division was composed of brigades and regiments that were subdivided into battalions of 3,360 men (4 battalions of 6 companies of 140 men each). Each of the six companies was organized by function: four were composed of *chasseurs* (fusiliers) with one company each of *voltigeurs* and *grenadiers*. *Chasseurs* were foot soldiers, equipped with .69 calibre Charleville (Charleroi) muskets that could fire two rounds per minute, if the soldiers were well trained, dexterous, and lucky. The standard was three rounds every four minutes, and reloading could feel interminable in the heat of battle. Soldiers still mounted their bayonets, as they had done historically, but the bayonet was more for the fear it inspired than its usefulness in close quarters. Musket range was about 170 yards, and accuracy left much to be desired.[35] Massed musket fire could be effective as a volley; but used by an individual soldier, a particular target would more likely be missed. *Grenadiers* in Napoleon's army were shock troops, the largest men whose name came historically from their assignment to handle extremely explosive grenades. Instead, for the most part, *grenadiers* were used to provide more strength and force to the infantry. *Voltigeurs,* members of the sixth company in a battalion, were skirmishers. Selected for their size and agility, Napoleon threw them into the contest first, either individually or in small groups, to dislodge and unbalance the enemy troops prior to the main attack. As expert marksmen, *voltigeurs* carried .69 calibre carbines and any other weapons of choice.[36] Somewhere among the troops of the battalion, there would also always be a band.

Mounted troops during the Napoleonic wars were divided into light cavalry (*chasseurs à cheval, hussars,* and *dragoons)* and heavy cavalry (*cuirassiers*). Light cavalry, according to Napoleon, was to remain unattached from any infantry corps because its use was to support the advance guard, rear guard, and flanks of the army as needed. Mobility was of the essence, so Napoleon prescribed that the light cavalry, whether officers, noncommissioned officers, or soldiers, would always sleep fully clothed. In the fray, they were a reckless lot, "with shako over the ear, sabre trailing, face disfigured and divided into two by an immense scar; upturned moustaches half-a-foot long, stiffened with wax . . . and with this what an air!—the air of a swaggering ruffian."[37] Their equipment necessarily had to be light, but they would be armed with a carbine and bayonet, a saber, and two pistols. The total weight could be no more than 11 pounds. Again, Napoleon was prescriptive about their actions and even how their horses should be treated: "The [men] will be trained to cross rivers by swimming beside their horses, grasping them by the mane, and holding the carbine above the water. The horses will be harnessed as simply as possible. They are expected to be able to drink while bridled and will be accustomed to watering only once a day."[38]

Heavy cavalry included the largest and most heavily equipped of Napoleon's *cuirassiers*. "It is in the heavy cavalry that the science of the mounted man should be carried to the highest degree," Napoleon had written to his stepson in 1806.[39] Again, no detail missed his attention, including the weight of their armor, how they could be equipped with carbines, how they would fire their carbines in spite of their voluminous protective steel breastplates, and who would serve as their orderlies. Because of the weight of their equipment, Napoleon also worried about their ability to fight when dismounted, and he detailed what they should do. "The *cuirassier* will be armed with carbine with bayonet, a pair of pistols, and a straight saber," he wrote in his report on the organization of the army. "He will carry fifteen cartridges around the pistol holders and will not have a cartridge box. When forced to fight dismounted, he will place them in his right pocket and he will receive from the pack fifteen additional cartridges, which he will put in his pocket. He will keep the hooded cape."[40] It was as though Napoleon was looking over their shoulders at each engagement.

When Napoleon invested himself in the reorganization of the French military, he left nothing to chance. Knowing that an army was at least partially at the will of its intelligence, Napoleon then reorganized the scouts. In 1806, he put forward a plan to have four regiments of scouts made up of four squadrons of 200 men each. Scouts had to have excellent vision and be no taller than five feet, so that they could ride horses whose height did not exceed four feet three and a half inches. No saddles would be issued, rather they would ride only on pads. They would have one coat, one vest, and one pair of breeches or trousers along with one multipurpose cloak. Everything that they carried needed to fit in one valise that could weigh no more than four pounds. They were never to be separated from their battalion, but they could be used in almost any manner. "The small size of the horses of scouts makes them especially capable of following infantry everywhere," Napoleon reported.[41] Furthermore, the army could save significant revenue by using smaller horses that they could more likely replace while on campaign. As mounted soldiers, scouts could also be used in the cavalry, if needed. The plan not only made military sense; it was exceedingly practical.

Finally, Napoleon's greatest pride was placed in his Imperial Guard that had replaced the consular guard of 1800–1804. The Imperial Guard, in spite of its name, had nothing in common with a palace guard or imperial bodyguard; rather it was a small, elite army including infantry, artillery, cavalry, and support. When Napoleon named it in 1805, the Imperial Guard stood at approximately 8,000 men. By 1812, it had grown to 80,000, of whom 56,000 were still effective. Members of the Guard were hand picked by the Emperor based on their service in at least three campaigns. They wore the best uniforms, had the best rations and equipment, were paid more highly than soldiers of the same grade in the regular army, and were rarely committed to battle. Hence, they were often called the "immortals" because the Emperor carefully spared their lives. As veterans, however, Napoleon set them aside because they had already proven themselves, and he kept them as his most important reserve. Each time when they were committed, until Waterloo, the Guard was decisive in the outcome.[42]

The Grand Army was a complex organization, and the ingredients of Napoleon's success also included the Emperor's commitment to good field security, the speed and mobility of his troops, the ability to assemble and concentrate his men, unity of command, and his uncanny rapport with his soldiers. In combination, the ingredients were a chef's delight.[43] Regardless of what the term "field security" might connote, what Napoleon meant was fine-honed deception. As Napoleon prepared for any campaign or potential engagement, he went to extraordinary lengths to mask the strength of his troops and to veil their objective. For what seemed like whim, he might detach a division; his cavalry might veer in another direction or create a screen to protect his real troop maneuvers. The enemy, he believed, should never know precisely what was occurring. To keep them unsettled and unbalanced was precisely what he intended to do. Napoleon also made sure that he controlled his own press and that his intelligence was as powerful as possible. An unwary local might be unceremoniously grabbed, bundled up, and interrogated. Post boxes and couriers might be searched and letters confiscated. Nothing was safe as the Emperor's troops advanced.

A second ingredient of war was Napoleon's mastery of speed and mobility. He could move men more quickly than any of his opponents even contemplated, and he could inspire them in the process. Napoleon recounted in his correspondence what his *grognards* (Imperial Guard) had said about his demands: "The Emperor has discovered a new way of waging war; he makes use of our legs instead of our bayonets."[44] In fact, Napoleon expected his men to be ready for action, bayonets mounted, when the forced march ended near the field of battle that he had carefully selected. On the eve of the battle, Napoleon would be there in his faded green coat and uniform of a corporal of the Guard. They saw him; they heard him. They felt his commitment. During the evenings long before the battle began, he had calculated time and space. He had planned his contingencies, and he had factored into his calculations the element of time. To the enemy, it was the element of surprise. "Strategy is the art of making use of time and space," he had said.[45] To Napoleon, these were not just computations of the hypothetical; they were real expenditures of men and *matériel*.

Napoleon's third ingredient for war has been called "assembly and concentration" based on Napoleon's often-misunderstood maxim that "the army must be kept assembled, and the greatest possible force concentrated on the field of battle."[46] The maxim is, in fact, a two-part program. As Napoleon moved his troops into position, he always maintained mobility. He recognized that even he might have read the enemy's position incorrectly. When he stated that the army must be assembled, his real message was that all of the corps and divisions should be within a reasonable and measured distance from where the battle would occur, so that they could be concentrated when the time was right. In fact, he used a standard of two days march (certainly no more than three days) when he positioned the men whom he might need. The measure of two days, however, could also be deceiving in a quintessential Napoleonic manner: to the enemy it would appear that his men were two days away, but under conditions of forced march, the modern equivalent of a *blitzkrieg*, troops could be on the battlefield within one day. In this manner, the element of surprise would always be his.

Napoleon's fourth and fifth ingredients of successful warfare were unity of command and the rapport that he had with his soldiers. We have already touched upon the meaning of unity of command in an earlier section of this chapter, but it is worthwhile mentioning again. Its success lay in the scale of battles that could still be managed by the Emperor himself. With his prodigious memory for detail and inventiveness, unity of command was a deciding factor in his victories. But the principle of unity of command also carried the elements of defeat. When battles grew larger, distances grew longer, multiple armies were fielded by the coalitions against Napoleon, and communications did not undergo any significant change, unity of command was impossible.

We Shall Not Rest

Just as Napoleon's tactics may defy analysis, there is at least one ingredient of Napoleon's warfare that will also never be fully understood. In spite of the length of the Napoleonic wars and in spite of their cost, the majority of French soldiers were extraordinarily loyal to him. Whether it was the legend of "the little corporal," the belief that no musket ball had been made that could harm him, or his strong presence with his troops, Napoleon could always rouse his men, gain their immediate support, and be assured that they would follow him. Even his archrival, British commander Arthur Wellesley, Duke of Wellington reported: "I used to say of him that his presence on the field made a difference of 40,000 men."[47]

Who were these men whom Napoleon commanded? They were volunteers and conscripts, the latter having come out of a draft system that dated back to the closing years of the Revolution. The draft, as it remained after 1798, applied to all men aged 20 to 25, although they were required to register at 18. Exemptions included heads of households, married men, only sons, seminarians, doctors, the disabled, and those who were deemed physically unfit, including all men whose height was less than five feet.[48] In practice, young men were called up in a lottery by the youngest each year. In military terminology, those inductees were the class of that particular year. As was standard in most armies of Europe, revolutionary law had also provided for the purchase of substitutes. Napoleon continued the practice, although he allowed only 5 percent of the draft quota in any year to be filled by men whose services had been purchased by others.[49] Given the extent of the Napoleonic wars, one might think that Napoleon's armies conscripted nearly every able-bodied Frenchman. On the contrary, Napoleon called, on the average, 73,000 men per year until the last critical years of the empire when the numbers of young men called into service increased dramatically. In general, the number of inductees was less than one-tenth of those who were eligible.[50]

New recruits and inductees went almost directly from their villages, towns, and country fields into the Napoleon army, potentially to the front. They learned their drills within a week, sometimes on their way to their engagement. Napoleon did not concern himself with what might be seen as a lack of preparation because he merged his new conscripts into an army that was already trained as a finely tuned military machine. Furthermore, his troops were commanded by veterans who had served with him previously and whom he trusted. His system was based on an important principle that he continued from the wars of the Revolution—the *amalgame.* Fresh recruits would always be merged into the existing army of veterans. According to statistics, one out of every two men in the army of 1805 had fought at Marengo (1800) in the Second Italian Campaign, and one in four had served during the wars of the Revolution.[51] According to Napoleon, the army itself was the best training ground for his men.

The life of a soldier in Napoleon's army was a series of hopes and challenges. As far as the army was concerned, it was one of the only occupations in France where talent and merit could provide immediate access to promotions, additional pay, and privileged treatment, for example, assignment to the Imperial Guard or receipt of the sinecures that came from military promotions and imperial titles. As far-fetched as it may sound, Napoleon's soldiers believed that a marshal's baton could be found in every soldier's knapsack.[52] The truth was far less glamorous: noncommissioned officers rarely achieved a rank higher than lieutenant, and promotions above the rank of colonel were conferred solely at the Emperor's recommendation. Yet, men knew that they could be noticed and that birth and family were no longer the deciding factors in their prospects for a better future. Each time a decoration was granted on the battlefield, as infrequently as the event might have been, the legend grew.

Napoleon encouraged that belief by learning the names of his men and committing the names and faces so much to memory that he could recognize them years later. He also took great pleasure in reviewing his soldiers and in speaking before them on the eve of battle or on the day of a victory. "You know what words can do to soldiers," he had written to one of his generals in 1800.[53] There was incredible truth in that statement. When he had first marched into Italy, he had already felt the power of his promises. As he stood before his assembled troops at the foot of the Alps in 1796, his words had resonated with his men:

> Soldiers, you are ill-fed and almost naked. The government owes you a great deal, but it can do nothing for you. Your patience and courage do you honor but give you neither worldly goods nor glory. I shall lead you into the most fertile plains on earth. There you shall find great cities and rich provinces. There you shall find honor, glory, riches. Soldiers of the Army of Italy! Could courage and constancy possibly fail you?[54]

Throughout his campaigns and even after his first exile, his words never failed him, and they continued to inspire the men who followed him. To have the Emperor present "excited their exertions," and accounts tell of Napoleon's remarkable reception even by *les Marie-Louise,* 16-year-old boys who had been recruited in the waning days of the Empire to fill the ranks.[55]

Besides the promise of glory, the army offered acceptable rations, although the military did not always provide them. According to regulations, each soldier could expect one pound of bread, four ounces of meat, two ounces of dried vegetables, and one ounce of brandy per day. When troops were supplied with their allowance, their daily food intake was better than most Frenchmen and eminently better than the food that French women and children were eating. But, Napoleon attempted to avoid convoys that cluttered the roads and camps, so the promise often exceeded reality. There was a fine line that Napoleon and his commanders walked. The Emperor had bragged that the French soldier was the only soldier who could "fight on an empty stomach." But, he also knew that the health of his men had to be preserved. It was axiomatic that a "soldier's health [had to] come before economy or any other consideration."[56] Yet, Napoleon always wrestled with the problem of supply for his men, and in the case of rations, he continued to support experimentation. By 1809, fundamentally because of pressures from the military, canning was perfected. A Parisian confectioner named Nicolas François Appert succeeded in using boiling water to preserve animal and vegetable matter in glass bottles. Appert's invention, however, was too late and too costly to supply the growing numbers of soldiers in Napoleon's armies; nonetheless he received a coveted prize from the French government.

As life in the military held promise for Frenchmen, it was not an easy existence. Infantrymen on campaign were required to carry their muskets as well as 58-pound packs containing the following items: "sixty rounds of musket ammunition, rations for a week, a spare pair of pants, two shirts and two extra pairs of boots."[57] Reports indicated that their mass-produced boots were a constant problem because the soles had been glued on rather than stitched. After a battle, they frequently scoured the field for better-made boots freed by the deaths of their enemies or allies. When times were difficult and the campaign was extended, soldiers still needed the bare minimums. "There are five things the soldier should never be without," Napoleon admonished his commanders, "his firelock, his ammunition, his knapsack, his provisions for at least four days, and his entrenching tool."[58] On the retreat from Russia, however, even those requisites were lacking.

Although Napoleon stated firmly that a commander must consider the needs of his soldiers, it was also part of his nature to win at all costs. Men had to be prepared to die willingly and gloriously. "Troops are made to let themselves be killed," he had said.[59] At the battle of Wagram in 1809, for example, casualties were 32,000 men or nearly 20 percent of the French forces that were engaged. When he wrote to the Empress Joséphine the following day, he remarked, "My losses are high; but the victory is decisive and complete."[60] He had taken 100 guns and 12 flags. He noted that he was sunburned, but everything had gone well. No one, not even Napoleon, would have argued about the cost of the wars that he fought. He needed soldiers for his armies, and in some ways his need became a vicious circle. As he expanded beyond existing French territory into what came to be called his satellite kingdoms, he could conscript additional men into the army; but he also unleashed nationalism, and he confirmed the resolve of his enemies to end his empire. At the worst of times in 1813, in a letter to Clemens von Metternich of Austria, it is hard to see any amount of concern Napoleon shared for his sol-

Table 5.2 French Casualties by Year, 1803–1814

Year	Killed in Action or Died of Wounds	Died in Hospital	Prisoners and Disappeared	Hospitalized Long Absent	Totals
1803	0	1,000	500	500	2,000
1804	1,000	5,500	2,500	1,000	9,000
1805	2,000	7,000	unknown	5,000	14,000
1806	5,000	16,000	2,000	13,000	36,000
1807	7,500	33,000	2,000	4,000	46,500
1808	2,500	16,000	1,000	24,500	54,000
1809	19,000	32,5000	14,000	12,500	78,000
1810	9,000	33,000	11,500	4,00	57,500
1811	7,500	23,500	3,500	7,000	41,500
1812	9,000	26,000	154,000	20,500	210,000
1813	16,500	51,500	124,000	72,500	264,500
1814	7,000	52,000	53,000	66,000	178,000
Date uncertain	500	4,500	2,000	5,500	12,500
Total	86,500	302,000	369,000	236,000	1,003,500

The figures above do not include 150,000 troop casualties from recently annexed departments of France and 300,000 casualties of foreign troops that served alongside French troops. Casualties of soldiers on the battlefield and in the hospital collectively were 388,500 of whom 70 percent were from disease, exposure, or complications of wounds and injuries. In total, the count was a million men. Other historians have raised the number to 1.4 or 1.5 million Frenchmen lost in the Napoleonic wars. Casualty counts are much higher when the French revolutionary wars are added into these figures.

This table was adapted from Jacques Houdaille, "Le problème des pertes de guerre," *Revue d'Histoire Moderne et Contemporaine* (1970), 17: 418, by Owen Connelly in *The French Revolution and Napoleonic Era, 233.*

diers. Whether it was braggadocio or not, Napoleon wrote: "A man like me doesn't notice a million deaths."[61] "In war," he said, "men are nothing, one man is everything."[62] Table 5.2 provides statistics on the cost in human lives of the Napoleonic wars from 1803 through 1814.

Was Napoleon an enigma when it came to his soldiers? While his comments sometimes sound contradictory, his message was reasonably consistent. He intended to do the best that he could for his soldiers on campaign. He would lead them to fertile plains; he would take them beyond the reaches of France to extend the Empire; he would bring them glory and rewards. But, they had to be prepared to pay the price for his dreams. Peace would become a chimera, and their tours of duty would be extended. Forced marches would take their toll. As the scale of battles increased, casualties would increase. "We shall not rest until we have planted our banners on the territory of our enemies," he wrote on the way to Austerlitz.[63] What they did not know was that for many of them, their graves would be dug as their banners were planted.

In spite of his ultimate defeat on the field at Waterloo, Napoleon's warfare remained unmatched by any single army of his time. Wellington again had the last word: "Napoleon was a grand *homme de guerre* (man of war), possibly the greatest that ever appeared at the head of a French army."[64] If he never was "Napoleon the Great," then who was this man who has so fascinated history? Napoleon's imperial dreams and military exploits against the powers of Europe are the subject of the next chapter.

Notes

1. Napoleon to Chaptal, Minister for Foreign Affairs, February 9, 1803, quoted in *Napoleon's Letters: Selected, Translated, and Edited by J. M. Thompson* (London: Prion, 1998), 79.

2. Napoleon (1820), quoted in Lucian Regenbogen, *Napoléon a dit: aphorisms, citations et opinions* (Paris: Les Belles Lettres, 1996), 28.

3. Napoleon (1796), quoted in ibid., 25.

4. See, for example, J. M. Thompson, *Napoleon Bonaparte* (Phoenix Mill, U.K.: Sutton Publishing Ltd., 2001).

5. David G. Chandler, *The Campaigns of Napoleon: The Mind and Method of History's Greatest Soldier* (New York: Macmillan Publishing Co., Inc., 1966), xxix. Chandler noted that French casualties in World War I were 1,360,000 men or 340,000 per year in a war that was far shorter than the Napoleonic contest. Chandler noted: "It is useful to keep the casualty question in proper perspective in any attempt to evaluate Napoleon's responsibility as a war lord."

6. Chandler, *Campaigns*, xxxiv ff.

7. Owen Connelly, *Blundering to Glory: Napoleon's Military Campaigns* (Wilmington, Del.: A Scholarly Resources Imprint, 1987), 1.

8. Generals who are frequently mentioned by Napoleon include Alexander the Great of Macedonia (356–323 B.C.), Julius Caesar (c. 100–44 B.C.), Prince Eugene of Savoy-Carignan who fought for the Austrian Empire (1663–1736), Frederick the Great of Prussia (1712–1786), Gustavus Adolphus, King of Sweden (1594–1632), Hannibal of Carthage (247–183 B.C.), and Marshal-General Henri de la Tour d'Auvergne, Vicomte de Turenne who fought for Louis XIV in his extensive wars (1611–1675). For Napoleon's remarks about

each of these generals, *The Mind of Napoleon: A Selection from His Written and Spoken Words, Edited and Translated by J. Christopher Herold* (New York: Columbia University Press, 1955), 224–30 and *Napoleon on the Art of War,* ed. Jay Luvaas (New York: The Free Press, 1999), 30–41.

9. *The Military Maxims of Napoleon,* translated from the French by Lieutenant-General Sir G. C. D'Aguilar (London: Freemantle and Co., 1901), 44.

10. Napoleon to General Lauriston, December 12, 1804, quoted in *Napoleon's Letters,* 90.

11. Napoleon on "The Great Captains," quoted in *Napoleon on the Art of War,* 30.

12. F. M. Kirchiesen, *Memoirs of Napoleon I* (London, 1929), 254–55, quoted in Chandler, *Campaigns,* xxxv–xxxvi.

13. Napoleon to Berthier, August 28, 1805, quoted in *Napoleon's Letters,* 111–12.

14. Memorandum on Allocations to General Songis, August 16, 1799 and Napoleon to Citizen Chaptal, November 29, 1803, quoted in *Napoleon's Letters,* 83, 53.

15. Pieter Geyl, *Napoleon: For and Against* (New Haven, Conn.: Yale University Press, 1963), 16.

16. H. A. L. Fisher, *Napoleon* (Oxford, U.K.: Oxford University Press, 1967), 17.

17. Chandler, *Campaigns,* 134.

18. Owen Connelly, *The French Revolution and Napoleonic Era* (Chicago: Holt, Rhinehart, and Winston, Inc., 1991), 231.

19. *Correspondance,* XXIX: 159, quoted in Chandler, *Campaigns,* 146.

20. According to Connelly, "Guibert recommended the *ordre mixte,* or attack with some battalions in column (50- to 60-man front) and others in line (three ranks), with some battalions moving from column to line for greater fire power, as they closed with the enemy. For the latter maneuver, he had the first three ranks move ahead while those behind moved up on their left and right flanks." (*Blundering to Glory,* 13.)

21. David Gates, *The Napoleonic Wars, 1803–1815* (London: Arnold, 1997), 8.

22. Connelly, *French Revolution and Napoleonic Era,* 231.

23. Napoleon to Joseph (1805) and a Conversation in 1813, quoted in *Mind of Napoleon,* 206–07.

24. Napoleon to Prince Cambacérès, Arch-Chancellor of the Empire, June 18, 1813, quoted in *Napoleon's Letters,* 286.

25. *Army Bulletin* (March 2, 1807) and Conversation with General Caulincourt (August 17, 1812), quoted in *Mind of Napoleon,* 204–05.

26. Geyl, *Napoleon: For and Against,* 252.

27. Alistair Horne, *How Far from Austerlitz? Napoleon, 1805–1815* (New York: St. Martin's Press, 1996), xxii.

28. Connelly, *Blundering to Glory*, 62.

29. Conversation (1804), quoted in *Mind of Napoleon*, 47.

30. T. C. W. Blanning's recent work titled *The Eighteenth Century: Europe, 1688–1815* (London and New York: Oxford University Press, 2000) argues convincingly that peace was never a possibility under Napoleon.

31. *Napoleon on the Art of War*, 8.

32. Napoleon wrote, "Anything not profoundly contemplated in details will produce no results." (Regenbogen, *Napoléon a dit*, 25.)

33. Napoleon to Eugène (June 7, 1809), *Correspondance* XIX: 81, quoted in *Napoleon on the Art of War*, 78.

34. Gates, *Napoleonic Wars*, 8.

35. Horne, *How Far from Austerlitz?* 83.

36. See "Army, French" in Owen Connelly, ed., *Historical Dictionary of Napoleonic France, 1799–1815* (Westport, Conn.: Greenwood Press, 1985), 23 and Connelly, *French Revolution and Napoleon*, 228–29.

37. General Baron de Marbot, quoted in Horne, *How Far from Austerlitz?* 90.

38. "Project d'une nouvelle organization de l'armée," *Correspondance*, XXXI: 455, quoted in *Napoleon on the Art of War*, 50.

39. Napoleon to Eugène (13 March 1806), *Correspondance*, XII: 183, quoted in ibid., 54.

40. "Projet d'une nouvelle organization de l'armée," *Correspondance*, XXXI: 456–57, quoted in ibid., 55.

41. Note Concerning the Organization of Regiments of Scouts (July 9, 1806), *Correspondance*, XII: 527–28, quoted in ibid., 48–49.

42. "Garde imperiale," Jean Tulard, ed., *Dictionnaire Napoléon* (Paris: Librairie Arthème Fayard, 1987), 776–77. As the wars continued, the Imperial Guard was divided into the Old Guard, Middle Guard, and Young Guard, based on the time of induction.

43. The phrase "ingredients of Napoleonic War" comes from Chandler, *Campaigns*, 144–61.

44. *Correspondance*, XI: 336 quoted in ibid., 148. Men of Napoleon's Old Guard were also called *les grognards*. While the word means a "grumbler" or someone who is continually displeased, the name was attached to the Guard in an amicable, bantering manner. Members of the Guard, who had paid their dues in previous battles, often complained about their conditions (albeit better than other soldiers) and how the Emperor treated them. Napoleon knew that he could always count on them, joked about their grumbling, and even encouraged them sometimes.

45. Chandler, *Campaigns*, 161.

46. *Correspondance*, XXXI: 418, note 40, quoted in ibid., 153.

47. Earl P. H. Stanhope, *Conversations with the Duke of Wellington* (London, 1899), 9, quoted in ibid., 157.

48. Later during the Napoleon wars, height was reduced to 4'9". Even then, one in four men was rejected as unfit to serve. According to J. M. Thompson, the average height of British soldiers was 5'5", and only one out of 16 was rejected for service. See Thompson, *Napoleon Bonaparte*, 283.

49. Connelly, *French Revolution and Napoleonic Era*, 229, note 2. The price varied with the department and the year—on the average 500 francs in 1800, 2,000 in 1805, 2,800 in 1809, 3,500–5,000 in 1813–1814.

50. Connelly, *French Revolution and Napoleonic Era*, 228–29 and Connelly, *Blundering to Glory*, 74.

51. Thompson, *Napoleon Bonaparte*, 283.

52. Chandler, *Campaigns*, 161.

53. Napoleon to General Brune (1800), quoted in *Mind of Napoleon*, 214.

54. Proclamation to the Army of Italy (April 10, 1796), quoted in ibid., 214.

55. Arthur Wellesley, Duke of Wellington, quoted in Thompson, *Napoleon Bonaparte*, 285; see also Chandler, *Campaigns*, 157.

56. Notes to Chaptal (n.d.) and Correspondence (1813), quoted in *Mind of Napoleon*, 281, 219.

57. Horne, *How Far from Austerlitz?* 93.

58. *Military Maxims of Napoleon*, 33.

59. Conversation (1817), quoted in *Mind of Napoleon*, 211.

60. Napoleon to Joséphine, July 7, 1809, quoted in *Napoleon's Letters*, 210.

61. Alan Forrest, *Conscripts and Deserters: The Army and French Society during the Revolution and Empire* (New York: Oxford University Press, 1989), 19.

62. Note (August 30, 1808), quoted in *Mind of Napoleon*, 219.

63. Thompson, *Napoleon Bonaparte*, 286.

64. Ibid., 285.

Symbols of the French Revolution under the *Directoire*, 1796. Around the allegorical figure of Liberty, who is coiffed with a liberty bonnet, are the symbols of revolutionary France: a cornucopia representing the plentiful harvest, symbols of engineering and medicine showing French skills, a rooster representing vigilance and courage, the fasci representing prowess in war surmounted by Victory who is carrying the flag of the French people *(Peuple Français)*. Courtesy of the Bibliothèque nationale de France, Paris.

Bonaparte as General-in-Chief of the Army of Italy, 1796. Courtesy of the Bibliothèque nationale de France, Paris.

Bonaparte at the Bridge at Arcola in the First Italian Campaign, 1797. Courtesy of the Bibliothèque nationale de France, Paris.

"The King of Brobdignag (King George III) and Gulliver (Napoleon)." In this wonderful period cartoon set in 1803, the larger-than-life George III examines the smaller-than-life Napoleon. "My friend Grildrig, you have made a most admirable panegyric upon yourself and country, but from what I gather from your own relation & the answers I have with much pains wringed & extorted from you, I cannot but conclude you to be one of the most pernicious, little odious reptiles that nature ever suffer'd to crawl upon the surface of the Earth." Courtesy of the Bibliothèque nationale de France, Paris.

"Diverse Projects for Attacking England," 1803. If Napoleon were to attack England, then he would have to use everything within his means: balloons to ferry equipment, horses, and men; landing craft; battleships; and even a forerunner of the Chunnel. Courtesy of the Bibliothèque nationale de France, Paris.

The Battle of Austerlitz, December 2, 1805. Courtesy of the Bibliothèque nationale de France, Paris.

Napoleon as the Savior of France, 1806. According to the caption, France, which was surrounded by monsters ready to devour it, was saved by Napoleon, whom the gods sent. Neptune provided the horses to draw his chariot, Minerva protected him, and the cyclopes forged his weapons to make him eternally invincible. Courtesy of the Bibliothèque nationale de France, Paris.

CODE NAPOLÉON.

SA MAJESTÉ L'EMPEREUR ET ROI MONTRE A L'IMPÉRATRICE-REINE LES ARTICLES DU CODE CIVIL, QU'IL VIENT DE TERMINER.

Napoleon presenting the Civil Code to Joséphine, 1806. Courtesy of the Bibliothèque nationale de France, Paris.

"From the Highest to the Lowest . . . or Causes and Effects," 1814. As Napoleon overstretched his Empire from Madrid to Moscow, his stilts snapped. At Fontainebleau, he abdicated. Courtesy of the Bibliothèque nationale de France, Paris.

"The Pear was Ripe," 1815. In an interesting drawing from 1815, Napoleon's profile is seen in the leaf attached to the pear. The caption continued: "The [overripe] pear that fell is Napoleon." Courtesy of the Bibliothèque nationale de France, Paris.

CHAPTER 6

WAR MAKES RATTLING GOOD HISTORY

For a decade France had not known peace. From April 1792, when France declared war on Austria beginning the wars of the French Revolution, until March 1802, when France and Britain concluded the Peace of Amiens, peace had been no more than a five-letter word. The French Republic had experienced the threat of foreign and émigré troops on its soil, and French ports had been blockaded. However, during that decade, French soldiers had also been successful: the borders of France had been expanded to the Rhine on the northeast and to the Alps on the east and southeast. The French dream of natural frontiers was realized.[1] Three constitutions had been designed, two Italian campaigns against the Austrians had been fought, Napoleon had challenged the British in Egypt, although the French presence there was short-lived, and he now wore a Consul's mantle.

The End of the Second Coalition (1800–1802)

The decade of war from 1792 until 1802 had ended, for the most part, because Napoleon had set his sights upon such an objective. To achieve peace with France's enemies had required two stages: first, the French had to defeat Austria on the battlefield and second, peace had to be negotiated with Britain. In the first case, after the coup of Brumaire and promulgation of the Constitution of the Year VIII in 1799, Napoleon had designed a strategy against Austria that allowed for significant contingencies. He put his armies into order, mounted his horse, and returned to northern Italy. On the continent, of the countries that had participated in the Second Coalition against France, only Austria remained at war, and French armies were still positioned along the Rhine in Germany and in Austrian-controlled northern Italy.[2]

Napoleon's strategy for forcing Austria to make peace hinged on several objectives that were linked by space and time. In fact, his plans were complex. They relied on French General Jean-Victor Moreau's ability to push the Austrian troops east coupled with Napoleon's successful crossing of the Alps, the timely assistance of a corps of Moreau's army (General C. J. Lecourb), and General André Massena's continued resistance to Austrian troops around Genoa. Tactically Napoleon wanted to remove Austrian troops from northern Italy; strategically he wanted a decisive engagement to force Austria to make peace. What Napoleon needed was the element of surprise, impeccable timing, and an almost impossible achievement from Massena.

Obsessive about details, Napoleon even gave personal attention to the element of surprise. He would appear faithful to the new French constitution that separated the functions of consul from commander-in-chief. In such a governmental structure, Napoleon would not look as though he were preparing an army for himself. Should Austrian intelligence discover troops amassing near Dijon, they would be identified with Napoleon's chief of staff, General Alexandre Berthier, who was, in fact, assembling and equipping the 60,000 men whom Napoleon needed for the campaign. Just as Napoleon had intended, the Austrians looked away, expecting a traditional assault to be made toward Vienna. In the meanwhile, Napoleon studied maps and mastered each element of an alpine crossing. The Austrians remained unaware that even the name, Army of the Reserve, was a deception.

As French troops crossed the Alps, legend was in the making. Although the campaign began in May, the weather was severe, and ice and snow made the crossing difficult.[3] Regardless, Napoleon saw himself as Hannibal, and if the campaign were successful, Napoleon intended to be remembered in that manner. In reality, the crossing was far less romantic. Berthier had made sure that the soldiers were well equipped with snowshoes, provisions, and extra clothing, but he could not guarantee everything. For example, their uniquely designed artillery sleds were too cumbersome, and they resorted to hollowed-out logs to drag field cannon across paths that had only known foot soldiers and cavalry in the past. According to Napoleon's guide, even Napoleon resorted to expediency. As he traversed the ice-choked slopes and narrow paths, first Napoleon gave up his horse, then he mounted a mule. Then on short descents, he simply dismounted, sat down, and used ice and the seat of his pants to carry him down the steep slope. In five days, Napoleon and his men had managed the crossing. On May 30, the Army of the Reserve was on the plain of Lombardy. Two days later, French soldiers were welcomed into Milan, where Napoleon recreated the Cisalpine Republic (soon to become the Republic of Italy).

Since the crossing had been successfully completed, the remainder of Napoleon's plans needed to fall into place. To the north, a series of victories pushed the Austrian forces away from Switzerland just as Napoleon had hoped, but Massena could not hold Genoa. Daily rations for Massena's men had been reduced to a few ounces of horsemeat and morsels of sour bread made of bran, oats, straw, and cocoa. His men were starving to death, and Massena preferred to negotiate an agreement rather than to accept unconditional surrender. Although Napoleon was initially enraged over Massena's capitulation, the French soldiers were allowed to leave Genoa under escort, but still carrying their weapons. On another day they would fight again.[4] For all of Napoleon's earlier strategy, plans had gone awry. Not only had Genoa been lost, but reinforcements from the Army of the Rhine had not arrived. Furthermore, Napoleon began to make mistakes. He underestimated the Austrians, and he miscalculated the 71-year-old Austrian field marshal's resolve. Reports were misleading, maps were inaccurate, and problems with supply kept Napoleon's army less than fully prepared. Even more important, as of June 13, Napoleon's scouts and light cavalry could not locate the Austrians. With no information, Napoleon convinced himself that the elderly Austrian commander, Field Marshal Michael Friedrich Melas, was withdrawing without seeking a fight. This was Napoleon's gravest error.

At 6:00 A.M. on Sunday morning June 14, 1800, the Austrian army made itself known. Artillery sounded the reveille; the engagement had begun. To the French, the surprise was complete: not only did armies rarely engage each other so early in the morning, reconnaissance still seemed to confirm that Melas was withdrawing rather than preparing to fight. Yet, through the dust emerged three columns of 31,000 men supported by 100 cannon. By midmorning, the French were paying dearly for their lack of preparation, and they were still outnumbered two to one. Napoleon strengthened his right, committed all of his troops including his reserve, and desperately tried to recall General Louis-Charles Desaix, whose men had been dispatched earlier to watch for the Austrians on their withdrawal. By early afternoon, Desaix had not arrived, and the badly mauled French pulled back. The Austrian commander, who felt assured of victory, retired from the battlefield, assuming that his chief of staff would complete the rout.

At 3:00 P.M., Desaix's men and artillery arrived; they had heard the sound of battle and marched toward it. Napoleon immediately committed them to the field. Along with the fortuitous explosion of a munitions wagon and a daring cavalry assault, Desaix's arrival had changed the course of the battle. The Austrians, who had appeared victorious in midafternoon when Field Marshal Melas retired, lost 6,000 men while 8,000 were taken prisoner, including the Austrian commander's chief of staff. On the field at Marengo also lay General Desaix, whose arrival had saved the day, but whose life had been lost in the process.[5]

Without question, the battle of Marengo shares its stories and legends with the entire Second Italian Campaign; and when Napoleon wrote the account of Marengo for his *Army Bulletin* of June 15, he fashioned his own particular history. Later critics of Napoleon, in fact, noted that *Army Bulletins* were no less than pure propaganda. It became a joke to say, "He lies like a *Bulletin*." At the time of Marengo, however, victory was theirs, and Napoleon's detractors were few and far between. According to Napoleon's version of Marengo, only the timing of the Austrian assault had been a surprise, rather than the assault itself, and Desaix's arrival was part of the plan, although the timing had been a real test of French endurance. When Desaix's men appeared on the battlefield, what invigorated the soldiers was the presence of their First Consul who "revived the *morale* of the troops."[6] According to Napoleon, it was almost as though Desaix had not been there. According to another much more trivial story, a new dish was also inaugurated the evening of the battle. Napoleon's chef created Chicken Marengo by de-boning a fresh, pilfered chicken with his sabre, and cooking it as a casserole in a tomato base with the herbs and spices of the region. Allegedly it became an instant favorite with Napoleon.[7]

Three days after the battle of Marengo, Napoleon began his return to Paris. Regardless of the decisiveness of the victory, the Austrians did not ask for a permanent peace. Napoleon was disappointed that the Second Coalition had not been brought to a quick conclusion, but his prowess as a commander had been confirmed again. In Paris, he went back to governing, and Moreau and the Army of the Rhine remained in Germany as the truce held all summer. In November when the armistice had not turned into a final peace, Napoleon ordered that hostilities be reopened, and in December at Hohenlinden, Moreau defeated the main Austrian armies in a crushing blow. Finally in February 1801, France and Austria signed the Peace of Lunéville, confirming anew the conditions of the Treaty of Campo Formio that had ended the First Italian Campaign in 1797. France controlled the entire left bank of the Rhine, compensation was assured for rulers who had lost territory, Tuscany was placed under the control of the Duke of Parma whose land had been annexed to the Cisalpine Republic, and the King of Naples was restored. The treaty also recognized the French sister republics that had been established during the two campaigns: Cisalpine (Italian), Helvetic (Swiss), Ligurian (Genoese), and Batavian (Dutch).[8] Napoleon had substantially altered the map of Europe, and he was a power to be reckoned with. He had also learned some lessons from the battle of Marengo: never to violate his principles of keeping a reserve and concentrating his troops, never to underestimate the power or intentions of his adversaries or their ability to surprise him, and always to remember the "psychological advantage of producing fresh troops 'out of the hat' toward the close of a hard-fought day."[9]

The continent fell under a hush, but the British still held out even though there was nothing left of the Second Coalition that Prime Minister William Pitt had organized. Everyone knew that as long as Pitt remained in power, it was unlikely that any final peace could be negotiated. Then came Pitt's resignation in early March 1802, and the door was opened for negotiations. Almost immediately Napoleon's brother Joseph Bonaparte went to the bargaining table with Lord Cornwallis (known to Americans for his loss at Yorktown) representing the British government. Their work was simplified by agreements that had been reached the previous October and by Napoleon's insistence that the negotiations move quickly. There was ample reason: the Army of the Orient was in peril of expulsion from Egypt. In such a case, the French government would lose any bargaining power it had. Fortunately for Napoleon, by the time news of the final French capitulation reached Britain, the preliminaries for the Peace of Amiens had been signed and the conditions were set.

As history has shown, in the Peace of Amiens (March 27, 1802) lay the seeds of 12 more years of war. According to the provisions of the treaty, Britain was required to restore all conquests that had been taken from France or its allies since hostilities had begun. Britain could retain only Ceylon and Trinidad. British troops were to leave Elba, and Malta was also to be evacuated and returned to the Knights of St. John. In return, France was to abandon Egypt (already a fact) and not to interfere in the affairs or independence of Naples, Portugal, or the Batavian Republic (Holland). Independence for the Ionian Islands on the Adriatic Sea was guaranteed, and provisions were set for a commercial treaty between the two countries. Without such a treaty, it was likely that worldwide economic sparring between France and Britain would never end.[10] While the Peace of Amiens guaranteed an end to the international war, the British government resented losing nearly all of its conquests and feared that the French would regain control of the Mediterranean when Malta was evacuated. Hence, Britain did not hasten to evacuate the strategically located island. France, therefore, had an excuse for future hostilities. On the other side, Napoleon kept garrisons in Naples and refused any overtures for a commercial treaty, in spite of its urgency. Without such a treaty, the British believed that he could cordon off most of Europe from British trade, as he had been trying to do. Regardless of their signatures, neither side was satisfied with the provisions.

An Uneasy Peace Becomes the Third Coalition (1803–1805)

Whether Napoleon ever intended to have an extended or permanent peace remains a question debated by historians, but Napoleon *did* profit during the period of peace by focusing his mind on the details of government, domestic peace, the economy and industry, his colonial schemes, and the frontiers of France. In those brief months, the French annexed Elba, Piedmont, Switzerland, and Parma making them into fully participating departments of France; and Napoleon planned to make Louisiana, which he had acquired from Spain in 1801, into the "breadbasket for the sugar islands of the French West Indies."[11] When Napoleon's designs for a new empire in the Mississippi valley evaporated, the French sold the Louisiana Territory to the United States for 80 million francs ($15,000,000). The money was to be committed to a new contest against Britain, whenever that might occur. Designs on the east were not easily abandoned, and evidence shows that the French continued to look with interest on Egypt and Syria, as well as on India.

Britain was not amused by Napoleon's activities that seemed to flout the Peace of Amiens, and in April 1803, the British ambassador was withdrawn from Paris. The French had already sent out signals that there was nothing permanent in their agreement, and Napoleon began to build his new army—the Army of England—at Boulogne on the English Channel. Britain was to blame, Napoleon said, and he railed against the Perfidious Albion that had not yet evacuated Malta. By May, French and British ships in the Channel were firing at each other, and Napoleon ordered the arrest of all British nationals in France, whether or not they were residents. Three other events made war on the continent inevitable: French armies moved into Hanover to extend French control to central Germany; Napoleon executed the Duc d'Enghien with premeditation, although there was no evidence to link him to the Cadoudal Plot;[12] and in 1805, Napoleon raised the Iron Crown of Lombardy to his head, naming himself King of all Italy. With these acts, Napoleon succeeded in offending the pope and alarming the King and Queen of Naples over the Kingdom of Italy, challenging Holy Roman Emperor Francis II over the reorganization of Germany, threatening Tsar Alexander I over France's potential incursions into the Baltic, and continuing his armed rivalry with Britain. Among the troubled kingdoms, only Naples remained allied with France, although Queen Marie Caroline minced no words when she called the Emperor "the Corsican Bastard."[13] As members of an old dynasty, the Bourbon rulers of Naples thought of Napoleon as an upstart; their loyalty was purely a function of circumstance.

The question was what would happen next. Would the British take action? If not, how would Napoleon tame the Perfidious Albion? Napoleon believed that to end the British menace there were only three routes: a direct assault on the island kingdom, a blockade that would strangle British trade so fully that the government would be forced to capitulate, or an assault on Britain through its back door in the Mediterranean. Napoleon had already tried the latter, so he preferred one of the other strategies. As Napoleon considered a blockade, the seeds of what came to be called the Continental System were sown. Already in 1803, Napoleon had closed all French ports to British or British-borne colonial goods. Even neutral shipping was not exempt. In reply, Britain had declared a blockade of all French ports on the English Channel and North Sea. Within the next year and a half, the British extended their blockade to the Adriatic and across northern Europe from Brest to the Elbe River. By 1806, Napoleon made the blockade as systematic and binding as he was able to do without strong French naval support. The Continental System, engineered to wreck British trade and to bring the government to the bargaining table, however, would take time.[14] The third strategy became his choice. He planned an assault on England across the Channel.

As Napoleon reviewed his options, he believed that the most expedient surrender of Britain could be achieved by a surprise landing, followed by an attack on London and its subsequent capitulation. Again, detail was everything. One hundred fifty thousand men were to be organized as the Army of England, and flat-bottom boats were to be built with mounted mortars at their bows and sterns. Instructions were prepared for the invading troops, and orders were given to find English-speaking interpreters to accompany the soldiers on their assault. Millions of francs were spent on roads to the Channel ports, and Napoleon concocted a scheme to draw the British navy away from England in time for the crossing. "The Channel is a mere ditch," Napoleon wrote to Cambacérès. "[It] will be crossed as soon as someone has the courage to attempt it."[15] The English prepared as well, establishing watchtowers on the coast and taking notes on French maneuvers. Cartoons, sometimes in jest and sometimes with a serious tone, showed Napoleon's troops reaching England under the sea (a forerunner of the Chunnel), across the sea via a mammoth bridge or a flotilla, and above the sea in a massive balloon corps that could carry even horses and artillery.[16]

In reality, Napoleon's plan was quite simple. He planned to combine the various French squadrons to compose a fleet of 40 ships of the line. Then he would send them off to the Caribbean to draw the English fleet after them. Without the English fleet to hinder Napoleon's operations, he would ferry his army to the opposite coast for the assault. Key players included Admiral Pierre Villeneuve's squadron at the port of Toulon in the Mediterranean and Admiral Ganteaume's squadron that was harbored at Brest, near the mouth of the Channel. As Napoleon planned the maneuver, it was chancy at best. Could the French admirals join up to conduct the feint successfully? Could they draw the British to the Caribbean and then hasten back to the Channel in time to carry out Napoleon's invasion? While Villeneuve initially did his part, Napoleon reviewed the tides, the vagaries of Channel sailing, the chances of his invasion of England, and the war clouds that were brewing throughout Europe. Napoleon began to reconsider his plans; however, he continued to wait for Villeneuve's squadron to reach Boulogne. He pestered Villeneuve to make haste, chastised him for taking the time to construct a Franco-Spanish fleet after leading the British on their chase to the Caribbean, and finally demanded that Villeneuve sail north, threatening to end his career. Focused on the Channel, Napoleon still always had his eyes on the impending contest on the continent. On September 3, 1805, Napoleon was unwilling to wait any longer for Villeneuve, and he told his advisors that the prime moment to invade England had been lost. He turned the Army of England away from the Channel; it was no more. Napoleon's troops were rechristened the Grand Army, and their new objective was Austria.

With 200,000 soldiers and a reserve of 40,000 men, the Grand Army was a formidable force when it crossed into Germany. As it turned out, their march was no less than a *blitzkrieg* as Napoleon's carefully regimented soldiers marched an average of 20 miles per day. At the head, middle, and rear of each brigade, members of the military band were placed drumming the cadence of the march; and for five minutes every hour, the troops rested to the sound of music. The pace, measured later, was three miles per hour. By early afternoon of each day when the march was completed, the men foraged, ate, or rested.[17]

As the Grand Army penetrated into Germany, Napoleon's intelligence reported that the Austrian commander was still unaware of precisely what the French were doing. Field Marshal Karl Mack was moving west toward Napoleon's armies, but he did not know the strength of the French army or its exact location. The Black Forest, along with Napoleon's cavalry cloak and his complete press blackout (what Napoleon called his field security) had provided him with a superb advantage. Until too late, Mack did not realize that his army had been caught. At Ulm, he had blundered into a situation that was impossible. He was surrounded, and the means of escape had been blocked. "The unhappy General Mack," as he called himself to a French commander, surrendered 30,000 men, including 20,000 cavalry, 60 guns, and 40 regimental flags.[18]

Napoleon then moved toward Vienna, expecting the remaining Austrian troops and their Russian allies to assemble there to defend the Austrian capital. Instead, after armed sparring took place outside Vienna, the Austrians declared the city open to the invading armies. Vienna had been spared battle, but it had fallen. Then on December 2, 1805, Napoleon met the Austrian troops under Archduke Charles (Karl) and the Russian army which, as yet, had played no significant role in defending the Third Coalition. In the meanwhile, the British navy under the command of Admiral Horatio Nelson had found Villeneuve's fleet and had annihilated it off the Cape of Trafalgar.[19] Britain had established itself as mistress of the seas, but Napoleon was becoming master of the continent.

What Napoleon needed was a victory that would smash his opposition. He faced criticism in Paris for the economic downturn, the weather that had begun gloriously in September had turned to continuous cold and freezing rain dampening the spirits of his men, and a gloriously completed campaign would further solidify his one-year-old Empire. To assure himself of victory, he needed to draw his enemies into his snare. As he reconnoitered the area north of Vienna, he chose the place of his battle. It was one of his primary principles to select the battlefield and then to force his opponent to use it. In this case, the location was Austerlitz. "Gentlemen, examine this ground carefully," he was reported as saying, "it is going to be a battlefield; you will have a part to play on it."[20] In the meanwhile, Napoleon moved his troops around, sometimes using his cavalry to cloak their maneuvers and sometimes leaving units visible for the deception. Tsar Alexander I, who had replaced General Mikhail Kutuzov commanding some 86,000 Russian troops, was drawn into the snare. Napoleon's deception looked real to the tsar who had finalized his plan on December 1. The tsar gave orders to strike south against the French right flank, march on the Vienna Road to sever Napoleon's supply line, attack the rear of the French army, and force its retreat into the hands of Archduke Ferdinand of Austria. Kutuzov counseled Alexander I against his plan, but other advisors believed that Napoleon's army was smaller than it was, that it was far less concentrated, and that it was particularly weak at certain points.

On December 2 at 7:00 A.M., Alexander I launched the attack. Sensing that Napoleon's south flank was the weakest, he poured his men against General Louis-Nicholas Davout's troops that were, in fact, far less concentrated than they should have been. In doing so as the day proceeded, Alexander I terminally weakened his own center, while Napoleon had the time to strengthen Davout's position. It was midday, however, when Napoleon's armies were finally in a position to reduce the Russian flank and center. The location had been chosen carefully, and as the French center under Nicholas-Jean Soult shifted south, the Russian soldiers first found themselves pounded into the marginally frozen marshes at their rear and then hammered and hammered again. The area, known as Goldbach Brook and Satschan Pond, became a "bloody killing ground."[21] There was nowhere for the Russians to go. Forward, they were cut to pieces by close-range artillery. Behind them were the formerly frozen marshes and lakes that had been diced by artillery fire. The weight and number of retreating troops further fractured the ice, turning the lakes and marshes into drowning pools from which there was no escape. As the day proceeded, the French gained dominance on the Pratzen Heights in the center of the line of operations. The Austro-Russian center and right flank, severely weakened by Alexander's commitment of troops against Davout, retreated under direct assault toward the village of Austerlitz. By sunset, there was no hope, and a ceasefire was sounded. See Figure 6.1 for a map of the battlefield at Austerlitz.

The Russian army had lost 25,000 men, at least 10,000 who were killed. Alexander I had even committed his own Chevalier Guard, resulting in heavy casualties among his nobly born soldier-elite; but the Russian tsar would not consider terms. Alexander I simply removed his troops from the battlefield and returned to Russia. The Austrian Emperor, however, had no recourse, and he immediately asked for an armistice. Less than a month later on December 26, 1805, the Peace of Pressburg was signed. Brutal and humiliating in its terms, the treaty stripped Austria of territory on the south and west of the kingdom, including Venice, Istria, and Dalmatia which were added to the Kingdom of Italy and the Tyrol which was added to Bavaria. Württemberg and Baden, allies of Napoleon, also received land. In addition, Napoleon became a kingmaker, naming the rulers of Württemberg and Bavaria to that title.[22] There was no question that Napoleon was sending a message to Austria. Francis was ruler of a second-rate power, and Napoleon drove the message home by figuratively rubbing salt in his wounds. Napoleon was pleased with what had transpired. The battle had been won on the anniversary of Napoleon's coronation as Emperor. And, as the sun had risen over the field of Austerlitz and the fog had melted away, his power had never been greater. His health was good, and he was sleeping well.[23] He was 36 years old.

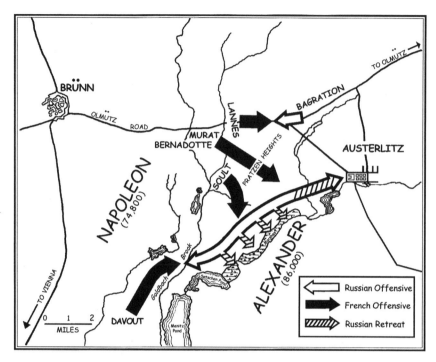

Map 6.1 Battle of Austerlitz, December 2, 1805

Intermission and the Fourth Coalition (1806–1807)

Napoleon had won the campaign of 1805 both strategically and tactically, and he lost no time continuing his reorganization of Europe. In order to do so, the Treaty of Pressburg provided him with an intermission.[24] In early 1806, Napoleon established one particular ground rule for his allies: to waffle in loyalty was unacceptable. On that note, Napoleon sent Massena into the Kingdom of Naples to punish the Neapolitan King and Queen for their very ill-conceived welcome of an Anglo-Russian force during the Third Coalition. There was no choice for Ferdinand IV and Marie Caroline except to flee to Sicily, and Napoleon brought his diplomat-brother Joseph Bonaparte to their throne. In northern Europe, he manipulated the Dutch into abandoning their republic, which had been loyal to the French since 1795, and installed his brother Louis on the throne of the Kingdom of Holland. Elsewhere, he engaged in imperial matchmaking to add legitimacy to his dynasty; for example, his stepson Eugène, viceroy of Italy, married the daughter of the king of Bavaria. In Cleves and Berg, Napoleon's sister Caroline reigned with her husband Marshal Joachim Murat, and Napoleon's sister Elisa was named princess of Lucca and Piombino in Italy.

As a final act in 1806, Napoleon completed the reorganization of the German states that he had begun after the Peace of Lunéville. When he was finished, he had created the Confederation of the Rhine (*Rheinbund*) from hundreds of German duchies, principalities, and kingdoms that had been nominally under the control of the Holy Roman Emperor. Francis, Emperor of Austria, had also worn that crown. But, with the creation of the *Rheinbund*, there was nothing left of the Holy Roman Empire; it had ceased to be "holy, Roman, or an empire." On August 6, 1806, Holy Roman Emperor Francis II abdicated (retaining his sole title of Francis I, Emperor of Austria), and over a thousand years of history ended. Germany now followed French influences and French demands—from a rewritten constitution to the promise of 63,000 men for the French armies.

Napoleon then turned his interest to Prussia, which had been noticeably absent from European affairs for nearly a decade. Yet, Napoleon knew that the Prussian king, Frederick William III, had toyed with joining the Third Coalition. The battle of Austerlitz had changed his mind, and he had thoroughly distanced himself from his wounded Austrian neighbor. In fact, in mid-December 1805, before the Treaty of Pressburg had even been signed, Frederick William had allowed himself to be courted by Napoleon who gave him the right to occupy Hanover in northern Germany. Acceptance of the offer came with a price. Two months later Napoleon demanded that Frederick William III make the arrangement formal. While Hanover was ceded to Prussia, in return, Hanoverian and Prussian ports had to be closed to British commerce, and Prussia agreed to recognize certain grants of territory to France and her allies. Prussian neutrality was becoming less and less of an option for the king. Napoleon intended to force Prussia into a direct contest with Britain. While both sides stalled for time, Napoleon negotiated with Britain to attach Sicily to his brother's Kingdom of Naples. He offered Hanover as a plum to the British—in spite of the fact that Prussian troops occupied the north German territory and that it had been ceded outright to Frederick William III earlier that year. Although French negotiations with the British over Hanover and Sicily were conducted in secret, Prussia received word of Napoleon's duplicity. A Fourth Coalition was in the making.

Great Britain and Prussia now shared a common duplicitous adversary, and in July 1806, Russia and Prussia also came to an agreement. The terms of the Russo-Prussian pact were reciprocal: Prussia would not engage in any attack on Russia, and Russia would aid Prussia in the event of a French attack. War was on the horizon. With a war party advising him at court, and jealous and aging commanders spoiling for battle, Frederick William III agreed to war. He pictured himself as a new Frederick the Great, and he demanded that Napoleon remove French troops from southern Germany. Napoleon replied by requesting that Prussia disarm and return to détente with the French. "The idea that Prussia could take me on single-handed is too absurd to merit discussion," Napoleon wrote to his Foreign Minister in September 1806. "She will go on acting as she has acted—arming today, disarming tomorrow."[25] While Napoleon thought that the idea of a contest with Prussia was absurd, he refused to let Frederick William III continue his sabre rattling. When the Prussians did not demobilize, he sent an ultimatum to disarm no later than August 8, and he moved his troops forward. On October 14, less than a week after the ultimatum expired, Napoleon pressed the Prussian troops into battle at Jena. Nearby at Auerstädt in a much bloodier battle, the Duke of Brunswick's Prussian soldiers engaged Marshal Davout's men. When the twin battles were concluded, the Prussian troops fell back, but there had been heavy casualties on both sides. Routed and hounded, the Prussians were no protection for Berlin, which was in French hands by October 25. The king fled to East Prussia to await further news. In all, Prussian losses were 25,000 casualties, with 140,000 prisoners and 2,000 cannon captured. The campaign had taken 33 days, and Frederick William III had proven to be a miserable successor to the illustrious Frederick the Great.[26] Although Napoleon had described the Prussian king as a "good fellow,"[27] Napoleon did not intend to let him off easily. Prussia would pay for its mistakes, and the French now dominated northern Germany.

Russia, nonetheless, remained at bay; and in order to isolate the continent from Britain, it had to be defeated. The question was where the battle would take place. As a realist, Napoleon pictured the contest on the plains of East Prussia with Austria behind him and Russia to the east. In such an event, Napoleon had to assure the safety of his troops.

His strategy was to enlist the Poles whose hopes of freedom were powerful. Their anger had not cooled against the Russians who, along with Austria and Prussia, had completed the partition and dismemberment of the Polish kingdom in 1795. As much as the Poles wanted independence from their occupation, Napoleon was unwilling to go so far. But, he never told them what their reward might or might not be. With the support of Polish troops regardless of his lack of promises, Napoleon contrived to force the Russians into a situation from which they could not extricate themselves. He kept the British occupied in the Middle East and therefore unable to help Russia, and he fielded an army that he believed the Russians could not defeat. At Eylau in February 1807, the French and Russian armies met. While Napoleon had fundamentally set the conditions for their contest, he could not control everything. In a blinding snowstorm with an Arctic wind that kept temperatures well below freezing, they fought savagely against each other until the Russians withdrew. The field had been more than a foot deep in snow, hiding frozen streams and ponds. Casualties were horrific—possibly as high as one in three French soldiers—and 23 generals were dead or seriously wounded. French Marshal Michel Ney, who had been there, described the scene, "What a massacre! And, without results." The Russians had not asked for a truce; they had not acknowledged defeat. The battle of Eylau had not been decisive. It was the first time in half a decade that the Grand Army did not seem invincible.[28]

After the battle of Eylau, the Russian and French troops engaged each other intermittently, and Napoleon remained watchful until spring when Russian General Levin August von Benningson committed a fatal mistake. Benningson was found, potentially bottled up just west of Friedland with a river behind him and few means to remove his troops to the east, if he should need to do so. As soon as Napoleon was aware of Benningson's error, under conditions of forced march, Napoleon concentrated 80,000 troops against the Russian commander's 58,000. Even when the battle began, Benningson did not know the scale of his opposition. The battle of Friedland turned out to be a massacre. The town was torched, "and into the river the Russians were butchered, drowned, and burned alive."[29] Casualties were between 18,000 and 20,000 Russians, and the French had captured 80 guns. The Emperor noted that he had been feeling well; it was, after all, the anniversary of Marengo. With Benningson's army lost, Tsar Alexander I had no other recourse than to ask for peace. Less than a month later, the former belligerents met at Tilsit to confirm their agreement and to set its provisions. There, between July 7 and July 9, 1807, two treaties were signed ending the Fourth Coalition. The scene was theatrical, and each of Napoleon's adversaries attempted to play to the Emperor.

The summit, as it has been called, actually took place on a splendidly constructed, elegantly decorated, enclosed raft floating in the Nieman River. The enclosed chamber, the size of an apartment, was "surmounted by two weathercocks; one displaying the eagle of Russia, the other the eagle of France."[30] Within the sheltered compartment, the initial meeting between Napoleon and Alexander lasted three hours, away from any witnesses or commentators. Frederick William III, who had not been invited to the raft, watched on the rain-soaked riverbank unable to influence the settlement that dismembered his kingdom. Napoleon intended to make the Prussian king remember the absurdity of his joining the Fourth Coalition. In the process, Alexander took advantage of the situation and willingly sold out his former ally. The result was a reversal of alliances: Napoleon and the Russian tsar would control the fortunes of Europe, one on the west and the other on the east. The two found each other to be insufferably alike as they parceled out Europe. Later, Napoleon wrote to Joséphine, "I am satisfied with Alexander, and he must be satisfied with me. If he were a woman, I think I would make him my mistress."[31]

When the conditions were finalized, the Treaties of Tilsit contained the following documents. First, there was a Franco-Russian treaty that created a Duchy of Warsaw for the Poles. Constructed from former Prussian-held Polish lands, the duchy was to be governed by the King of Saxony rather than being an independent state. The treaty also guaranteed Russian mediation of the dispute between Britain and France and French mediation of the dispute between Russia and Turkey. If the dispute between France and Britain could not be resolved, the tsar was to assist France in gaining Portugal and the Baltic states as partners in the Continental System. A Franco-Russian military alliance was also created to provide mutual support for each other's diplomatic needs, but more significantly, it guaranteed separate diplomatic spheres for the new allies. Second, the Treaties of Tilsit contained a series of secret articles that provided for Russian territorial cessions to France and guarantees of reparations to Ferdinand IV of Naples, who had earlier lost this throne. Third, a Franco-Prussian agreement was concluded. The agreement slashed Prussian territory in half, required Prussia to join the Franco-Russian alliance against Great Britain, and assessed a significant indemnity.[32] Just as Napoleon had humiliated Austria in the Treaty of Pressburg, the French made an intractable enemy of Prussia at Tilsit. Napoleon returned to Paris content with his work and also content with himself. During the campaign, his personal life had taken on new pleasures when he met and seduced Maria Walewska, the Polish beauty who had been given to him almost as a gift. It was extraordinary, but as soon as officials in Warsaw had detected Napoleon's interest in Maria Walewska, they quickly removed her very elderly husband from the city, leaving her free for Napoleon's advances. From the campaign of 1806–1807, the Emperor would remember Polish loyalty, although it came with the continued hope of independence, Maria Walewska's personal loyalty to him that continued for years, and a child whom he later fathered with his devoted Polish mistress.[33]

The Peninsular War and the Fifth Coalition (1807–1809)

Almost before the ink was dry on the Treaties of Tilsit, Napoleon was fully embroiled in new activities. The situations had been forced upon him, he believed, through circumstances that were initially beyond his control. Great Britain continued to obsess him, particularly as British goods found their way into Europe through Portugal, the Papal States, and other less guarded ports on the continent.[34] Napoleon decided that there was little else that he could do except to close those ports by force. His main objective was the Iberian Peninsula, the geographic home of Spain and Portugal. Spain had been a French ally since 1795; Portugal, however, was a long-term, committed trading partner of the British. In order to close the Portuguese ports, Napoleon would have to rely on his alliance with Spain because his field army could not cross into Portugal without penetrating Spanish territory. As he laid his plans, there was no way for him to know that the contest would last until his abdication or that casualties would tally 240,000 men (100 per day). Nor could he know that his men would learn firsthand the savagery of guerrilla warfare. The Peninsular War, as those eight years of nearly constant warfare came to be called, was Napoleon's "ulcer," his Spanish debacle, "the unlucky war [that] ruined me."[35]

On July 19, 1807, Napoleon began his actions against Portugal. He required the maritime kingdom to close its ports under threat of military occupation. When Portugal refused, Napoleon appointed his longtime friend General Andoche Junot to command an invasion force of the country. In order to invade, however, Napoleon needed to guarantee safe passage across Spain for Junot's troops. He quickly negotiated such an arrangement, along with the authority to post a reserve of 40,000 men on the Spanish border. Crossing through Spain and Portugal, Junot's "armed parade" reached Lisbon in November with almost no opposition, although the Portuguese royal family had been whisked away only hours earlier by British ships that ferried them to Brazil. Even without armed engagements, the toll to capture Portugal was high. French troops quickly learned that they could not live off the land because the peasants had left them close to nothing and they could trust no one. Disease, malnutrition, and exposure—instead of musket balls—claimed French lives. Nonetheless, Portugal was under French control. The ports were closed, and Junot established himself in splendid fashion as he reorganized the government on a French model.

Spain, however, was not such a simple matter. Spain was a French ally, yet it was also allowing leakage of British goods onto the continent, and it had to be stopped. The situation in Spain was critical because the government itself was such a problem. According to one historian, it was "degenerate [and] wildly ineffective, wasteful, graft-ridden, top-heavy with officials, burdened with pensioners, and unofficially bankrupt."[36] Spain was ruled *de facto* by Prince Manuel Godoy, who was also known as the Prince of Peace. Officially, however, King Charles IV governed, but he was known only for his fascination with hunting and his periodic bouts of insanity. His wife, Queen Maria Luisa, was intimately involved with the Prince of Peace and wielded a certain amount of power behind the scenes; and Ferdinand, the crown prince and future heir, was habitually conspiring against his family while trying to eliminate Godoy's authority. If that were not enough, Napoleon found the Spanish to be poor allies. They had done little to support his wars, failed to fulfill their monetary promises, provided a poor complement to his navy, and nearly joined the Fourth Coalition against France. While the royal family conspired against each other, Napoleon made secret promises to Godoy for his support. After the arrangement was sealed, it was only a matter of time until Napoleon planned to topple the regime, reorganize the Spanish state, administer it efficiently, and have access to its troops and resources for the French Empire. Napoleon's intentions, however, were unknown to Godoy.

In a series of initially disconnected incidents, Napoleon precipitated the events that brought his brother Joseph to the throne of Spain and prompted the Peninsular disaster. In March 1808, Napoleon decided to make the French presence in Spain permanent. He sent Murat and 40,000 soldiers, accompanied by the Imperial Guard and a military band, through the countryside into Madrid where they were to be stationed. The French troops were splendidly attired, and they marched in parade formation. Their reception was festive and promising—but only because the Spanish had misread Napoleon's signals. In the interim, Crown Prince Ferdinand had overthrown his father and requested Napoleon's assistance to shore up his kingdom. At the same time, the overthrown Charles IV and a very angry former Queen Maria Luisa petitioned the French emperor for assistance in restoring them. It would have been a comedy if the results had not been so serious for the Spanish kingdom. Napoleon demanded that both sides meet with him at Bayonne on the French border to sort things out. Then by force, he required them to abdicate permanently, and he named his brother Joseph Bonaparte to the throne. The appointment of Joseph was not just a surprise to the Spanish; it was astonishing, because most of the Spanish populace had expected Napoleon to support Ferdinand's usurpation and to legitimize it.

So, on May 2, 1808, when French cavalry placed the last of the Spanish royal children under custody, the city broke out in rebellion. Residents of Madrid (Madrileños) attacked Murat's troops with everything that they could find: chamber pots, cooking utensils, furnishings, roof tiles, paving stones, and anything else available. Napoleon had known that such a revolt was possible, and he had counseled Murat to do everything to keep order. A whiff of grapeshot was not out of the question. The cannons were fired at point-blank range, and cavalry swept the streets. According to stories, the Mamelukes (Napoleon's Moslem troops who had been with him since Egypt) responded even more brutally, although there were fewer than 100 of them in action that day. They dismounted, charged dwellings, pulled Spanish men, women, and children from their homes, beheaded them, and rolled their heads down the stairs and through the streets. To the Spanish, Dos de Mayo (the second of May) became the "day the demon emperor of the French set Moslems on the Christians of Madrid."[37] The following day, Murat rounded up the most visible leaders of the uprising and executed them by firing squad.

In July, this same city—Madrid—was to be the place of Joseph Bonaparte's coronation as King of Spain. Napoleon, who had not been present during any of the previous events, was still unaware of the extent of the troubles. "No one has told your majesty the truth," Joseph reported to Napoleon, but the Emperor was not listening.[38] As events took place, only 11 days separated Joseph's arrival in Madrid from his departure. Rebels (to the Spanish, they were freedom fighters) had organized the countryside, forced French troops to capitulate at Bailén, and then threatened Madrid. King Joseph I had no choice but to flee from his new capital. In Portugal, a similar situation occurred. The future Duke of Wellington forced Junot to capitulate after his defeat at Vimiero (Convention of Cintra). French troops in Spain were imprisoned; French troops in Portugal were repatriated by the British to France. For all intents and purposes, the entire Peninsula had been lost, and Napoleon needed to respond quickly and decisively.

Napoleon knew that he needed to take personal command of the situation in the Peninsula. But, in order to be absent from France, he first had to make sure that his alliance with Russia was firm and that he would have sufficient troops east of the Rhine to oversee his central European holdings. He also knew that Austria was rearming with the assistance of Great Britain, so he met with Tsar Alexander at Erfurt to confirm the promises that had been made at Tilsit. In a somewhat strained meeting, the two emperors agreed to maintain their alliance. By November 1808, Napoleon was crossing the Ebro River into central Spain with 300,000 troops. He had brought with him veteran troops and the elite of his commanders. He intended to leave nothing to hazard, and a month later, with significant casualties, he was in Madrid placing Joseph back on the throne. Then, learning of new British incursions into Spain from Portugal, he rushed to Vallodolid with French troops to defeat the British and force them out of the Peninsula.[39] Before he could conduct another victory, however, he had new difficulties to address. He learned that his own sister and the very unlikely duo of Talleyrand and

Fouché were plotting against him. Should he die in Spain, they intended to ignore the constitution and put his brother-in-law Murat on the imperial throne. Yet, in two and a half months in the Peninsula, Napoleon's presence in Spain had restored Joseph to the throne and had eliminated the opposition of Spanish troops. The British were on the run, and he felt confident enough to return to Paris to deal with the succession plot and his critics. Furthermore, he needed to prepare against a new Austrian threat. In Spain, however, the guerrilla war was just beginning in earnest. Napoleon, however, never returned in person to the Peninsula. In fact, it is quite likely that, until the end, he always underestimated its importance to the Empire.

When Napoleon arrived in Paris, morale appeared lower than he had ever seen before because of the scarcities occasioned by the Continental System and continuing conscription. The stock market was falling, and desertion was reported to be high. Young men allegedly mutilated themselves to avoid service in Spain and Portugal.[40] In his own court, he also had to deal with Fouché and Talleyrand, engineers of the succession plot. It was Talleyrand who bore the Emperor's wrath. Whether he was dismissed or forced to resign, the Foreign Minister's days were over as a French diplomat. In a heralded and widely reported meeting, Napoleon leveled on him a litany of charges and abuses. Talleyrand really did not care, because he had lost faith in Napoleon's judgment from the time of the Treaties of Tilsit. He had already been feeding information to the Russian tsar, and he was currently collaborating with the Austrians, unknown to the Emperor. Regardless of the confrontation, Talleyrand stayed in Paris, living off the rewards he had earned earlier from Napoleon. When Napoleon later reflected on Talleyrand's career and his duplicity, the Emperor chastened himself. He should have had him shot, he reported, because Talleyrand was nothing more than "dung in silk stockings."[41]

Napoleon did not know precisely when the Austrians would be prepared for their new contest against him, but he took no chances. Leaving troops in Spain and Naples, he assembled an army of 260,000 troops with 29,000 cavalrymen, supported by 311 cannon, for the new campaign. Archduke Charles of Austria, however, had not waited for Napoleon's first move, and he had declared war in March. A coalition between Britain and Austria was finalized early in April. Pressures for war had been unrelenting, and Archduke Charles had mobilized an army of 340,000 men. Within the previous few years, the scale of war had changed dramatically. The Austrian commander reported that he would have preferred to have 700,000 men when the hostilities opened.[42]

Once the campaign was launched, the battles moved quickly. On April 9 the Austrians crossed into Bavaria. Within two weeks, Napoleon took command of the French army and defeated a portion of the Austrian army at Eckmühl, with Austrian casualties at 50 percent of their forces. Napoleon then advanced toward Vienna. At Ratisbon, however, the impossible occurred. A ricocheting and spent cannon ball wounded the Emperor. His foot injury was painful but far from life threatening, so Napoleon made sure that his troops saw him still riding among them.[43] Just as the men of the Grand Army had shown that they were no longer invincible at Eylau, Napoleon's cloak of invincibility had been removed. In May, Napoleon met the Austrians at Aspern and Essling on the Danube. For the first time in his campaigns, he seriously rushed his preparation for the river crossing, and the toll was devastating. Pontoon bridges failed, coordination was incomplete, and the full army was never reassembled. An Austrian eyewitness reported, "In every street the fight raged; in every house, in every ditch. Carriages and carts were obliterated by musket fire."[44] In the melee, Napoleon also lost two of his most prized commanders, among them the first of his marshals to die in combat.[45] After two days of slaughter between the armies, Napoleon withdrew. It was a draw, and surprisingly Archduke Charles did nothing to follow up. The mistake ultimately cost the Austrians the war.

In six weeks, Napoleon was in control again. No preparation would be rushed, and he had gone back to his insistence on detail. He had assembled nearly 200,000 men and more artillery than at any other time of the campaign. In the meanwhile, Archduke Charles had regrouped on an unassuming plain near a small town called Wagram across the Danube. Sorely lacking in vigilance, the Austrians did not know that Napoleon was constructing everything possible to cross the river and to force the Austrian field marshal into battle—but on Napoleon's terms. By 6:00 P.M. on July 5, 1809, Napoleon had used everything his engineers had constructed—20 pontoon bridges, rafts, landing craft, and gunboats to protect them—and he had assembled 188,900 men and 488 guns on the north bank to face Archduke Charles. The Austrians could count 140,000 men and 450 guns, and they awaited Archduke John with an additional 12,000 troops.[46]

On July 6, in sweltering summer heat with raw recruits mixed with his veterans in a multinational army, Napoleon fought the battle of Wagram. Tactically he took advantage of his sheer numbers and the speed with which he could take advantage of any opportunity on the battlefield. Toward 4:00 P.M., Archduke Charles realized that he could no longer hold back the onslaught of French forces, and he began to withdraw his men corps by corps. "The enemy is flying in disorder," Napoleon reported the next day. "My losses are high; but the victory is decisive and complete."[47] But, Napoleon was incorrect. Archduke Charles still had 80,000 men whom he could have deployed, but he did not turn to engage them as Napoleon probably would have done. On July 12, the Austrian field marshal requested a truce, to which Napoleon hastily agreed. The French Emperor did not want to continue the contest either. At Wagram, Napoleon had learned that his armies were not made of the mettle and skill of Austerlitz and that he could not always rely on his multinational troops who did not have the same personal loyalty to him as the French. Looting and desertions had increased, and he had lost too many men for his own comfort. Napoleon finally dictated the peace on October 14, after he had given an ultimatum to Francis I of Austria. By the Treaty of Schönbrunn, the Austrians were assessed 85,000,000 francs in indemnities, the army was restricted to 150,000 men, and Austria's boundaries were altered radically. In total, because of the territorial adjustments, Austria had lost 3.5 million of its inhabitants.[48]

Besides the Fifth Coalition that Napoleon had just concluded, the Emperor had also been forced to deal with other challenges to his European dominance. A British expeditionary force had landed in the Low Countries, although it had been beaten back into the marshes where the invading soldiers fell victim to swamp fevers and disease. Wellington had invaded Spain again, but the British troops had been forced to retreat to Lisbon. In Italy, mountaineers in the Tyrol had rebelled, but the Emperor's stepson Eugène had subdued them. When Pope Pius VII continued to challenge Napoleon's authority and even excommunicated him, Napoleon placed the Papal States under further French authority and, in a fit of pique, sent troops to "arrest that monk." "I am aware that one should render unto God the things that are God's," wrote Napoleon, "But the Pope is not God."[49] Pius VII was initially placed under house arrest in Savona, and later he was moved to Fontainebleau because

Napoleon feared that the British might try to rescue him.[50] Surprisingly, there was little immediate fallout from Napoleon's actions toward the supreme pontiff. Only the economic blockade of Europe had not fulfilled its aim. Nonetheless, Napoleon was pleased with himself, and he proceeded with his plans to create a dynasty that would truly be his. On December 15, 1809, by a *Senatus consultum,* Napoleon dissolved his marriage to Joséphine. It remained only for Napoleon to complete negotiations for a new bride who could provide him with the son that he desperately wanted. See Figure 6.2 for a map showing the extent of the Napoleonic Empire, 1810–1812.

The Russian Campaign and the Sixth Coalition (1810–1813)

Although momentarily Europe appeared to be at peace, such was not the case. The Peninsula remained in ferment as the guerrilla war became increasingly unmanageable and as British threats from Portugal grew more intense. Napoleon, however, was preoccupied—perhaps for one of the very few times of his life. Instead of returning to the Peninsula, he sent Massena, whose military successes were legion. But, even Massena did not want to go into the Peninsular hellhole, where rebels and other enemies of the French were known to dismember the bodies of fallen troops and hang them in trees as reminders. One never knew when a Spanish beauty or her dowager aunt might be hiding a lethal weapon in her skirts. It was even dangerous to take communion in a Spanish cathedral because the priest might have poisoned the host (bread or wafer), and children often lured French soldiers into ambushes. The contest in the Peninsula was fought only partially on the principles of European warfare. For the rest of the time, guerrilla war (meaning "little war" to distinguish it from the traditional, pitched battles of armies) became a daily occurrence, and the phrase entered the European vocabulary. Among the more interesting memoirs of the Peninsular War are Laure Junot's descriptions. See the biographies at the end of this volume for more information on Mme Junot, who saw firsthand the horrors of guerrilla warfare.

Napoleon's preoccupation was Marie Louise, his new bride, who was destined to bear a son less than a year later. The Emperor was pleased with his choice. "Let me thank you for the fine present you have

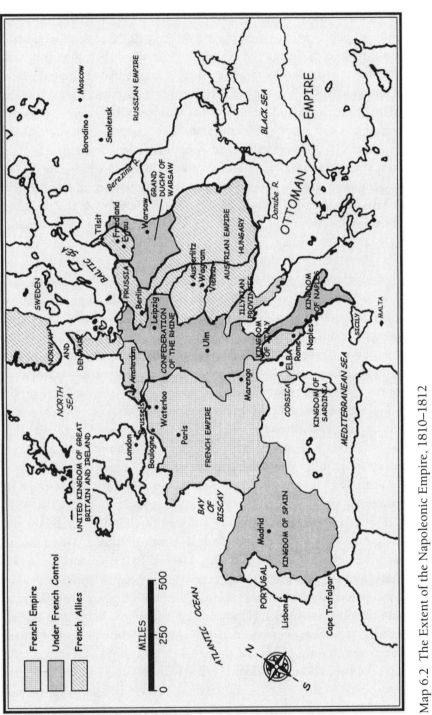

Map 6.2 The Extent of the Napoleonic Empire, 1810–1812

given me," Napoleon wrote to her father, Francis I of Austria.[51] While remaining in Paris with Marie Louise during 1810–1812, he kept his finger on the pulse of Europe, manipulating his allies, toying with Britain and the United States over freedom of the seas, and laying plans to deal with his erstwhile ally Russia. Furthermore, he was forced to deal with anti-French hostilities within the Empire. They were caused by increased taxes to support the incessant wars, additional levies of food and equipment, and accelerated draft quotas. The Continental System had not yet brought the "nation of shopkeepers" to its knees, but Napoleon's economic warfare had caused a serious recession and labor unrest in Britain. On the other hand, Napoleon's allies also felt the squeeze. Only the wealth from smuggling had made the hardship any less damaging. Goods were scarce, and French industry had not yet taken up the slack as Napoleon had promised. Among the most notorious of Napoleon's smuggler allies was the Emperor's own brother, King Louis of Holland, who refused to have his adopted country sacrificed on the altar of economic warfare. Just as Napoleon knew the details of any campaign, he also grasped the economic realities of allowing Britain access to the continent and of allowing Louis to fashion his own diplomacy in opposition to the Empire. In May 1810, Napoleon clamped down on Holland. "I am tired of protestations and fine phrases," he wrote to his brother, who had refused to support French levies and to close Dutch ports. Napoleon simply dethroned Louis, annexed the territory, and with the flourish of his pen, concluded his last memorandum with a postscript, "I will never write to you as long as I live."[52]

While Napoleon wrote fewer letters and seemed less interested in international affairs, he was, nonetheless, watchful. Only a month after he had removed his brother from the throne of Holland, he fired Fouché, his longtime Minister of Police. He had grown tired of having Fouché conduct his own personal diplomacy. His old co-conspirator from the days of the coup of Brumaire had been caught negotiating with Britain over the potential British annexation of Holland. Enough was enough! Two months later in August, Napoleon began seriously to play the United States against Britain over international shipping, the rights of neutrals, and the meaning of freedom of the seas. Great Britain had created the Atlantic confrontation, Napoleon argued, with its Orders-in-Council that placed all neutral shipping in harm's way. As always, Britain was to blame; he said that he had only responded in kind with his Berlin and Milan

Decrees that blockaded European ports. Napoleon offered a solution: if the United States would refuse Britain's overtures and avoid British ports, it would be welcomed on the continent as a neutral and its shipping would prosper without seaborne danger. Slowly but surely, Napoleon began to construct the scenario that created the War of 1812 between the United States and Great Britain. In the end, the war was too small and too inconsequential to serve as the second front that Napoleon needed to take Britain's eyes, troops, and commitment away from Europe. For Napoleon's strategy, see Document 8: *The Continental Blockade.*

As of 1810, Napoleon's major problem was Alexander I of Russia. The tsar's commitment to the settlement at Tilsit had become marginal; and in some cases, the tsar flagrantly ignored the provisions. While Napoleon pleaded innocence, he also had moved well beyond the provisions of Tilsit. Napoleon continued to foment war against Russia in the Middle East, and in 1810, Napoleon annexed Oldenburg because the duchy refused to abide by the Continental System. The annexation was a personal affront to Alexander I, whose brother-in-law ruled it. Furthermore, Napoleon continued to posture about Polish independence, and Napoleon's marriage to Marie Louise of Austria appeared to be the forerunner of an Austrian alliance to replace Napoleon's bond with Russia. If any single event brought about the Russian campaign, however, it was Alexander's decree of December 31, 1810 allowing unimpeded colonial shipping into Russian ports. Except in name, Alexander had withdrawn from Napoleon's blockade. "If we are prepared to close the continent against the English," Napoleon wrote to his Foreign Minister, "there will be peace."[53] If not, the pathway was also clear. As with Holland, enough was enough!

By December 1811, Napoleon was convinced that Alexander would not comply with French demands, and he put in place the final details of a Russian campaign.[54] As he gathered his troops for a field army that ultimately numbered 610,000 men, he also gathered the data that he needed for success. Even his imperial librarian played a role. "Please send me a few good books," he wrote, "those that are best worth consulting—on the topography of Russia, especially of Lithuania—marshes, rivers, forests, roads, etc."[55] Napoleon had no reason to doubt his prospects for victory, because the French Empire thoroughly dominated the European continent. From 83 departments in 1791, France had grown to 130 departments by 1812, and France's land area had doubled.

Napoleon's satellite kingdoms included Italy, Naples, Spain, and West-phalia. His allies also included the Confederation of the Rhine, the Swiss Confederation, Denmark/Norway, Prussia, and Austria.[56] Supremely self-confident, Napoleon continued to correspond with Alexander I, needling him over the failures of the Treaties of Tilsit and blaming him for the impending crisis. "Your majesty has shown a lack of trustfulness, and (if I may say so) of sincerity," he wrote to the tsar, "You have spoilt all your prospects [for peace]."[57]

At the time Napoleon wrote to Alexander, French troops had already crossed into Russia, but Napoleon had scarcely seen the enemy. His plan, however, was predicated on superior force, a quick entry into Russia, and a decisive battle that would force Alexander's hand. Week after week, the French troops penetrated Russian territory, skirmishing from time to time, but finding the Russians gone by the next dawn. Behind his armies, Napoleon was forced to garrison each Russian city as a protection for his supply line. Summer heat, disease, and the grueling march thinned his ranks, and his men became demoralized. At Smolensk, the French armies finally met the Russians, but before anything decisive could occur, they withdrew. It seemed that nothing could force the Russians to take a stand. Finally at Borodino, General Kutuzov made the choice to hold his ground along a four-mile, partially fortified line of hills on the way to Moscow. There, Napoleon enlisted his men and 600 artillery pieces to bring down the Russian army. All he could do, however, was to force the enemy troops back from their original position, but the Russians stood firm again. Flanking maneuvers failed, and Napoleon resorted to assault after assault. It was a battle of attrition. When evening fell and hostilities ceased, over four square miles were strewn with the dead. Even though enemy troops had not been sent fleeing from the encounter, Napoleon announced a major victory. In the meanwhile, the Russians quietly retired, leaving the way open to Moscow without opposition. "The trophies of this incomplete victory," reported one of Napoleon's generals, were "seven to eight hundred prisoners and twenty broken cannon."[58] The French were approximately 525 miles into Russia, three months had already passed, and, in reality, no decisive battle had yet been fought.

On September 14, 1812, Napoleon entered Moscow and almost immediately fires broke out. For nearly a week blazes lighted the sky, although the French troops tried valiantly to extinguish them. Supplies were woefully scarce, and even roofs over their heads were in short supply. As the French troops established themselves, Napoleon wrote to the tsar, "The beautiful and superb city of Moscow exists no more. Three quarters of the houses have been burned. I have made war on Your Majesty without animosity."[59] Napoleon had worked hard to make the letter sound reasonable, so he expected a reply from Alexander or, at the least, from General Kutuzov; but the Russians had agreed upon silence. They had drawn the French 600 miles into Russia, not through a plan, but simply because they had found no other option. Unwilling to fight Napoleon on his terms, they had chosen to retreat, taking their supplies, their people, and their Russian pride with them.

In October, Napoleon realized that the Russians did not intend to sue for peace. The weather had begun to change, and it was clear that Moscow would not be an appropriate garrison for the winter. When the Russians attacked Murat's cavalry on October 18, Napoleon laid out his new plans. The French troops would move back toward Smolensk across territory that had not been ravaged by war. They would pass the winter there and await a new season to destroy the opposition. With Napoleon's withdrawal from Moscow, opportunity fell into the hands of the Russians, and Kutuzov took the offensive to drive the French forces back on the route that the Russian commander chose. He pressed them back along the scorched earth of their initial invasion. Ruthlessly, painfully, and without pity, the Russians went after them. By the time Napoleon's armies stood their ground to cross the Berezina River, fewer than 100,000 men remained (one-sixth of the invasion force). Stragglers were left where they fell, frostbite and gangrene claimed their victims, and the icy waters of the Berezina took hundreds more. When the French army finally reached the Duchy of Warsaw, leaving Russia permanently behind, the number had been cut in half again. See Document 9: *Diary of a Napoleonic Foot Soldier.*

In December before the retreat was complete, Napoleon left his men to return quickly to Paris. According to rumors, the French Emperor had died in Russia. The rumors had taken on such veracity that a crazed, former inmate had nearly overthrown the government and Napoleon realized that he needed to be in Paris in person to prove that he was alive. He could take no chances on losing his seat of power even though "Generals Mud and Winter" had cost him so dearly in Russia. In one of his most famous *Army Bulletins,* Napoleon admitted that the Russian campaign had ended badly. True to form, he reported that his "health had never been better."[60] Although the Grand Army had retreated from Russia, Napoleon refused to acknowledge any role played by the Russian armies in the retreat. He wrote, "the enemy was consistently defeated, and never captured a single flag or a single gun. My losses are real, but the enemy can take no credit for them."[61] Statistics for both sides included the corpses of 430,707 men and 230,677 animals that were buried or burned where they fell.[62] The wounded, deserters, and prisoners more than doubled the number of casualties.

As 1813 dawned, Napoleon's two-front war came home to haunt him. Although reversals had taken place during the previous year solidifying French control of Spain, King Joseph I, Napoleon's brother, found himself foundering again. He evacuated Madrid and Valladolid, and finally he took a stand at Vitoria. Wellington's force was an Anglo-Portuguese and Spanish army numbering 95,000 men. Flanking Joseph's scattered and ill-directed soldiers, Wellington's men had little opposition. The French seemed incapable of doing anything right, and French troops simply fled. At the same time, Napoleon's reconstituted Grand Army of 170,000 men held its own in central Europe. In fact, at the battles of Lützen and Bautzen in May 1813, Napoleon achieved separate victories over the Russian and Prussian forces. The allies, however, wanted the contest to end. They turned to Napoleon's father-in-law, Francis I of Austria, who was not part of the Sixth Coalition yet. In his role as mediator, he proposed an armistice and laid out ground rules for peace. Regardless of the fact that French armies were undergoing reverses in Spain and that they were outnumbered in Europe, Napoleon refused to relinquish any of his conquests.

War or peace, Napoleon said, "did not depend on the cession of any part of [French] territory." War had been fueled by "the jealousy of the powers and the passions fomented by English cunning."[63] Again, the British were at fault, according to Napoleon, so there was no way he would engage in peace talks. As a result, the armies of Europe assembled. The main allied field army was composed of 240,000 Russian, Austrian, and Prussian troops. The allies of the Sixth Coalition could also count on the King of Sweden's 120,000 men, Prussian Field Marshal Gebhard von

Blücher's 95,000 men, and Benningson's Russo-Polish army of 60,000 men. They vowed to maintain a unified command under Prince Karl Philip von Schwarzenberg, and, regardless of circumstances, never to be drawn into battle alone against Napoleon. Napoleon could almost match their numbers with the Grand Army that he had increased to 250,000 men (although many were very young recruits), along with General Nicholas-Charles Oudinot's 70,000 soldiers, and 70,000 troops committed from the *Rheinbund.* In August, Napoleon defeated Schwarzenberg at Dresden, but the Austrians withdrew without giving the Grand Army an opportunity to inflict further casualties. At Leipzig, on October 16–18, 1813, the "Battle of the Nations" pitted 370,000 allied troops against Napoleon's 220,000. Napoleon could assemble no more men as the battle raged. The Bavarians changed sides, and Napoleon feared encirclement. Carefully, Napoleon began a phased and orderly withdrawal.

With his army still intact, Napoleon crossed the Rhine in November 1813, and the allied powers attempted anew to approach the French Emperor by offering him peace based on the natural frontiers of France. Napoleon again refused, although he knew the severity of his situation. "The point can be put in a nut-shell," he wrote to his brother Joseph, "France is invaded. All Europe is in arms against her, but more particularly against me."[64] But, Napoleon continued to fight, and according to historian Owen Connelly, he "fought the most brilliant campaigns of his life in early 1814."[65] He was, however, fighting exclusively a defensive war, and he had no grand strategy. Again, the allies attempted to negotiate. Even though the allied armies had entered French territories, they were prepared to allow French boundaries to be redrawn to the map of 1792. Napoleon again declined the offer by countering with one of his own. Although Napoleon had been able to hold off each of the allied armies on its own, by March 1814, they had joined to try to defeat him. He mobilized Paris, called up as many troops as he could, and intended to move forward to defend the capital from his position near Fontainebleau. He knew that the allies had 200,000 troops for the assault on Paris. He also knew that they were likely to reach the French capital before he could send support.

At 2:00 A.M. on March 31, 1814, the war of the Sixth Coalition finally ended. Citizens, national guardsmen, cadets from military academies, and a demoralized, leftover French army had been pressed back to the heights of Montmartre overlooking Paris. It was useless to hold out, and Marshal A.-F. Marmont, who was defending the city, defected with his troops. Without waiting for imperial orders, the commander of the remaining French troops surrendered. At Fontainebleau, Napoleon's other marshals and generals also refused to cooperate with the Emperor, and Napoleon was forced to abdicate.

Even then, Napoleon did not recognize the severity of what had occurred. On April 4, he abdicated in favor of his son, assuming that the French Empire would be spared. The allies, however, held all of the cards. Outside of Paris, nearly all of the French armies had given up their positions or were in such desperate situations that it was only a matter of time until they would capitulate. The allies demanded unconditional surrender, and two days later, Napoleon complied: "The Allied powers having proclaimed that the Emperor Napoleon is the only obstacle to the re-establishment of peace in Europe, the Emperor Napoleon, faithful to his oath, declares that he renounces, for himself and his heirs, the thrones of France and Italy."[66] On April 11, 1814, the provisions of the Treaty of Fontainebleau were set. Napoleon was granted sovereignty over the 86-square-mile island of Elba where he was also to hold the title of Emperor. He was also provided a substantial, annual stipend and allowed a military retinue of 600 men to accompany him into exile. As had been offered earlier, the boundaries of France were defined as of 1792. Savoy, Avignon along with other former papal territories in the south of France, and parts of Belgium and the Rhineland remained French. It is extraordinary that the treaties were so generous after more than a decade of war had consumed European powers on the continent and in their sometimes far-reaching territories. The settlement for Napoleon and France could have been far worse.

On the evening of April 12, a few days before Napoleon was to depart for Elba, he took the vial of poison that he had worn around his neck since the retreat from Russia and he drank its contents. The two-year-old mixture of opium, belladonna, and white hellebore made him violently ill, but he did not die. "What a task it is to die in bed," Napoleon said to the men who surrounded him.[67] Neither a sabre nor a cannon ball could kill him on the battlefield, and fate spared him one more time. The French and Napoleon had entered their twilight years—or had they? A legend was in the making.

Notes

The title of this chapter: "War Makes Rattling Good History" comes from Thomas Hardy's *The Dynasts*, quoted in Alistair Horne, *How Far from Austerlitz? Napoleon, 1805–1815* (New York: St. Martin's Press, 1996), xx.

1. Historically, France considered its natural frontiers to be the Channel (*La Manche*), the Bay of Biscay (Atlantic Ocean), the Pyrenees, the Mediterranean Sea, the Alps, and the Rhine River. Those natural frontiers framed France, creating what the French chauvinistically called their God-given hexagon. Natural frontiers had been a preoccupation of French wars since at least the time of Louis XIV, a century and a quarter before Napoleon.

2. The two field armies were the Army of Italy under General André Massena and the Army of the Rhine under General Jean-Victor Moreau. Both men were seasoned veterans and two of the finest French commanders. During the wars of the French Revolution and Napoleonic period, French armies were typically named for the region of their objective or where they served. For example, the Army of the Orient had been engaged in the Egyptian Campaign, and the Army of England was created at Boulogne to attack Britain. Beginning in 1805, when Napoleon was in command of a particular army, it was also called the Grand Army (see Chapter 5).

3. Napoleon to Cambacérès and Lebrun, *Correspondance* (1801), quoted in J. M. Thompson, *Napoleon Bonaparte* (Phoenix Mill, U.K.: Sutton Publishing Ltd., 2001), 161.

4. Owen Connelly, *Blundering to Glory: Napoleon's Military Campaigns* (Wilmington, Del.: A Scholarly Resources Imprint, 1987), 64; and David Chandler, *The Campaigns of Napoleon: The Mind and Method of History's Greatest Soldier* (New York: Macmillan Publishing Company, Inc., 1966), 285.

5. Chandler, *Campaigns of Napoleon*, 286–98.

6. Thompson, *Napoleon Bonaparte*, 164–65.

7. For a standard recipe for Chicken Marengo, see Irma S. Rombauer and Marion Rombauer Becker, *The Joy of Cooking* (New York: The Bobbs-Merrill Company, Inc., 1975), 427.

8. Connelly, *Blundering to Glory*, 71; "Lunéville, Treaty of," *Historical Dictionary of Napoleonic France, 1799–1815*, ed. Owen Connelly (Westport, Conn.: Greenwood Press, 1985), 316; and "Lunéville," in David Chandler, *Dictionary of the Napoleonic Wars: The Soldiers, Strategies, Armaments, Movements and Battles That Shaped Events During Napoleon's Reign* (New York: Macmillan Publishing Company, 1979), 256–57.

9. Chandler, *Campaigns of Napoleon*, 301.

10. "Amiens, Treaty of," *Historical Dictionary of Napoleonic France*, 16; and "Amiens," in Chandler, *Dictionary of Napoleonic Wars*, 10–11.

11. Connelly, *Blundering to Glory*, 71–72.

12. See Chapter 2 of this book, note 24.

13. Owen Connelly, *The Epoch of Napoleon* (Malabar, Fla.: Robert E. Krieger, 1972), 67.

14. Thompson, *Napoleon Bonaparte,* 227. Thompson's discussion of the Continental System contains one of the best datelines of this system of economic warfare between Great Britain and France. Officially dated from 1806, the Continental System did not officially end until Napoleon's abdication and repeal of the various laws that created it.

15. Ibid., 230.

16. J. Christopher Herold, *The Age of Napoleon* (Boston: Houghton Mifflin Company, 1987), 254.

17. Chandler, *Campaigns of Napoleon,* 390–92.

18. *Correspondance* XI: 342, quoted in ibid., 402.

19. For a short account of the Battle of Trafalgar, see Herold, *Age of Napoleon,* 239–44. See also "Trafalgar," in Chandler, *Dictionary of Napoleonic Wars,* 448–50, which includes a map of the position of each ship of each fleet.

20. General de Ségur, *Histoire et Mémoires* (Paris, 1837), 279, quoted in Chandler, *Campaigns of Napoleon,* 412.

21. Connelly, *Blundering to Glory,* 88.

22. "Pressburg, Treaty of," *Historical Dictionary of Napoleonic France,* 403–04; and "Pressburg," in Chandler, *Dictionary of Napoleonic Wars,* 348.

23. Napoleon to Joseph, December 3, 1805, quoted in *Napoleon's Letters: Selected, Translated, and Edited by J. M. Thompson* (London: Prion, 1998), 115.

24. Roger Dufraisse, *Napoleon* (New York: McGraw-Hill, Inc., 1992), 95.

25. Napoleon to Talleyrand, September 12, 1806, quoted in *Napoleon's Letters,* 138.

26. Chandler, *Campaigns of Napoleon,* 502.

27. Napoleon to Joséphine, October 13, 1806, quoted in *Napoleon's Letters,* 141.

28. Horne, *How Far from Austerlitz?,* 224–25.

29. Connelly, *The Epoch of Napoleon,* 68.

30. General Savary (as quoted by Bourienne), in Chandler, *Campaigns of Napoleon,* 586.

31. Herold, *Age of Napoleon,* 187.

32. "Tilsit, Treaties of," *Historical Dictionary of Napoleonic France,* 473; and "Tilsit," in Chandler, *Dictionary of the Napoleonic Wars,* 441–42.

33. After their first meeting at a ball in Warsaw, it was clear that Napoleon was smitten with Maria Walewska, who was married to an elderly Polish nobleman. He continually wrote to her, pledged his faithfulness, and pleaded with her to join him. Maria Walewska, who was equally enamored by the man who had tamed Europe, met Napoleon in Paris in 1808, then in Vienna in 1809, and in Paris again in 1810. Their child was born on May 11, 1810. Napoleon never forgot her, and their son Alexandre was provided for in the Emperor's *Last Will and Testament.*

34. For reasons of space, it is not possible to chronicle the problems of Pope Pius VII. French troops initially occupied the Papal States in February 1808 to shut out British goods. The situation grew increasingly difficult thereafter.

35. Emmanuel Dieudonné, comte de Las Cases, *Memoirs of the Life, Exile, and Conversations of the Emperor Napoleon* (New York: Worthington Company 1890) 2: 134.

36. Owen Connelly, *The French Revolution and Napoleonic Era* (Chicago: Holt, Rinehart and Winston, 1991), 246.

37. Ibid., 248.

38. Ibid., 249.

39. Sir John Moore, who commanded the British forces, found himself opposite Soult rather than Napoleon. In January of 1809, he reached Corunna, having been hounded across the mountains by French troops. Although Moore was killed in the Peninsula, most of his troops were safely removed by the British Navy.

40. See Alan Forrest, *Conscripts and Deserters: The Army and French Society during the Revolution and Empire* (New York: Oxford University Press, 1989) for further information.

41. Connelly, *French Revolution and Napoleonic Era,* 253.

42. Horne, *How Far from Austerlitz?,* 260–61.

43. Ibid., 350.

44. Austrian eyewitness quoted in ibid., 267.

45. Jean Lannes (1769–1809) had joined the French military in 1792. He was among the first 14 marshals named by the Emperor in 1804, and he was rewarded with the title Duke of Montebello in 1808. At Aspern-Essling, a cannon ball massively fractured his leg, which had to be amputated. A few days later, he died of gangrene. Lannes had seemed as invincible as the Emperor, having been wounded more times than any other marshal. As rarely as Napoleon showed serious emotion, he genuinely mourned the death of one of his earliest friends.

46. Horne, *How Far from Austerlitz?,* 273; and Connelly, *Blundering to Glory,* 142.

47. Napoleon to Joséphine, July 7, 1809, quoted in *Napoleon's Letters,* 210.

48. "Schönbrunn," in Chandler, *Dictionary of Napoleonic Wars,* 404; and Horne, *How Far from Austerlitz?,* 283.

49. Napoleon to the Ecclesiastical Committee and to Prince Borghèse, March 16, 1811 and May 21, 1812, quoted in *Napoleon's Letters,* 247 and 267.

50. Connelly, *French Revolution and Napoleonic Era,* 260.

51. Napoleon to Francis, Emperor of Austria, March 29, 1810, quoted in *Napoleon's Letters,* 232.

52. Napoleon to Louis Napoleon, December 21, 1809 and May 23, 1810, quoted in ibid., 227, 235.

53. Napoleon to the French Minister of Foreign Affairs November 4, 1810, quoted in ibid., 242.

54. Napoleon called the Russian Campaign the Second Polish War of Independence. The first, he said, had been fought at Friedland and concluded at Tilsit with the creation of the Duchy of Warsaw.

55. Napoleon to Barbier, December 19, 1811, quoted in *Napoleon's Letters*, 263.

56. Connelly, *French Revolution and Napoleonic Era*, 261.

57. Napoleon to Alexander, July 1, 1812, quoted in *Napoleon's Letters*, 270.

58. Horne, *How Far from Austerlitz?*, 316.

59. Connelly, *French Revolution and Napoleonic Era*, 323.

60. Ibid., 326.

61. Napoleon to Frederick VI, King of Denmark and Norway, January 5, 1813, quoted in *Napoleon's Letters*, 278.

62. Ibid., note, 279.

63. Napoleon to the Minister of War, September 27, 1813, quoted in ibid., 291.

64. Napoleon to Joseph, January 7, 1814, quoted in ibid., 296.

65. Connelly, *French Revolution and Napoleonic Era*, 335.

66. Napoleon to the Allied Powers, *Correspondance*, XXVII: 355–56, quoted in Chandler, *Campaigns of Napoleon*, 1002.

67. General Armand de Caulaincourt quoted in ibid., 1002.

CHAPTER 7

THE LEGEND OF THE EAGLE

Vive l'Empereur!

On April 20, 1813, Napoleon left Fontainebleau for Elba. He embraced members of his Old Guard, kissed the eagle-topped French regimental standard that was presented to him, and prepared for the exile that had been meted out by the powers of Europe. For 10 months—from early May 1813 until March 1, 1814—he was Emperor of Elba. He could do what he pleased. He reorganized nearly everything about the island, conducted his own coronation, designed a flag and livery for his kingdom, restructured the economy, built a system of education and social welfare, and reinvigorated industry. His mother and his sister Pauline visited him occasionally; his Polish mistress Maria Walewska and their three-year-old son joined him briefly. His Empire was comprised of 12,000 residents of Elba, and he had an army of 1,600 men and a navy of five ships. But, it was a far cry from Fontainebleau and the battlefields that had consumed nearly two decades of his life.[1]

The English Commissioner on Elba, Neil Campbell, was fascinated with what had become of Napoleon. "I have never seen a man in any situation in life with so much personal activity and restless perseverance," he wrote in his recollections.[2] Yet, few others in Europe noted Napoleon's impatience, his boredom, his annoyance, and his lack of resignation to his fate. Marie Louise and his son had not joined him in his exile. *L'Aiglon* or "The Young Eagle," as the King of Rome was called, was being reared in an enemy court because the former French empress had returned to her Austrian roots. Furthermore, Napoleon's 2 million-franc stipend that was guaranteed by the Treaty of Fontainebleau had not arrived. Louis XVIII, so recently restored to the French throne, appeared to be both hopeless and hapless when it came to understanding the postrevolutionary French. He was obese and gout-ridden. He had even been dubbed "Louis, the Unavoidable" by the allies, because there had been no one else to place on the throne of France. He had restored the Catholic Church and increased taxes. The rolls of the unemployed lengthened, the revolutionary tricolor ceased to fly over France, and he had imposed censorship to silence his critics. As Napoleon looked across the Mediterranean Sea that separated Elba from France, he chose his new path.

While the Congress of Vienna met to redraw the boundaries of Europe by eliminating the vestiges of the French Revolution and by wiping away the excesses of the Napoleonic period, Napoleon simply slipped away from Elba. He boarded the *Inconstant,* disguised as a British warship, and sailed for France, followed by seven smaller vessels carrying his troops. It was a legend in the making, and Napoleon was not disappointed by what occurred. Landing near Cannes, Napoleon and his men headed north to restore the First French Empire. Near Grenoble, royal troops met the Emperor; there, they refused to fire on him. After a momentary silence, "Vive l'Empereur! Vive l'Empereur!" greeted Napoleon's ears, and municipal officials opened wide the doors to the city. As Napoleon traversed the French countryside, troops fell in behind him. At Auxerre, Michel Ney, who had promised to bring him back to Paris "in an iron cage," gave up his oath. He was a Napoleonic marshal, after all, who had fought unfailingly with the Emperor. He would take his chances on a restoration of Napoleon I. Three weeks later, Napoleon was back in Paris, issuing a new constitution. He was heartened by the support of the French people: "In spite of all that is past, you see the people return to me," he reported to a close associate, "there is sympathy between us."[3] But, war clouds were immediately on the horizon.

The powers of Europe, meeting in Vienna, agreed not to allow Napoleon to retake his throne. Britain pledged troops and resources to defeat him, and the allies reestablished themselves as a military coalition. They planned a concerted assault on Napoleon and France, and even before he entered Paris, they outlawed Napoleon as "an Enemy and Disturber of the Tranquility of the World."[4] Napoleon's response was a letter to the sovereigns of Europe in which he pledged "an unqualified respect for the independence of other peoples."[5] Whether Napoleon's words were sincere or another example of propaganda did not matter because allied troops were already assembling near Brussels: Wellington with a multinational army of 107,000 men and Blücher with 123,000 Prussians. Austrian and Russian troops from across the continent were scheduled to join them later. The allied plan was to take Paris and crush French resolve one more time. Potentially the allies could field more than three-quarters of a million men if they could work together again. On the other side, Napoleon's quickly constructed Army of the North was composed of 128,000 men, some from the Restoration Army of Louis XVIII, some new recruits, and the majority seasoned veterans and men who had always followed Napoleon. In total, counting his field army, 300,000 troops were at Napoleon's disposal, and he had begun to mobilize the National Guard. The scale of the contest was immense, and the challenge was real. For further information about the Duke of Wellington, see the biographies at the end of this volume.

As it came to be, there was no grand strategy to the Waterloo Campaign. It was, in fact, painfully simple, and it hinged on well-proven principles of warfare. Napoleon had to be victorious over each of the armies that faced him, and he had to do so before they united and before additional allied forces joined them. As he had done before, he planned to use time and space to his advantage.[6] Quickly and quietly, he amassed his men almost under the noses of the allies. He hoped to count on their lack of attention and their errors, and Wellington immediately proved him correct. Just as Napoleon had contrived, the British and Prussian commanders did not concentrate their troops. They were on their own, and opportunity belonged to Napoleon. On June 16, the French met the Prussian advance at Ligny. There, the 72-year-old Prussian commander stood firm and refused to let the French get the best of him. His efforts, however, were unavailing. In desperation late in the day, Field Marshal Blücher personally led the charge against Napoleon's Imperial Guard. In the melee, his horse was killed beneath him; he was knocked unconscious and nearly trampled.[7] The Prussians had lost 34,000 men (casualties and deserters), and there was nothing they could do except retreat. Although Blücher was still missing on the battlefield, the Prussians began to retreat due north instead of to the east toward their line of communications as Napoleon had expected. The direction of the retreat was one of the most fortuitous decisions of the entire campaign, because rather than widening the gap between the allied armies, the retreat narrowed their distance.

Twenty miles away at Quatre Bras, also on June 16, Marshal Ney had attacked Wellington's army. Ney's orders were to control the cross-roads and block Wellington's movement toward Blücher. Initially every-thing was set for victory; Ney was positioned well and had numeric superiority. But, he did not press his troops to start the battle. By the end of the day after furious fighting, the tardy assault and miscommuni-cation about an entire corps left Ney with a draw. Casualties were nearly equal. Although Ney recovered the advantage, he did not resume fight-ing until a day later on the afternoon of June 17, when he believed that he would finish off Wellington's army. Unknown to the French, Welling-ton had already moved his troops, except for some cavalry and rear guard, toward the ridge at Mont-St.-Jean, just south of Waterloo. It was a rude surprise to both Ney and Napoleon when they discovered the British commander's feint. Wellington's forces were now a much more organized and established foe, and the Prussians were within ample dis-tance to support them.

Ney's lethargy and misjudgment had, for all intents and purposes, allowed Wellington to choose the battlefield for the next encounter on June 18. Yet, there was still nothing to suggest to Napoleon that victory would not be his. Napoleon had artillery and troop superiority—72,000 men to Wellington's 68,000 men—and he had sent Marshal Emmanuel Grouchy to pursue the Prussians after Ligny. Overlooking the field at Waterloo, he confidently told his men that they would sleep in Brussels that night.

Across a three-mile stretch of slightly undulating hills and along a line of fortified farms, Wellington had established his defensive position. Wellington chose to be patient; he would await Napoleon's assault rather than opening the battle. Not until nearly the middle of the day did Napo-leon send his troops forward. He had chosen to let the water-soaked ground dry and harden to maintain his artillery superiority, including the deadly ricocheting capacity of his solid shot. In the final analysis, however, the choice was "a moment lost," and the time could never be recovered.

The battle of Waterloo began with a diversionary bombardment and attack on the left (at the Château of Hougoumont). The diversion had been designed to draw Wellington's troops to reinforce the chateau and weaken the center of the Anglo-Dutch line. Then, Napoleon planned for French troops to make their major assault on Wellington's

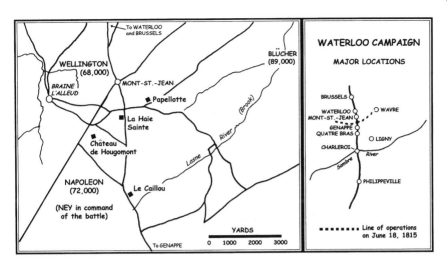

Map 7.1 The Waterloo Campaign and the Battle of Waterloo, June 18, 1815

center, press through, and take Brussels. From the beginning, however, the battle of Waterloo did not proceed as planned, and military historians, who have studied the contest in minute detail, can find innumerable causes. It appeared that French commanders, including Napoleon, were bent on forgetting the Emperor's principles of warfare—one by one. Besides the late timing of the assault, Napoleon did not know the lay of the land. Almost immediately at Hougoumont, the French were forced to strengthen their position besieging the fortified farm, rather than concentrating on breaking the enemy line as was their objective. Furthermore, the French line of operations was not maintained as it should have been; it wavered and curved across the battlefield. Later Ney mistimed his assault on the center, squandered men in assault after assault, and sent cavalry without infantry support against British squares. Grouchy, on whom Napoleon counted, failed to keep the main Prussian forces from aiding Wellington, and when Napoleon needed Grouchy's men most, the marshal never marched toward the sound of the drums. Principle after principle of warfare was lost.

The worst occurred late in the afternoon of June 18 when three Prussian corps arrived. Napoleon responded by strengthening his right against the Prussians. He furiously sought Grouchy, and then he hastened to support Ney's final assault. The French troops were now numerically inferior, they could not be concentrated any further, and

Napoleon committed the remainder of his Reserve. Toward 8:00 P.M., the last of the Imperial Guard met the British. Surprised and massively outnumbered, they retreated, and with them the French army broke and fled. It was a harrowing scene; the battle was over. At Genappe, south of the battlefield, French troops continued to flee before the Prussians. It was ghastly.

> Between the houses of the village, the road ran downhill to a bridge across the river Dyle. The bridge was only eight feet wide, just enough for a single wagon. The army poured into the top of the street and was carried down the hill by its own momentum: but it could only filter slowly out across the bridge at the bottom. First the bridge and then the whole of the street was blocked, and thousands upon thousands of men were crushed among the forage and baggage wagons which had halted there. In terror of what they imagined was coming behind them, men tried to cut their way through, horsemen slashed with their swords, infantry used their bayonets, shots were fired. They killed and maimed each other without making any progress: the living were only hampered by the dead.[8]

For the wounded on the battlefield, during the night, the looting and killing continued. The next morning, peasants collected clothing that had not been taken during the night; and sightseers, sometimes with perfumed handkerchiefs over their noses, gathered to look at the carnage. Finally, nearly 24 hours after the battle had ended, the wounded were cared for as the field of battle was cleared.[9]

The French army was in disarray and the battlefield provided grisly reality, yet Napoleon called Waterloo only a "disastrous skirmish." In denial about the extent of the defeat, Napoleon planned to raise a new army, even if he had to "drag the guns [with] carriage-horses," commandeer weapons from former Royalists, and continue the campaign to save and restore France. "There is still time to retrieve the situation," he wrote to his brother Joseph on June 19.[10]

This time Napoleon was wrong. Although his Minister of War was rallying troops to defend Paris and some 117,000 men were available, the French legislative body refused to support Napoleon. They had decided to save France themselves, rather than to put their trust in the once legendary Emperor. By June 21, Napoleon was in Paris pleading with his former marshals and ministers; but Fouché controlled the day, and Napoleon was forced to abdicate. He dallied at Malmaison

(Joséphine's former home), gathered some possessions and a new traveling library, and contemplated fleeing to America, which was his brother Joseph's destination. Instead, fearful that Blücher and the Prussians would capture him, Napoleon surrendered to the British on the *Bellerophon*. A day earlier, he had written to the Prince Regent of England, whom he regarded "as the strongest, the stubbornest, and the most generous of my foes." He had "put [himself] under the protection of British law" to avoid his less charitable enemies. He wrote, "Your Royal Highness: victimized by the factions which divide my country, and by the hostility of the European powers, I have ended my political career; and I come, as Themistocles did, to claim a seat by the hearth of the British people."[11]

Again, Napoleon was wrong. No gentleman's hearth awaited him. While he paraded on the deck of the British ship and engaged the ship's staff and crew in conversation, his fate was sealed even more surely. He was declared a prisoner of war to be transported to St. Helena where he would remain until his death. He was simply General Bonaparte, who had been defeated by the allies of Europe.

I Glimpsed an Eagle

Stendhal's novel, *The Charterhouse of Parma* (1839), arrived on the European scene one year before Napoleon's body was returned to Paris and nearly two decades after the Emperor's death. In the book, the reader meets Stendhal's young romantic character Fabrizio del Dongo at the time he heard the news of Napoleon's return from Elba in 1815. Europe was at war again. As Fabrizio contemplated his changing life, he looked up: "Suddenly, high in the sky to my right, I glimpsed an eagle—Napoleon's bird; it was soaring majestically toward Paris. I then resolved to offer that great man little enough but all I have."[12] Stendhal's fictional character then joined the Emperor's troops at Waterloo where he discovered war amid musket balls, cannonballs, smoke, and the fury of the battlefield. He had joined a man of destiny.

On May 5, 1821, the man of destiny died. Having been ill for months, Napoleon succumbed to what appeared at the time to be stomach cancer, the disease of his father.[13] He had grown pudgy, his stomach was distended, and he was in pain most of the time. He had given up most of his diversions—his walks, gardening, and card games of Piquet and Twenty-one. He had known that his life was drawing to an end; and only a few weeks before his death, he had dictated most of the significant passages of his last will and testament. The will was, for all those who read it, a statement of his life, his politics, and his legend. He wanted to be remembered as a good Catholic, a good father to his son and to the French people, a man whose largesse was unlimited, and a man who died "prematurely assassinated by the English oligarchy."[14] In the lengthy will and its codicils, he remembered each of his loyal retainers, specified rewards and pensions to the anonymous French soldiers who had given their lives and limbs for him, and chastised those who had deserted him. The will was, in fact, as much a personal memoir as many of his other writings. See Document 10: *Napoleon's Last Will and Testament.*

As news spread of Napoleon's death, responses were mixed. "What an event!" an admirer in Paris remarked. On the other hand, Talleyrand noted, "it is no longer an event, it is *only* a piece of news."[15] Talleyrand, however, was quite mistaken. As the years passed after Napoleon's death on St. Helena in 1821, the event was firmly imprinted on the collective memory of Europe and the sides lined up. There were writers, like Stendhal, who praised Napoleon; and there were those who saw him as an anti-Christ, a demon Emperor, an ogre, a bloody villain, a megalomaniac, and a tyrant who would not allow Europe to find peace. Others saw him as the son of the Revolution, a man who had unfortunately been corrupted by power before he could fully achieve his aim, and a modern Prometheus. Both a black legend and a more generous, sometimes hagiographic, legend defined the former Emperor.[16] In some cases, the legend came directly from the Emperor's exile. Always attempting to be in control, he had dictated voluminous memoirs to a handful of retainers who had gone to St. Helena with him. In total, only 27 people had been allowed to accompany Napoleon in his exile; yet, of those, 11 left memoirs or records that were published during their lifetimes or later. The first was published in 1822 immediately after his death.[17] See the biographies at the end of this volume for information on Las Cases who joined Napoleon during his exile and who published one of the best-known sets of memoirs of the Emperor.

Napoleon had also aroused the interest of a wealth of nineteenth-century writers: Leo Tolstoy, Lord Byron, Sir Walter Scott, William Makepeace Thackery, Thomas Hardy, Samuel Taylor Coleridge, William

Wordsworth, Percy Bysshe Shelley, Alexandre Dumas, Heinrich Heine, François René Chateaubriand, Honoré de Balzac, and Victor Hugo. Later Rudyard Kipling, George Bernard Shaw, and Anatole France joined the list.[18] Even musicians were not immune. During his lifetime Ludwig van Beethoven had dedicated a symphony to Napoleon and then withdrawn the dedication, and in 1880 Pëtr Tchaikovsky had composed the *1812 Overture* chronicling Napoleon's Russian Campaign.[19]

In Napoleon's expansion across Europe, he had also inspired nationalism—not so much because he wanted it, but because it was waiting to be born. The Poles cited him as their liberator, although he had never fulfilled his promises to them. Nonetheless, the Duchy of Warsaw existed to be the basis of the rebirth of Poland after World War I. Germans, like Johann von Goethe, found inspiration in his genius, and the Confederation of the Rhine became the foundation of modern Germany. By the mid-nineteenth century, Napoleon had been reborn as another *persona*. He had become a leader of the masses, the man who not only brought order out of the chaos of the Revolution, but who had brought the benefits of the Revolution to the descendants of his imperium. Representatives at the Congress of Vienna, who had attempted to expunge the Revolution and Napoleonic period from the map and memory of Europe, had done no such thing.[20]

Even existing political regimes were not exempt from Napoleonic influence. King Louis-Philippe (1830–1848), whose problems in France had increased in the 1830s although he had come to the throne of the French through revolution, attempted to capitalize on the resurgence of Bonapartism that he could not stem. In 1840, he authorized a meticulously planned exhumation of Napoleon's remains from the unmarked grave on St. Helena and then staged an elaborate funeral for Napoleon in Paris. He was responding to Napoleon's will that had left a simple message: "I wish my ashes to rest beside the Seine, in the midst of the French nation I have loved so dearly."[21] The ceremony was extravagant as six horses pulled the hearse carrying Napoleon's remains under the Arc de Triomphe and down the Champs-Elysées. To the sound of cannon and bells, the hearse crossed the Seine and delivered Napoleon to the site of his final resting place. Briefly in Louis-Philippe's Paris, the declining economy and labor disputes were forgotten. Old soldiers pinned on their medals of the Legion of Honor and shared war stories. A resurgence of nostalgia greeted the popular imagination. The theatrics, however, were not enough to save Louis-Philippe's throne, and France returned to revolution in 1848.

Historical memory was not lost on Hitler who tried a similar, although less grandiose, maneuver in 1941. While Napoleon's remains rested on the banks of the Seine, Napoleon's son had never been reunited with him. In an effort to bring the French into his fold, Hitler sent back to Paris the ashes of Napoleon's son, who had been interred in Austria over a century earlier. L'Aiglon, who was also called the Duke of Reichstadt in his mother's homeland, was soon buried near Napoleon's massive sarcophagus at Les Invalides.[22] Interestingly, Hitler's very politically charged action did not have its desired outcome. No imperial aura miraculously surrounded the Führer for returning what the French believed was theirs anyway. Writers, however, began to compare Napoleon and Hitler, particularly for the extent of their empires. "The resemblances are too striking," wrote Pieter Geyl, whose Napoleon: For and Against was published in 1949. By 1942, German tanks and troops were extending themselves from North Africa to the gates of Moscow, and Hitler had created the Third Reich through centralization, censorship, and the powerful manipulation of public opinion. For all of the superficial comparisons and parallels, Geyl did not push the comparison. "History does not repeat itself," he reported.[23] Similarly, in Henry Kissinger's less than flattering portrayal of Napoleon in A World Restored, he firmly asserted that Napoleon was no Hitler.[24] Although Europe could not live at peace with Napoleon, he had not built his empire on the exclusion and annihilation of designated peoples.

In conclusion, it may be fitting to turn one more time to Napoleon's own words. "I have closed the gaping abyss of anarchy, and I have unscrambled chaos," he told Las Cases in 1816. "I have cleansed the Revolution, ennobled the common people, and restored the authority of kings. I have stirred all men to competition, I have rewarded merit wherever I found it, I have pushed back the boundaries of greatness."[25] Leaving aside Napoleon's penchant for hyperbole, his reconstruction of France and the French codes had been immense; he had endorsed the revolutionary principle of civil equality, and no one refused to accept the Legion of Honor during his lifetime. He had also planned to create a federation of Europe: "a European code; a court of European appeal, with full powers to redress all wrong decisions, as ours redresses at home those of our tribunals. Money of the same value but with different coins;

the same weights, the same measure, the same laws, etc."[26] He had, in fact, made impressive strides to that end—adding 28 departments to France in a period of 10 years from territory annexed from the Dutch, Germans, Piedmontese, Italians, and Swiss. It is not surprising that nearly every article published recently on the European Union references Napoleon's plan. Yet, the Treaty of Maastricht had something quite different in mind. Napoleon's federation of Europe would have been dominated by the French; while the European Union is based on common citizenship, a common economic and foreign policy, a monetary union, and equality of states within the union, *no* country is to have hegemony over the others.[27] Napoleon would have been incapable of accepting that model.

In the final analysis, Napoleon was both ahead of his time and behind in recognizing the extent of the changes that had swept across France because of the French Revolution and across Europe because of his armies, occupations, and annexations. He stood with one foot firmly planted in the past and one solidly placed in the future. He was both the model of an eighteenth-century enlightened despot and the creator of the modern powerful, centralized state. In fact, his reign was filled with contradictions that he might not have escaped if peace had been assured. Napoleon's gigantic undertaking had failed, and with it his personal ambition remained unfulfilled.[28] But, the French never erased his presence. Although there is only one street named for him in Paris (*rue* Bonaparte), the city itself is a monument to the Emperor: Les Invalides, the Vendôme column, the Arc de Triomphe, the home of the Legion of Honor, monuments to his loyal marshals in Père Lachaise Cemetery, the names of the splendid boulevards, the avenues that radiate from l'Etoile (the location of the Arc de Triomphe), and a score of other reminders. Even his detractors could not ignore his accomplishments. "The Emperor took a hand in everything; his mind never rested," wrote Chateaubriand in his *Memoirs*. "Bonaparte is not great by virtue of his words, speeches, his writings, or by virtue of a love of liberty; he is great in that he created a solid and powerful government, a code of laws adopted in various countries, courts of law, schools, and a strong, active and intelligent administration on which we are still living."[29] While Chateaubriand had been scandalized by the casualties that France had incurred during the wars, he also lived in a world that had changed dramatically, in many ways for the better. Graveyards had indeed grown, but

Napoleon's soldiers had remained loyal, even choosing to fight with him for a second chance.

In 1813, even before the legend had been firmly established, one of Napoleon's own men had indicated to the Emperor who he was. He said: "Ah! Sire, some say you are a god, others, that you are a devil, but everyone allows you are more than a man."[30] The statement still rings true.

Notes

1. See Norman MacKenzie, *The Escape from Elba: The Fall and Flight of Napoleon, 1814–1815* (New York and Toronto: Oxford University Press, 1982).

2. Alistair Horne, *How Far from Austerlitz?: Napoleon, 1805–1815* (New York: St. Martin's Press, 1996), 357.

3. "Conversation of Napoleon at the Tuileries with Benjamin Constant, during the Hundred Days," in David L. Dowd, *Napoleon: Was He the Heir of the Revolution?* (Hinsdale, Ill.: Dryden Press, 1957), 12.

4. Owen Connelly, *The French Revolution and Napoleonic Era* (Fort Worth: Holt, Rinehart and Winston, Inc., 1991), 342.

5. Napoleon to the Sovereigns of Europe, April 4, 1815, quoted in *Napoleon's Letters: Selected, Translated, and Edited by J. M. Thompson* (London: Prion, 1988), 313.

6. Among his famous quotes is the following: "Space we can recover, time never." See David Chandler, *The Campaigns of Napoleon* (New York: Macmillan Publishing Co., Inc., 1966), 149.

7. Horne, *How Far from Austerlitz?*, 370.

8. David Howarth, *Waterloo: Day of Battle* (New York: Galahad Books, 1968), 198–99.

9. Ibid., 208–16.

10. Napoleon to Joseph, June 19, 1815, quoted in *Napoleon's Letters*, 314.

11. Napoleon to the Prince Regent of England, July 14, 1815, quoted in ibid., 315.

12. Stendhal, *The Charterhouse of Parma* (New York: Random House, 1999), 27.

13. J. M. Thompson, *Napoleon Bonaparte* (Phoenix Mill, U.K.: Sutton, 2001), 402. Sten Forshufvud and Ben Weider, however, have conducted extensive research in an effort to prove that Napoleon was poisoned. According to *The Murder of Napoleon* (1982) and later research based on samples of Napoleon's hair, the most likely assassin was the Count of Montholon who also resided at Longwood on St. Helena and who had ample opportunity. Historians, including David Chandler and Alan Schom, now view poisoning as the cause of his death. Other historians, including most French historians, remain convinced that stomach cancer was the cause of death. A recent French response

can be found in *Le Monde hebdomadaire* (November 5, 2002) citing a study conducted by Pierre Chevalier at the Laboratoire pour l'utilisation du rayonnement électronique (LURE) at Orsay, France.

14. Jean-Pierre Babelon and Suzanne d'Huart, *Napoleon's Last Will and Testament* (New York and London: Paddington Press, Ltd., 1977), 36–90.

15. Horne, *How Far from Austerlitz?*, 378.

16. Geoffrey Brunn, *Europe and the French Imperium, 1799–1814* (London and New York: Harper & Brothers Publishers, 1938), 250; and Jean Tulard, *Napoleon: The Myth of the Saviour* (London: Weidenfield and Nicholson, 1984). See also Sir Walter Scott, *The Life of Napoleon Bonaparte, Emperor of the French* (New York: Leavitt and Allen, 1858). The original biography was published in nine volumes in 1827.

17. Susan Conner, "St. Helena and the Napoleonic Legend," in *Napoleonic Military History: A Bibliography*, ed. Donald D. Horward (New York: Garland Publishing, Inc., 1986), 539–79. See also Chapter XXIV, "St. Helena" in Volume IX of *The Cambridge Modern History* (Cambridge: Cambridge University Press, 1969).

18. This list is drawn from Connelly, *The French Revolution and Napoleonic Era,* 350, note 16; and Frank McLynn, "Bliss was that dawn: Another year, another batch of books about Napoleon," abstract of an article in *The New Statesman* (December 17, 2001).

19. Beethoven's symphony *Eroica* was first dedicated to Napoleon until the composer learned that the First Consul had crowned himself Emperor. Tchaikovsky's *1812 Overture* lays out the Russian Campaign through the national anthems of Russia and France. During his Empire, however, Napoleon never used "La Marseillaise."

20. As much as possible, the provisions of the Congress of Vienna laid out *status quo ante*. See Norman Hampson, *The First European Revolution, 1776–1815* (New York: W. W. Norton, 1969), 175 ff. By the Second Treaty of Paris, France returned to prerevolutionary boundaries (losing even more territory than Napoleon had gained for the French state). France was required to pay an indemnity, and an occupation army remained on French soil. Elsewhere, as the boundaries of Europe were redrawn, restoration and legitimacy were key words, but the Congress of Vienna also sought to build a strong buffer against France. Territorial exchanges benefited the victors of the Napoleonic wars.

21. Babelon and d'Huart, *Napoleon's Last Will and Testament,* 36.

22. Roger Dufraisse, *Napoleon* (New York: McGraw-Hill, Inc., 1992), 155.

23. See Pieter Geyl, *Napoleon: For and Against* (New Haven and London: Yale University Press, 1949), 8; and Desmond Seward, *Napoleon and Hitler: A Comparative Biography* (New York: Simon & Schuster, Inc. Touchstone Book, 1988), 9–16. Geyl concluded that comparisons between Napoleon and Hitler made Napoleon appear far less "evil" than the black legend had painted him. Seward argues that their parallels are very strong: "What united them at their zenith was the demonic process of corruption by power."

24. Henry Kissinger, *A World Restored* (Gloucester, Mass.: Peter Smith, 1973), 331.

25. Conversation (1816) quoted in *The Mind of Napoleon: A Selection from His Written and Spoken Words, Edited and Translated by J. Christopher Herold* (New York: Columbia University Press, 1955), 332.

26. "Dictation of Napoleon to Las Cases at St. Helena, August 24 1816," quoted in Geyl, *Napoleon: For and Against,* 16.

27. Treaty of Maastricht, printed by the European Documentation Center, http://www.uni_mannheim.de.

28. Geyl, *Napoleon: For and Against,* 446.

29. François-Auguste-René, vicomte de Chateaubriand, *The Memoirs of Chateaubriand,* ed. Robert Baldick (New York: Alfred A. Knopf, 1961), 296, 301.

30. Narbonne to Napoleon (1813) quoted in George Gordon Andrews, *Napoleon in Review* (New York: Alfred A. Knopf, 1939), 280.

BIOGRAPHICAL SKETCHES: SIGNIFICANT PERSONS IN THE AGE OF NAPOLEON

Fouché, Joseph (1760–1820)

Joseph Fouché was among the best known of Napoleon's ministers, having served as Minister of General Police from the time of Napoleon's coup d'état on 18 Brumaire until September 1802 and again from June 1804 until July 1810. Quintessentially a policeman, Fouché was known for having his eye on everything. He oversaw governmental censorship, controlled the press, and created a secret police. He was widely feared for the information he collected and the way he used it to ferret out spies, conspirators, opposition leaders, other ministers, and even generals.

Born the son of a merchant sailor, Fouché studied for the ministry, although he was never ordained. He entered politics, voted for the death of the king, and served in the provinces during the Jacobin period, routing out counterrevolutionaries and overseeing mass executions. In July 1794, he was among the Thermidorians who overthrew Robespierre, and he continued to survive during the Directory period as a military agent, plenipotentiary, and ambassador.

At the time of Napoleon's coup, Fouché had recently returned to Paris as Minister of General Police, a position he continued under the First Consul. The position was broadly defined: the surveillance of public opinion; the suppression of crimes and misdemeanors; provisioning (internal commerce); overseeing traffic, streets, and health; and monitoring foreigners and émigrés. When Fouché described what he did, he said simply that he had been designated "to observe everyone and everything." Within a year he was known for the speed with which he brought to justice the authors of the Infernal Machine plot, who had attempted to kill Napoleon. Using the press, posters, and agents on the street, his police machinery was ubiquitous; and he soon became known for his legion of police informants (*mouchards* or snitches) who were paid out of a special fund that he managed allegedly from gambling and prostitution. By the fall of 1802, he had files on nearly everyone in politics, including two of Napoleon's brothers. Napoleon determined to bring him into check; and with peace assured by the Peace of Amiens, Fouché's position was eliminated.

Less than two years later, Fouché's expertise was needed to deal with the Cadoudal Plot that threatened Napoleon and his government. Clandestinely, efficiently, and meticulously, his agents infiltrated the plot. The result was a massive purge of royalist opposition and one potential military rival to Napoleon, along with the death of the duc d'Enghien. Even though Fouché did not support the death of the duc d'Enghien, Napoleon rewarded Fouché for his work. His position as Minister of General Police was re-created, and he quickly moved again to establish his network of police, secret police, agents, and spies throughout the Empire. By 1809 he was a power to be reckoned with; and while Napoleon was on campaign in Austria, he called up the National Guard and assigned its command to one of Napoleon's marshals to repel the British troops that had landed at Walcheren. Napoleon awarded him the title of duc d'Otrante, but Napoleon knew that he could not allow one of his ministers to raise an army that might ultimately be used against him. In July 1810, using his own agents, Napoleon had proof that Fouché was dealing with the Bourbons. Fouché fled, remaining for the most part out of politics until Napoleon's Hundred Days when interestingly he returned to his position with the Emperor. As soon as the defeat at Waterloo was known, Fouché went to work choreographing Napoleon's second abdication, a role that provided him with a position under the restored Louis XVIII. He remained there only briefly until he was sent in an official capacity to Dresden and finally to Trieste where he died.

Joséphine [Marie-Joseph-Rose de Tascher de La Pagerie de Beauharnais] (1763–1814)

Reigning empress of France from 1804 until her divorce from the Emperor in December 1809, Joséphine married Napoleon in 1796 when he was General Bonaparte, commander-in-chief of the Army of Italy.

Although she had been called Rose throughout her life, at Napoleon's request she became Joséphine. The early years of their marriage were stormy, but by 1799, Joséphine had settled into a comfortable role as doyenne of the court and confidante to her husband.

Described as a stunning Creole from the West Indies (Martinique), Joséphine first married a viscount and bore him two children by the time of the Revolution. The viscount, who was a political liberal, served in the revolutionary government until term limits returned him to military service. Although he initially gained rapid promotions, his victories were short-lived, and he was drummed out of the army, arrested, and executed in 1794. Very quickly, Joséphine had also been imprisoned and then widowed. When the Jacobins fell from power, the widow Beauharnais remained in Paris with her two children, frequenting salon society and being linked amorously with several of the members of the Directory. It was in that society that Napoleon met her. Unaware of her alleged sexual liaisons, Napoleon found her to be one of the most fascinating beauties of the day. Furthermore, he believed her to be rich and politically savvy when he asked her to marry him in March of 1796, just prior to his departure for northern Italy.

During the first months of their marriage, Napoleon wrote lovesick letters to Joséphine, sometimes twice daily. She was "the flame that burned incessantly" at his heart, his "tormentor," and his love. He wore his infatuation on his sleeve and all but drove his commanders crazy with his incessant references to Joséphine. As far as she was concerned, while Napoleon was on campaign, she preferred to be among her friends and companions in Paris, including her young amour Hippolyte Charles. She only joined Napoleon in Italy when forced to do so. During Napoleon's Egyptian campaign, her indiscretions and infidelity finally came to haunt her. He took a mistress in Egypt and returned to France in 1799 planning to divorce Joséphine. Her children's pleas and her tears drove him to reconciliation.

By 1804 she had become empress of France, a role that she fulfilled impeccably, although Napoleon's family never approved of their marriage. With her Old Regime manners and style, she oversaw the *système* that merged Napoleon's new nobility with the émigrés who had returned after amnesty was granted to them. When Napoleon was on campaign, Joséphine was now tucked away at her estate at Malmaison, outside of Paris. Never again was there any suspicion of infidelity, but Joséphine also did not bear Napoleon the heir that he desired and he was always piqued at her overspending. After a number of his own affairs, the last being Napoleon's relationship with Maria Walewska in 1809, and several illegitimate children, Napoleon made plans to divorce Joséphine. As 1810 dawned, Napoleon was free to remarry. According to witnesses to the events, Napoleon's separation from his empress was filled with tears. Napoleon, after all, had grown to rely on her constancy, her tasteful manners, and the quiet role that she played behind the throne. She retained her title and received a grant of 3 million francs per year, along with several properties including Malmaison. She retained a staff of 36 persons and all of the art and furnishings that she and Napoleon had previously collected for the estate.

In the end, Joséphine finished her days at Malmaison where she died on May 29, 1814, while Napoleon was in exile on Elba. According to witnesses at St. Helena, her name was still on Napoleon's lips in the days just prior to his death in 1821.

Junot, Laure-Adélaïde-Constance Permon, duchesse d'Abrantès (1784–1838)

Laure Junot, who married one of Napoleon's companions and friends, was a participant in revolutionary salon society in her youth and one of the best-known members of Napoleonic court society during the First Empire. In the 1830s, she received renewed recognition as a novelist and memoirist. Her chatty, gossipy, and sometimes acerbic descriptions of the Napoleonic period were incredibly popular upon their publication, and they continue to be a staple for historians and writers even today.

Born into Byzantine nobility (although many generations removed), Laure Permon was raised in revolutionary salon society by her mother, a Corsican expatriate. Her mother's Parisian salon became a frequent respite for men like Saliceti, Bonaparte, and her future husband Jean-Andoche Junot. There, still in her teens, she met Napoleon who appeared somewhat short to her, almost buried in his knee-high military boots. He was forever Puss in Boots to her, and she was Loulou or Laurette to him. Later she recalled Bonaparte's alleged proposal of marriage to her mother, who was almost twice his age, as he attempted to solidify his position in Directory society. Mme Permon turned him down, and he moved on to Joséphine.

In 1800, Laure Permon married Junot, who was then Napoleon's aide-de-camp and commandant of Paris. The ceremony was lavish for the 16-year-old, who took on new pretensions as part of that circle of society. After participating in the opening of the imperial court, Mme Junot followed her husband to Portugal where he had been appointed ambassador. Her recollections of Portuguese society were less than generous, perhaps even mean-spirited. She found fashion ridiculous, etiquette lacking, and no one particularly handsome. Returning to Paris after the French defeat at Trafalgar, Junot began his tenure as governor of Paris (1806) where he continued to be extravagant, hot-headed, and not particularly distinguished. Mme Junot, however, became one of the most sought-after hostesses. In the meanwhile Junot returned to Portugal to expel its ruling family, and in the process earned his title as duc d'Abrantès, joining Napoleon's new nobility. When Junot failed to keep control of Portugal and was forced to capitulate at Cintra, he rejoined his wife in Paris.

Their marriage was strained, their debts were increasing, and both of them courted disaster in their personal relationships. Junot was linked to Caroline, Napoleon's sister, and Mme Junot became embroiled in intrigue and scandal with the Austrian foreign minister Clemens von Metternich. Enough was enough, and Napoleon demanded that Mme Junot accompany her husband to the Peninsula in 1810. Entering Spain, she commented on the despoliation of the guerrilla contest, and she experienced firsthand the horrors of war as she traveled with the French army to the borders of Portugal. In the ruins of Ciudad Rodrigo she even gave birth to her son. The Peninsula was far from her privileged life in Paris.

When Junot died in 1813 after a bout of insanity and a suicide attempt, the duchess became a recluse. When Napoleon returned to power in 1815, she refused to see him; and he made no efforts to reconcile with the woman whom he had dubbed the "Little Pest." During the Restoration (Louis XVIII), she overspent on everything, selling most of her belongings just to have flowers on her table. In 1830, with the assistance of Honoré de Balzac, she began her memoirs. Between the publication of her writings in 1831 and her death, she wrote over three dozen volumes. Although she frequently erred about particular facts because she had not kept careful notes, her works were immediately popular. No one seemed to be able to match her flamboyant use of language, interesting turns of phrases, candor, familiarity with imperial society—both military and civilian—and sometimes shocking analyses of people and events during the Empire. Nonetheless, she continued to overspend; and she died in poverty in Paris in 1838. Although the reader must always check her facts, *Les Mémoires de la Duchesse d'Abrantès* remain one of the most colorful portraits of the Napoleonic period. Among the early English translations are *Memoirs of Napoleon, His Court and Family by the Duchesse d'Abrantès* (1855) and *Secret Memoirs and Chronicles of the Courts of Europe: The Memoirs of Emperor Napoleon* (1901).

Las Cases, Emmanuel Augustin Dieudonné, comte de (1766–1842)

Sharing Napoleon's exile on St. Helena from 1815 until his expulsion from the island in 1816, the Comte de Las Cases was in the enviable position of having daily access to Napoleon as the former Emperor considered how he wished posterity to remember him. In 1823, less than two years after Napoleon's death, Las Cases published the *Mémorial de Sainte-Hélène*, based on Napoleon's dictations to him. The *Mémorial* was immediately well received and widely quoted by admirers of Napoleon, and it remains one of the most important contributions to the Napoleonic Legend even today.

According to contemporaries of Las Cases, his choice of exile on St. Helena with the former Emperor was unexpected. Almost everything in Las Cases' past would have placed him with the royalist cause. When the French Revolution began in 1789, Las Cases was far from a revolutionary. In fact, he was a marquis who owned significant land and had served in the Royal Navy. He was among the first of the émigrés to leave France, and he served the counterrevolution until his return to France after 18 Brumaire and Napoleon's amnesty. His life was undistinguished, and he went unnoticed publicly until the publication of an important work on geography that also restored his fortune. It was not until 1809, however, that he gained notice in the French military when he volunteered in the defense of Holland against the British (Walcheren). After receiving rewards for his service, Napoleon invited Las Cases to serve as chamberlain in the court of Marie Louise in 1810. He then went with the Emperor to Russia and retired to England during Napoleon's first exile. He returned shortly later and entered Napoleon's service during the Hundred Days.

When Napoleon announced his second abdication, Las Cases was in the first ranks to pledge his loyalty. He then volunteered with his 15-year-old son to "have the honor of experiencing the trials of exile" with the Emperor. Other members of Napoleon's companions in exile, however, found Las Cases less sincere than he purported. They described him stereotypically as a small man who had attached himself to a great man ultimately to profit from the relationship. Regardless of Las Cases' motives, his multivolume work became a best seller. Published first in 1831, the *Mémorial* went through a second printing that same year. The following year another edition came out, followed by a 28-volume version beginning in 1830. Other editions appeared in 1835 (2 volumes), 1840 (5 volumes), and 1842 (2 volumes). Following Las Cases' death, reissued versions were printed in 1862, 1894, 1935, and 1951.

The *Mémorial de Sainte-Hélène* follows Napoleon on his walks around Longwood estate on St. Helena, takes him back to his youthful inspiration by Rousseau, engages him in reminiscences about court life and the reorganization of France, and lays out some of the former Emperor's most famous maxims and quotations. According to the *Mémorial,* Napoleon brought order out of chaos; he was a military genius, a champion of peace, a victim of the British, and a tireless supporter of the French people. In the introduction, Las Cases set forward his position: "Circumstances extraordinary have long kept me near the most remarkable man that ever lived. Admiration made me follow. . . . The world is full of his glory, his deeds, and his monuments; but few know the true shades of his character, his private qualities, or the natural disposition of his soul." Las Cases intended to fill that void.

In 1831 Las Cases was elected to the Senate of France under the reign of Louis-Philippe. Much to his pleasure, in 1840 he took part in the massive ceremony placing Napoleon's ashes under the dome of Les Invalides in Paris. Less than two years later, he died.

Massena, André, duc de Rivoli, prince d'Essling (1758–1817)

André Massena was one of Napoleon's most celebrated commanders, whom he nicknamed "l'enfant chéri de la victoire" at the time of the First Italian Campaign. Massena's name remains indelibly linked with the Revolution and Napoleonic period; it was etched on the Arc de Triomphe, and one of the major boulevards of Paris bears it as well. Until

1810 and during very difficult circumstances, Napoleon considered him his finest marshal.

Born in Nice (in the kingdom of Sardinia) and orphaned early in life, Massena was reared by an uncle until he joined the French Royal-Italian regiment where he served for 14 years. Having achieved the highest noncommissioned rank because he was not a noble, he resigned at the time of the French Revolution to take his chances in the volunteer battalions of the French revolutionary army that promised more opportunities for advancement. In 1792 when French armies annexed Nice, he became a French citizen, and by 1793 he had been named brigadier general. He served with Napoleon in the First Italian Campaign, and then received command of the Army of Helvetia (Switzerland) where he defeated the Austro-Russian army and the Russian relief army at Zurich, protecting France from invasion by the forces of the Second Coalition. This battle was among the most significant battles of the revolutionary years because France's entire eastern front had been exposed. Massena served again with Napoleon in the Second Italian Campaign, holding Genoa long enough for Napoleon to cross the Alps and to gain an advantage over the divided Austrian armies. His health being poor, he retired from military service for five years.

Throughout Massena's distinguished military career, he was also known for his love of money and his interest in women. Occasionally Napoleon disciplined him; but for the most part, Napoleon tended to excuse him because his military skills were remarkable. As it turned out, Napoleon could count on him almost without fail. Although Massena voted against the constitution of the Life Consulate in 1802 when he was serving in the Legislative Corps of the French Government, Napoleon made him one of his first marshals of the Empire in 1804. He returned to the military in 1805 and continued in Napoleon's campaigns in Naples (1806), Poland (1807), and Austria (1809). In the latter, he served at Aspern-Essling in one of the bloodiest contests of the campaign on the banks of the Danube. For his efforts, he was named prince d'Essling, to be placed alongside the title duc de Rivoli that he had been granted earlier. Injured, arthritic, over 50 years of age, and having lost the sight in his left eye in a hunting accident, Massena looked forward to retirement by 1810.

Much to his protestations, however, Massena was named commander of the Army of Portugal when Napoleon chose not to return to the Peninsula to take on the English under Wellington. Badly supplied, with corps commanders who could not work in concert, Massena penetrated into Portugal only to find his army facing formidable redoubts and fortifications around Lisbon that made it impossible for him to expel the British from the Peninsula. Under the worst conditions, sniped at by the enemy, he turned to face the Anglo-Portuguese army on the border of Spain in 1811. In the throes of defeat, Napoleon replaced him but sent him to be governor of the military district and port at Toulon. Napoleon, however, was soon engaged in the Russian campaign, while his French troops in Spain were slowly pushed back into France.

After his disgrace in the Peninsula and the recurring blame that Napoleon placed on Massena, he never commanded a field army again. As governments changed during Napoleon's first exile, the first restoration under Louis XVIII, and the Hundred Days, Massena simply acknowledged the new government and served the ruling power. With the final restoration, Massena retired to Nice where he died in 1817. Later, when Wellington was asked about Massena's quality as a commander, his backhanded comment was, in fact, substantial praise; he answered, "We were pretty even."

Staël-Holstein, Anne-Louise-Germaine Necker, baronne de (1766–1817)

Mme de Staël was the daughter of Jacques Necker, the Swiss comptroller-general for Louis XVI, and a leading literary and political critic, novelist, and celebrated hostess in Paris and at her family estate of Coppet during the revolutionary and Napoleonic eras. Although she initially supported Napoleon, she also became one of his most intractable critics.

Born in Paris to Swiss parents, she was reared in France at the court of Louis XVI where her father had been recruited to deal with the near financial insolvency of the French kingdom prior to the Revolution. When her family returned to Switzerland in 1793 as the Revolution became more radical, she followed the events from afar and became an advocate of constitutional monarchy or a parliamentary system on the English model. Only after the Jacobins were removed from power did she return to Paris to side with the more moderate republican government that had replaced it in 1795. There in Paris she established a literary salon of renown where leading writers and thinkers gathered, including Swiss countryman Benjamin Constant, who served in the Tribunate under Napoleon's Constitution of VIII (1799) and with whom she had a long-term relationship.

Although Mme de Staël was already well known because of her family, her writing, and her ties to Constant, in 1800 she gained further notice with the publication of her book *De la littérature considérée dans ses rapports avec les institutions sociales.* Like the *Ideologues,* although she was not one of them, she believed in the doctrine of human perfectibility, but felt that it could be achieved only if liberty nourished it. Napoleon grew concerned as her political position became more republican and oppositional and her salon became more popular, even with members of his family, his generals, and his government officials. In 1802, her novel *Delphine* appeared to mixed reviews and further ire from the First Consul. Reflecting the roles of women in society, her female characters were diverse: some accepted the prescribed roles of the period, others attempted to manipulate their roles as women in order to find some happiness in being female, and Delphine perfected ruse and deception in order to participate among the educated and powerful members of society. Furthermore, the book contained recommendations on other social issues: in favor of divorce, against monastic vows and Catholicism, and always critical of the continuing centralization of power.

According to contemporaries, she was physically a large woman, witty, flamboyant, well read, and comfortable in male society; and Napoleon was always ill at ease in her company. By 1803, he found her criticisms too strident to ignore. He ordered her to leave Paris and not to reside any closer than 40 leagues from the capital. During the years when she could not reside in Paris, she traveled throughout Germany, spent time in Vienna, and retired to Coppet during her father's last illness. When her father's critical memoirs of France (1804) and her popular novel *Corinne* (1807) appeared, Napoleon was angry but took no action; but *De l'Allemagne* (*On Germany,* 1810) was unacceptable. Although he had initially approved its publication in France, he withdrew his support, condemned it, confiscated the manuscript, and destroyed ten thousand copies that were ready to be sold. The book, later published in 1813 from a salvaged draft, used Germany as an example to inspire France to greater creativity and intellectual growth. Napoleon viewed it as thoroughly anti-French, just as he viewed her entire circle of international philosophers, writers, and companions.

Although she had once attempted reconciliation with Napoleon, during the later years of the Empire reconciliation was an impossibility. Mme de Staël publicly supported Napoleon's French opponents and then the Bourbons after the Restoration of Louis XVIII. She also continued to write, and her later publications included *Dix années en exil* (*Ten Years in Exile*) and *Considérations sur la Révolution française* (*Considerations on the French Revolution*). Always a romantic, her works, however, did not engage in nostalgia for a past age. Instead, she became a model for writers who supported progress and who attempted to forge a pathway between Enlightenment ideology and romanticism.

Talleyrand-Périgord, Charles Maurice de, prince and duc de Bénévent (1754–1838)

One of the great survivors of the revolutionary and Napoleonic periods, Talleyrand was a consummate diplomat who served six different regimes and betrayed four, spied on his own country, and even conducted diplomatic maneuverings in spite of government orders to the contrary. As historian Harold Parker described him, "he was adept at abandoning sinking ships after slyly opening the scuttles."

Talleyrand, who was born into one of the oldest noble families of France, would have entered the military had a childhood accident not left him club-footed. Because his injury was so severe, his family chose the church as his vocation. From the age of eight, he began instruction in the Catholic Church, becoming the deputy deacon of St. Denis at Rheims in 1775, followed by additional appointments until he became bishop of Autun in 1789. Among the liberals of the early Revolution, Talleyrand resigned his religious posts in 1791 and was instrumental in nationalizing church lands and abolishing the vestiges of feudalism throughout France. Joining the diplomatic service, he attempted to keep Great Britain from joining the allies against France in 1792 and 1793. He was, however, denounced by the radicals in France after the Republic was declared and expelled from England. With almost nowhere to go, Talleyrand emigrated to the United States where he remained for two years as a kind of gentleman-merchant, traveling among French émigrés and newly made American friends. He returned to France in 1796 where he immediately began again to insinuate himself into circles of political power.

In 1797, Talleyrand became Minister of Foreign Affairs under the government of the Directory. Having resigned from that post in 1799 because he found the government terminally unstable, he assisted Napoleon in the coup d'état of 18 Brumaire and was rewarded with his reappointment as Minister of Foreign Affairs. Napoleon initially found him charming and capable, characterizing him as his ablest diplomat. As Napoleon's Foreign Minister, Talleyrand took very seriously his objective to negotiate peace throughout Europe, and he was instrumental in a number of Napoleonic achievements: the return of the émigrés, the Concordat of 1801 with the pope, the reorganization of northern Italy into the Italian Republic, the creation of the Life Consulate, and the severity with which Napoleon dealt with the Cadoudal plot (including the execution of the Duc d'Enghien). Napoleon used Talleyrand to negotiate the Treaty of Pressburg (with Austria) ending the Third Coalition, the Continental System, and portions of the Treaties of Tilsit that ended the Fourth Coalition (with Prussia and Russia). For his efforts, Talleyrand accumulated additional wealth and titles, including Grand Chamberlain of the Empire and duc de Bénévent (Benevento in southern Italy), Grand Chancellor of the Empire, and Grand Elector. He had also received the coveted Legion of Honor and had become one of the wealthiest men in France.

By 1807, however, Talleyrand grew weary of Napoleon's expansionist plans, and he left the ministry of Foreign Affairs although Napoleon still frequently consulted him. In 1808 as a representative at Erfurt with Napoleon, he began clandestine dealings with Alexander I of Russia whom he counseled to oppose the Emperor. He was soon added to Austria's payroll as an agent. In spite of his growing estrangement from the Emperor, Talleyrand continued to have a political presence in France. Although Napoleon must have known of Talleyrand's duplicity, perhaps not the extent of it, the Emperor interestingly did nothing about it. Talleyrand was, according to Mme de Staël: "so double-faced that if you kick him behind, he will smile in front." The public quarrels between Napoleon and Talleyrand became legendary, and the Emperor's sniping became more intense; but the fabled former diplomat seemed immune.

As the disastrous Russian campaign drew to a close, Talleyrand opened more serious negotiations with the allies. He publicly supported Napoleon's abdication that he had, in fact, choreographed by assuring that the French Senate would depose Napoleon. He briefly became president of the Provisional Government of France and then went to Vienna as France's representative to the Congress of Vienna, serving the Bourbon king Louis XVIII. During the Hundred Days in 1815, Talleyrand remained in Vienna. He then retired to his estates, only to be recalled to serve as ambassador to Great Britain under King Louis-Philippe in 1830. In that capacity, he assisted in the creation of modern Belgium.

Wellington, Sir Arthur Wellesley, Duke of (1769–1852)

The man who came to be known as the First Duke of Wellington was first a British soldier, then the commander who most brought about Napoleon's military defeat leading to the end of the Napoleonic era in France, and finally a leading British politician and diplomat during the first half of the nineteenth century.

Irish born and educated at Eton and a French military academy in Angers, Wellington initially seemed little fit for the military. Because of his wealth, however, he was able to move up in the army where he saw his first combat in 1794 when he served in the Netherlands. His service continued in 1797 in India where he seriously began to study military strategy and tactics while learning to be a good administrator. In India, in fact, his successes on the battlefield first brought him notice. He remained in India until 1805 when he returned to England, where he served in politics for the next three years.

The French began to notice Wellington only when he first led troops in the Peninsula. In 1808 he decisively defeated General Junot bringing about the expulsion of the French from Portugal. In 1809, he replaced Sir John Moore who had been killed at Corunna and defeated the French under Marshal Soult, in an attempt to topple the government of Joseph Bonaparte. In the brutal contest at Talavera, he held his own against French assault and received the title Viscount of Wellington. Shortly thereafter, however, the English were forced to withdraw from Spain into Portugal again.

Wellington's challenge to the French armies and to the Napoleonic Empire began in earnest in 1810, when André Massena was sent to the Peninsula with Junot and Ney as his corps commanders to expel the "English leopard." As the French penetrated into Portugal, their advance was first checked at Bussaco and then at the Lines of Torres Vedras that French reconnaissance had not discovered. The fortifications to the north and east of Lisbon proved to be impenetrable, as Wellington had intended them to be. Ultimately the French had no recourse except to withdraw, followed closely by the Anglo-Portuguese Army that sniped and engaged them in battle all the way into Spain. If Wellington had appeared to be an English gentleman whose wealth had gotten him where he was (as his men had earlier thought), the Peninsula War changed their perceptions. He had become "that Bugger who beats the French." The war, however, was far from over, and another year elapsed as Wellington's army pressed into Spain, defeated French Marshal Marmont (who had replaced Massena) at Salamanca, and moved to the border of France. In 1813, after receiving additional reinforcements, Wellington took Vitoria where his massive victory earned him the title Duke of Wellington and his baton as a field marshal of Britain. In 1814, as Napoleon abdicated for the first time, Wellington was still slogging his way north through France against continuing French opposition.

Most of Wellington's Peninsular Army was then hurriedly shipped to the United States in 1814, in the final throes of the American War of 1812, and Wellington returned to England. From there he went to Paris as ambassador and then to Vienna for the peace talks that were to settle the Napoleonic era, until Napoleon returned from Elba much to the surprise of the powers of Europe. Wellington was then charged with commanding a multinational army against Napoleon's troops. There on the field at Waterloo, Wellington defeated the French for the final time. Although Wellington remained British Commander in Chief until 1852 when he died at the age of 83, the remaining years of his life were spent in politics as prime minister, home secretary, foreign secretary, and advisor to Queen Victoria and Prince Albert.

As a military commander, Wellington was without question one of the best. He was a realist when on campaign and organized his troops to be self-sufficient in the Peninsula. Knowing that he could not always count on the Portuguese to be as resolute as his British soldiers, he incorporated them into a divisional structure alongside his men. From 1810 on, he also took few chances, planning strategies deliberately in advance with contingencies. He consistently strengthened fortifications where he had them; he preferred to draw the enemy into his snare rather than taking audacious offensives; and at Waterloo, he even picked the battlefield.

PRIMARY DOCUMENTS OF THE NAPOLEONIC ERA, 1799–1815

Document 1
Napoleon Bonaparte's Letter to His Brother Joseph,
Paris, June 22, 1792

Between Napoleon's sojourns in Corsica and his military commitment to France, he happened to be in Paris during the summer and fall of 1792. On June 20, a mob of Parisians stormed the Tuileries where the King and royal family were in residence. They wanted the King to withdraw his veto on several actions that they believed to be counter to the Revolution. Nearby Napoleon watched the confrontation. Realizing the seriousness of the contest between the King (supported by Lafayette and the National Guard) and the mob (supported by the Jacobins and the radicals), Napoleon described the events to his older brother. The King had done well to keep the mob from taking more power, but a dangerous precedent might have been set. Source: *Napoleon's Letters: Selected, Translated and Edited by J. M. Thompson* (London: Prion, 1998), 11–12. Reprinted by permission of Prion Books, Ltd.

M. de Lafayette has written to the Assembly, attacking the Jacobins. It is a strong letter, and many people think it a forgery. M. de Lafayette, most of the officers in the army, all sound people, the ministers, and the Paris Department are on one side: the majority in the Assembly, the Jacobins, and the populace are on the other. The Jacobin attacks on Lafayette have passed all bounds: they describe him as a rascal, an assassin, and an object of pity. The Jacobins are lunatics, and have no common sense. The day before yesterday seven or eight thousand men armed with pikes, hatchets, swords, muskets, spits and pointed stakes, marched to the Assembly to present a petition. From there they went on to the

King's palace. The Tuileries Garden was closed, and protected by 15,000 National Guards. The mob battered down the doors, forced an entrance into the palace, mounted cannon against the King's apartments, razed four gates to the ground, and presented the King with two cockades— one white and the other red, white and blue. They gave him a choice. 'Make up your mind,' they said, 'whether you will reign here, or at Coblenz.' The King showed up well.

He put on the *bonnet rouge* [red cap of liberty]: so did the Queen and the Prince Royal. They gave the King a drink. They stayed in the palace four hours. This event has provided plenty of material for aristocratic harangues at the Fueillants Club. Nonetheless, it is unconstitutional, and sets a very dangerous precedent. It is certainly hard to guess what will become of the country under the present stress of affairs.

Document 2
Supper in Beaucaire

Or

A Discussion between a Soldier of Carteaux's army, a Marseillais, a Man from Nîmes, and a Manufacturer from Montpellier, on the Events which have Occurred in the Former County, on the Arrival of the Men from Marseilles.

When Napoleon published *Supper in Beaucaire* in July 1793, he had already spent nine years of commissioned service in the military, but he had not been particularly noticed. His pamphlet, however, arrived on the French political scene at precisely the right moment. As history unfolded, *Supper in Beaucaire* along with Napoleon's noteworthy service at Toulon, brought him governmental attention and changed his life.

According to the story of Napoleon's fictionalized supper, a soldier [Napoleon] had arrived in the small town of Beaucaire on the last day of the regional fair. In a polemical and heated discussion, the soldier and his companions analyzed the causes of the counterrevolutionary revolt that was taking place in the south of France. Regardless of what the soldier said, one of his dinner companions [a man from Marseilles] persisted in his conviction that the centralized Jacobin government was the opponent of true revolutionary principles. In the end, the soldier won the debate, by convincing the man from Marseilles that his counterrevolutionary actions and those of his comrades were tantamount to a coalition with the enemy. As he finished, Napoleon's message was simple; regardless of other conditions, might would triumph.

In no way was *Supper in Beaucaire* an elegant statement of Jacobin positions, but it did catch the eye of Napoleon's Corsican compatriot Christophe Saliceti, who was serving the Jacobins in the south of France. Saliceti forwarded the pamphlet to Maximilien Robespierre's brother Augustin who had the pamphlet published and who made sure that the government was aware of Napoleon's military recommendations. Napoleon's first serious foray into political pamphleteering had netted an important result. Although Jacobin ascendance was short-lived (ending in July 1794), Napoleon's military reputation was assured.

The following is an edited version of the original focusing mainly on the soldier's [Napoleon's] words to the counterrevolutionary Marseillais. Because the original essay contained ellipses (. . .) as a literary device, I have chosen to avoid confusion by not using ellipses to point out sections that have been edited. Source: *Supper in Beaucaire* in *Napoleon Wrote Fiction,* Edited, Introduced and Translated by Christopher Frayling (Salisbury, England: The Compton Press, 1972), 119–35. Reprinted by permission of PFD on behalf of Christopher Frayling.

I found myself in Beaucaire on the last day of the fair. As luck would have it, I had as table companions for supper two Marseilles merchants, a man from Nîmes and a manufacturer from Montpellier. After a few moments spent in getting acquainted, they had found out that I had come from Avignon and that I was a soldier. The minds of my table companions, which all week had been fixed on the progress of trade as a means of making money, were at this moment fixed on the outcome of current events, on which the future of their livelihood depended. They wanted to find out my opinion, so that in comparing it with their own, they might adjust their views and assess prospects for a future, which would affect us all differently.

The Marseillais seemed to be particularly depressed. The evacuation of Avignon had taught them to have doubts about everything—all they had left was a considerable anxiety about their fate. Mutual confidence soon made us talkative and we embarked on a conversation more or less on these lines.

The Soldier [Napoleon] describes Carteaux's army as it forced the counterrevolutionaries out of Avignon:
The army was four thousand strong when it attacked Avignon. Today there are six thousand men, and before four days are out there will be ten thousand.

The army skirmished around the town, tried to force the gates by planting explosives and fired a few cannon to test the garrison's resistance. The Marseillais [counterrevolutionaries] numbered three thousand six hundred men. They had more artillery and [it was] of superior caliber; in spite of this they were forced to retreat. That astonishes you, but the reason is that only veteran troops can stand up to the uncertainties of a siege. They had to evacuate the town. The cavalry pursued them as they retreated. Many of their men were captured and they lost two cannon.

Then the Soldier turned directly to the men from Marseilles to make his point about their counterrevolutionary activities:

Your leaders are incompetent; beware of their predictions. You are naturally impetuous, you are being led to the slaughter by the same means that have destroyed so many people—by exciting your vanity.

You tell me that your army is at Aix with a great artillery train and good generals; well, whatever your army does, I assure you it will be defeated.

You had three thousand six hundred men—at least half of them have scattered. You have good generals, [but] I have yet to see them so I cannot comment on their talents. They will be bogged down in details and will not be supported by subalterns; [and] it will take them two months to organize their army even tolerably well.

You have some eighteen and twenty-four pounders [cannons] and you think yourselves undefeatable—you are following vulgar opinion, but the professionals will tell you, and inevitable experience will make it quite clear, that good four and eight pounders have as much effect in open warfare and are superior in many ways.

Your gunners are raw recruits; your opposite numbers are artillerymen of the line, whose skill makes them masters of Europe. What will become of your army if it concentrates on Aix? The army will be lost—it is a precept of military science that he who entrenches his position is sure to be defeated. Theory and practice agree on this point. You can be quite certain, then, that the choice which, seems the best to you, is in fact the worst.

What kind of dizziness can suddenly have possessed your people? What fatal blindness leads you to the slaughter? How can you possibly aspire to resist the entire Republic? Even if you force the Republic's army to fall back on Avignon, can you doubt that in a very few days fresh forces will come to replace it? Will the Republic, which makes the law for the whole of Europe, take it from Marseilles?

In collaboration with Bordeaux, Lyon, Montpellier, Nîmes, Grenoble, the Jura, the Eure and the Calvados, you embarked on a revolution. You had some chance of success—your ringleaders may have had dubious motives but you had an imposing show of force; on the other hand, now that Lyon, Nîmes, Montpellier, Bordeaux, the Jura and Eure, Grenoble and Caen have accepted the Constitution, now that Avignon, Tarascon and Arles have yielded, you must admit that your stubbornness is rather foolish. You are influenced by people who, having nothing to lose, involve you in their downfall.

The Marseillais then challenged the Soldier about the Jacobin government, its "blood-thirsty excesses," and soldiers in the Republican military, whom he called brigands.

The Soldier replied:

That is civil war; people cut each other to pieces, detest each other and kill other people they know nothing about. These soldiers whom you call brigands are our best troops and our most disciplined battalions—their reputation is above scandal.

You seem to think they go to extremes with you; on the contrary, they are treating you like misguided children. Do you think that Marseilles could have withdrawn the merchandise she had in Beaucaire without their consent? They could have sequestered the merchandise right from the start of the war. They did not wish to do that and thanks to them, you can go home in peace.

Your army, on the other hand, has killed, assassinated more than thirty people, invaded family privacy and filled the prisons with good citizens under the vague pretext that they were brigands.

You say that you fly the tricolor flag.

Paoli also hoisted that flag, in Corsica, to give himself time to deceive the people, to crush the true friends of liberty, in order to lure his fellow-countrymen into his ambitious and criminal schemes. He hoisted the tricolor flag, and he opened fire on ships belonging to the Republic. He drove our troops from their fortresses; he disarmed those who guarded them, and he organized riots in order to harass those Republicans who remained on the Island. He pillaged the storehouses, selling everything in them at giveaway prices in order to have money to sustain his revolt. He plundered and confiscated the belongings of the most well-to-do families because they supported the unity of the Republic, and he declared "enemies of the fatherland" all those who stayed in our armies. Before that, he had caused the failure of the expedition against Sardinia. And still he was shameless enough to call himself friend of France, and a good Republican, and still he deceived the Convention which repealed the order for his discharge.

We should no longer put our trust in words. We must analyze deeds, and you must admit that looking at yours, it is easy to show you to be counterrevolutionaries.

What effect has your movement produced on the Republic? You have led it almost to ruin; you have hampered our army operations. I do not know if you have been in the pay of the Spaniard and the Austrian, but they certainly could not have wished for a happier diversion. What more could you do if you were in their pay?

As the Soldier continued, other table companions joined in the challenge to the Marseillais.

The Man from Nîmes spoke first:

We abandoned the Marseillais the moment we saw that they sought counter-revolution, and that they were fighting over personal grievances. The mask fell as soon as they refused to promulgate the Constitution. That is why we forgave the Mountain [Jacobins] a few irregularities. We were acting in good faith—you [the Marseillais] were the ones who had a fox under your coat; we wanted a Republic and therefore had to accept a Republican Constitution.

The Merchant from Montpellier then joined in:

You have overthrown all the laws, all the conventions. By what right do you break up your Department? Was it Marseilles who established it? By what right has your city's battalion been trampling over the rest of the province? What makes you think now that this Department does not have the right to call upon public force to defend it? You have thus confounded every conceivable right, you have established anarchy and since you dare to justify your actions by the right of the strongest, you are nothing but brigands and anarchists.

You have set up a popular tribunal, and only Marseilles has elected it; it is contrary to every law. It can only be a bloody tribunal since it represents one faction. You have forcibly subjugated the whole of your department to this tribunal. By what right? Aren't you usurping the very authority you take such unjust exception to, where Paris is concerned? In Avignon, you have committed people to prison without authority, without a warrant, without an order from any administrative body. You have abused family privacy, ignored the liberty of the individual; you have cold-bloodedly ordered assassinations in public streets. You have revived those very scenes (whose horror you exaggerate in any case) which afflicted the early days of the Revolution: without inquiries, without trials, without knowing who the victims were, on the word of their enemies alone, you have arrested them, torn them from their children, dragged them through the streets and put them to the sword. You have sacrificed as many as thirty in this way. You have dragged the Statue of Liberty through the mud; you have publicly desecrated her. She has been the object of all manner of insults from lawless youths. You have hacked at the Statue with your swords, you cannot possibly deny it, since it was mid-day and more than two-hundred of your people were seen to be present at this criminal profanation.

The Soldier then summarized the positions of his table companions and questioned whether the counterrevolutionary activities would still continue:

Yes, it has been conclusively proved that the Marseillais have ruined several of our army operations, and wished to suppress liberty. The point is to find out what they can hope for and what course is still open to them.

The Man from Marseilles, still resistant to what the Soldier and his table companions have pointed out, pledges to continue to resist the Republican troops:

I must say we have fewer choices open to us than I thought, but one's strength is greatest when one has resolved to die and we have so resolved rather than bow again under the yoke of those men of blood who govern the state. You know that a drowning man clutches at every straw; so will we, rather than allow ourselves to be butchered. Yes, we have all taken part in this new revolution, so we would all be sacrificed to vengeance. We will always remember that monster who was nonetheless one of the principal members of the Club: he had a citizen lynched, pillaged his house, and raped his wife after making her drink a cup of her husband's blood.

The Soldier challenges his facts:

How disgusting! But is that a fact? I doubt it very much, for you know that no one believes in rape nowadays.

The Marseillais continues:

It is true! Rather than submitting to such people, we will fight to the last ditch. We will give ourselves over to the enemy.

The Soldier notes that the Marseillais cannot win against the stronger armies of the Republic and they must return to the Republic:

Believe me, Marseillais, shake off the yoke of the small number of scoundrels who lead you to counter-revolution, re-establish your constituted authorities, accept the Constitution, and give the representatives their liberty, so that they can go to Paris to intercede for you. You have been led astray; it is nothing new for the people to be deceived by a few conspirators and intriguers. In every age, the impetuosity and ignorance of the multitude has been the cause of most civil wars.

After further discussion, the Men from Marseilles begin to understand the magnitude of their errors—that they were led astray by a few counter-revolutionary leaders; that they were indoctrinated into believing that republican soldiers will treat them violently and maliciously; and that they have failed to understand the meaning of the Jacobin regime in Paris.

The Soldier concludes the discussion:

At last you are seeing reason. Why should not a similar change of attitude affect a large number of your fellow-citizens who have been misled and who are acting in good faith? Then [we] who wish to spare French blood, will send you some loyal and well-qualified man; we will come to an agreement, and, without a moment's delay, the army will go and make the [enemy] dance the Carmagnole beneath the walls of Perpignan, and Marseilles will still remain the center of gravity for liberty. You will just have to tear a few pages out of your history.

This happy prophecy put us back in good humor, the Marseillais gladly bought us several bottles of champagne, which completely dissipated all worries and cares. We went to bed at two o'clock in the morning, arranging to meet at breakfast the next day—when the Marseillais had plenty more doubts to express, and I many interesting truths to teach them.

Document 3
Napoleon's Letter to Joséphine, in Absence, April 3, 1796

When Napoleon left for his command of the Army of Italy, he had only been married to Joséphine for three days. During the weeks and months of the First Italian Campaign, he wore Joséphine's portrait on a ribbon around his neck and frequently showed it to his commanders. Outside of his military affairs, he seemed incapable of speaking of anything else. At the time when he met the attractive widow in Paris in 1795, he believed her to be wealthy and well placed in society to assist him in his career; furthermore, he was fascinated by Joséphine and by her physical charms. This letter, written in April, was followed by increasing pleadings to join him in Italy, most of which went unanswered. Later, he demanded her presence and sent two of his aides to Paris to bring her to Italy. She obsessed him; but at the same time, her thoughts were on Parisian society and additional extravagances. When Napoleon later learned of her infidelities, his ardor and passion cooled. Although Napoleon later said that she was the only woman he truly loved, he also noted, "Love is the occupation of the idle man, the distraction of the warrior, the stumbling block of the sovereign." (See Fisher, *Napoleon,* 147.) Source: *Napoleon's Letters: Selected, Translated and Edited by J. M. Thompson* (London: Prion, 1998), 8–20. Reprinted by permission of Prion Books, Ltd.

I have all your letters, but none has affected me like the last. Darling, do you think what you are doing, when you write to me in such terms? Do you suppose my position is not so painful already, that you must pile regret upon regret, and reduce my soul to distraction? The way you write! The feelings you describe! They are flames that scorch my poor heart. Away from you, my one and only Joséphine, there is no pleasure in life: away from you, the world is a desert in which I am all alone, without even the solace of expressing my feelings. You have robbed me of more than my heart: all my thoughts are about you alone. Whenever I am bored or worried with business, whenever I am troubled as to how things will turn out, whenever I am disappointed with mankind, and feel inclined to curse the day I was born, I put my hand to my heart: there throbs your likeness; I have but to look at it, and my love is perfect happiness, and there is pleasure in every prospect but that of long absence from my beloved.

What art did you learn to captivate all my faculties, to absorb all my character into yourself? It is a devotion, dearest, which will end only with my life. 'He lived for Joséphine': there is my epitaph. I strive to be near you: I am nearly dead with desire for your presence. It is madness! I cannot realize that I am getting further and further away from you. So many regions and countries part us asunder! How long it will be before you read these characters, these imperfect utterances of a troubled heart of which you are queen! Ah! Wife that I adore. I cannot tell what lot awaits me; only, that, if it keeps me any longer away from you, it will be insupportable, beyond what bravery can bear. There was a time when I prided myself on my courage; and sometimes, at the sight of misfortunes that fate might have in store for me, I would face in imagination unheard-of ills, without a frown, without a feeling of surprise. But nowadays, the mere thought that my Joséphine may be unwell, or that she might be taken ill—above all the cruel possibility that she may not love me as she did, wounds my heart, arrests my blood, and makes me so sad and despondent that I am robbed even of the courage of anger and despair.

Once I would tell myself that to die without regret is to be safe from any harm the world can inflict; but now the thought of dying without the certainty of your love is like the torments of Hell, the very image of utter annihilation. I experience all the feelings of a drowning man.

My perfect comrade, whom fate has allotted to make life's painful journey at my side! The day when I lose your heart, Nature will lose for me all her warmth and vegetation. . . . I cannot go on, dearest: my soul is so sad, my mind over-burdened, my body tired out. Men bore me. I could hate them all; for they separate me from my love.

I am at Port-Maurice, near Oneille [northern Italy]. I shall be at Albenga tomorrow. Both armies are on the move: we are trying to outwit one another. May the cleverer man win. I like Beaulieu; he manoeuvres well: he is a better soldier than his predecessor. I shall beat him, I hope, and in the grand manner. Don't be worried about me. Love me as you love your eyes. No, that is not enough: love me as you love yourself—and not yourself only, but your thoughts, your mind, your life, your all. Darling, I'm raving, forgive me. Nature is a poor recompense for such feelings as mine, or for the man you love.

Document 4
Napoleon's Legacy as Viewed from St. Helena

Among Napoleon's companions on St. Helena from 1815 through 1816 was the Comte de Las Cases. Although he was expelled from St. Helena in 1816 for smuggling letters to and from the island during his months with Napoleon, he kept careful notebooks of his conversations with the Emperor and dictations from Napoleon to him. Published in 1822, Las Cases' memoirs of Napoleon in four volumes became an instant success. The following selection summarizes Napoleon's legacy, as viewed in Napoleon's own words and Las Cases' comments. As will become immediately apparent, Las Cases was an admirer of Napoleon. Source: Emmanuel Dieudonné, comte de Las Cases, *Memoirs of the Life, Exile, and Conversations with the Emperor Napoleon,* 4 vols. (New York: Worthington, 1890), 1: 118–19.

The course by which Napoleon advanced to supreme power is perfectly simple and natural; it is single in history; the very circumstances of his elevation render it unparalleled. "I did not usurp the crown," said he one day to the Council of State, "I took it up out of the mire; the people placed it on my head: let their acts be respected!"

And, by thus taking up the crown, Napoleon restored France to her rank in European society, terminated her horrors, and revived her character. He freed us of all the evils of our fatal crisis, and reserved to us all the advantages arising out of it. "I ascended the throne unsullied by any of the crimes of my situation," said he, on one occasion. "How few founders of dynasties can say as much!"

Never during any period of our history, were favors distributed with so much impartiality; never was merit so indiscriminately sought out and rewarded; public money so usefully employed; the arts and sciences better encouraged, or the glory and lustre of the country raised to so high a pitch. "It is my wish," said he one day to the Council of State, "that the title of Frenchman should be the best and most desirable on earth; that a Frenchman traveling through any part of Europe may think and find himself at home."

If liberty seemed occasionally to suffer encroachments, if authority seemed sometimes to overstep its limits, circumstances rendered those measures necessary and inevitable. Our present misfortunes have, though too late, made us sensible of this truth; we now render justice, though also too late, to the courage, judgment, and foresight which then dictated those steps. It is certain that in this respect the political fall of Napoleon has considerably increased his influence. Who can now doubt that his glory and the lustre of his character have been infinitely augmented by his misfortunes?

Document 5
Napoleon Bonaparte's Letter to Talleyrand on Constitution Making, September 17, 1797

From Napoleon's headquarters in the First Italian Campaign, he sent this letter to Talleyrand, who was France's Minister of Foreign Affairs. In the letter, he considered what type of government should be formed once the Austrians were expelled from Italy. He first analyzed the English model that Montesquieu had described in *The Spirit of the Law* (*De l'Esprit des Lois,* 1748); then he made his own recommendations. Two years later, with Sieyès and others, he took the opportunity to create a constitution for France. The Constitution of the Year VIII, as Napoleon's first constitution was called, had neither the tidy division of powers that Montesquieu had recommended, nor did it place significant power in the hands of the legislative branch. Source: *Napoleon's Letters: Selected, Translated and Edited by J. M. Thompson* (London: Prion, 1998), 39–40. Reprinted by permission of Prion Books, Ltd.

For all our pride, our thousand-and-one pamphlets, and our blustering airy orations, we are extremely ignorant of the science of political conduct. We have never yet defined what is meant by the executive, legislative, and judicial powers. Montesquieu defined them wrongly: not because that famous man was incompetent to do otherwise, but because—as he admitted—his work was only a kind of description of conditions which had once existed, or still existed in his day—a summary of notes made during his travels or his reading. His gaze was fixed on the government of England: he defined, in general terms, the executive, legislative, and judiciary of that country.

But why, in point of fact, should it be thought a function of the legislative power to declare war and peace, or to regulate the amount and character of the taxes? The English constitution has reasonably enough entrusted the second of these functions in the House of Commons; and it is a good arrangement because the English constitution is nothing but a charter of privilege—a black picture, framed in gold. Since the House of Commons is the only body which, for better or worse, represents the nation, it is proper that it should have sole power to impose taxation: it is the only defense they have been able to devise against the insolent tyranny of the court party. But why, in a government whose whole authority emanates from the nation; why, where the sovereign is the people, should one include among the functions of the legislative power things which are foreign to it? There is only one thing, so far as I can see, that we have really defined during the last fifty years, and that is the sovereignty of the people. We have been no happier in settling what is or is not constitutional, than in allocating the different powers in the state. The French people [are] organized only in outline.

The governmental power, taken in the wide sense that I would give it, ought to be regarded as the real representative of the nation, governing in virtue of the constitutional charges and the organic laws. It falls naturally, it seems to me, into two quite distinct authorities. One of these is supervisory, but not executive: to this body what we nowadays call the Executive Power would be obliged to submit every important measure: it would be, if I may call it so, the legislative side of the executive. This great body would be in a real sense the National Council: it would control all that part of the administration and of the executive which our present constitution entrusts to the Legislative Power.

Thus the governmental power would consist of two authorities, both nominated by the people; and one would be a very large body, containing only such persons as had already occupied some of the posts that give men experience in the business of government. The legislative power would enact all the organic laws in the first instance, and would have power to alter them, but not at a few day's notice, as can be done now; for, once an organic law is placed upon the statute book, I think there should be no power to change it without four or five month's debate.

This Legislative Power, carrying no rank in the Republic, closed to outside influence, hearing and seeing nothing of what goes on around it, would have no ambitions, and would not inundate us with thousands of ephemeral measures, whose very absurdity defeats their own ends, and which have turned us into a nation with 300 law books in folio, and not a single law.

There you have, I think, a complete system of government, and one that finds its excuse in the present situation. It would really be disastrous if a nation of 30 million people, in this 18th Century, were unable to save the country except by recourse to arms. Violent remedies discredit the legislator. He who gives men a constitution ought to consider beforehand how it will affect them.

Document 6
Description of Napoleon by His Private Secretary Méneval

Méneval was only 24 years old when he began his service to Napoleon. During the years from 1802 through 1813, he chronicled Napoleon's activities, sometimes interjecting his own observations as is the case with this excerpt. Prior to serving as Napoleon's private secretary, he worked with Napoleon's brother Joseph. Later, when he became too ill to keep up with Napoleon, he was reassigned to Marie Louise. His memoirs are analytical but generally favorable to Napoleon. Source: Claude François Méneval, *Memoirs Illustrating the History of Napoleon I from 1802 to 1815,* 3 vols. (New York: D. Appleton and Company, 1894), 1: 108–11 and 414.

The First Consul came back late, and spent almost the whole day receiving people in his drawing-room. . . .

[The First Consul] was then in the enjoyment of vigorous health. He had recently been cured of an internal disease, from which he had begun to suffer greatly during the second year of the Consulate. This suffering was caused by an inveterate cutaneous infection, which had been driven into the system by the remedies he had taken, and of which the skilful doctor, Corvisart, had just relieved him. I have heard it said that during the siege of Toulon one of the gunners of a battery where Napoleon was, was killed. It was important that the firing should not slacken. Napoleon took the rammer and loaded the cannon several times. Some days later he was covered with a very malignant itching skin disease. He tried to remember when and where he could have caught this disease. It was then discovered that the artilleryman, from whose burning hand Napoleon had taken the rammer, was infected. In the carelessness of youth, and being entirely absorbed in his work, he had neglected to undergo any treatment. He contented himself with some remedies which only caused the outward signs of the disease to disappear, and the poison had been driven into his system, and caused great damage. This was the reason, it was added, of the extreme thinness and poor, weak look of Napoleon during the campaigns in Italy and Egypt.

[During the second year of the Consulate] Napoleon was moderately stout. His stoutness was increased later on by the frequent use of baths, which he took to refresh himself after his fatigues. It may be mentioned that he had taken the habit of bathing himself every day at irregular hours, a practice which he considerably modified when it was pointed out by his doctor that the frequent use of hot baths, and the time he spent in them, were weakening, and would predispose to obesity.

Napoleon was of mediocre stature (about five feet two inches), and well built, though the bust was rather long. His head was big and the skull largely developed. His neck was short and his shoulders broad. The size of his chest bespoke a robust constitution, less robust, however, than his mind. His legs were well shaped, his foot was small and well formed. His hand, and he was rather proud of it, was delicate, and plump, with tapering fingers. His forehead was high and broad, his eyes grey, penetrating and wonderfully mobile; his nose was straight and well shaped. His teeth were fairly good, the mouth perfectly modeled, the upper lip slightly drawn down toward the corner of the mouth, and the chin slightly prominent. His skin was smooth and his complexion pale, but of a pallor which denoted a good circulation of the blood. His very fine chestnut hair, which, until the time of the expedition to Egypt, he had worn long, cut square and covering his ears, was slipped short. The hair was thin on the upper part of the head, and left bare his forehead, the seat of such lofty thoughts. The shape of his face and *ensemble* of his features were remarkably regular. In one word, his head and his bust were in no way inferior in nobility or dignity to the most beautiful bust which antiquity has bequeathed to us.

Of this portrait, which in its principal features underwent little alteration in the last years of his reign, I will add some particulars furnished by my long intimacy with him. When excited by any violent passion his face assumed an even terrible expression. A sort of rotary movement very visibly produced itself on his forehead and between his eyebrows; his eyes flashed fire; his nostrils dilated, swollen with the inner storm. But these transient movements, whatever their case may have been, in no way brought disorder to his mind. He seemed to be able to control at will these explosions, which, by the way, as time went on, became less and less frequent. His head remained cool. The blood never went to it, flowing back to the heart. In ordinary life his expression was calm, meditative, and gently grave. When in a good humour, or when anxious to please, his expression was sweet and caressing, and his face was lighted up by a most beautiful smile. Amongst familiars his laugh was loud and mocking.

My portrait of Napoleon would be incomplete did I not mention the hat, without trimming or lace, which was ornamented by a little tricolour cockade, fastened with a black silk cord, and the grey surtout [overcoat] which covered the simple uniform of colonel of his guard. This hat and this surtout, which became historical with him, shone in the midst of the coats covered with gold and silver embroidery which were worn by his generals, and the civil and military officers of his household.

Nevertheless he liked to be surrounded with splendor and a kind of pomp. He often used to say to those on whom he lavished his money: "Be economical and even parsimonious at home; be magnificent in public." He followed this maxim himself.

Document 7
Napoleon's Observations on War

The following selection from Las Cases' *Memoirs of the Life, Exile, and Conversations of the Emperor Napoleon* written in 1816 provides a summary of Napoleon's observations on war, campaign plans, the element of accident, the army train, and the use of artillery and cavalry. Source: Emmanuel Dieudonné, comte de Las Cases, *Memoirs of the Life, Exile, and Conversations of the Emperor Napoleon,* 4 vols. (New York: Worthington Company, 1890), 4: 140–44.

The Emperor sent for me about six o'clock. He informed me that he had just been dictating a chapter on maritime rights. He spoke to me of some other works he had in view. I ventured to remind him of the fourteen paragraphs which he had already planned, and to which I alluded on a former occasion.

He read and corrected the valuable notes which he had dictated to the Grand Marshal on ancient and modern warfare, the different plans of composing and regulating armies &c. He afterwards entered into conversation, and, among other things, said: 'No series of great actions is the mere work of chance and fortune; it is always the result of reflection and genius. Great men rarely fail in the most perilous undertakings. Look at Alexander, Caesar, Hannibal, the great Gustavus, and others; they always succeeded. Were they great men merely because they were fortunate? No, but because, being great men, they possessed the art of commanding fortune.

Should the Emperor leave behind him his thoughts on these points, they will be truly invaluable. In the course of the evening, he pronounced his opinion on several military subjects; sometimes embracing the highest questions, and sometimes descending into the minutest details.

He remarked that war frequently depended on accident, and that, though a commander ought to be guided by general principles, yet he should never lose sight of anything that may enable him to profit by accidental circumstances. The vulgar call good-fortune that which, on the contrary, is produced by the calculations of genius.

He was of the opinion that infantry charged by cavalry should fire from a distance, instead of firing closely according to the present practice. He proved the advantage of this method.

He observed that infantry and cavalry left to themselves, without artillery, could procure no decisive result; but that, with the aid of artillery, all things else being equal, cavalry might destroy the infantry.

He added that artillery really decided the fate of armies and nations; that men now fought with blows of cannon balls, as they fought with blows of fists; for in battle, as in a siege, the art consisted in making numerous discharges converge on one and the same point; that, amidst the conflict, he who had sufficient address to direct a mass of artillery suddenly and unexpectedly on any particular point of the enemy's force was sure of the victory. This, he said, had been his grand secret and his grand plan of tactics.

The Emperor conceived that it would be impossible to form a perfect army without a revolution in the manners and education of a soldier, and perhaps even the officer. This could not be accomplished without ovens, magazines, commissaries, and carriages. There could be no perfect army, until, in imitation of the Romans, the soldier should receive his supply of corn, grind it in his hand-mill, and bake his bread himself. We could not hope to possess an army, until we should abolish all our monstrous train of civil attendants.

Document 8
The Continental Blockade

In 1810, Napoleon wrote the following letter to his Minister for Foreign Affairs to lay out the history of the continental blockade, to place full responsibility on Britain for the ongoing economic warfare, and to set forward some principles for dealing with American shipping. Napoleon's letter was a response to the American Non-Intercourse Act of 1809 and the British Orders-in-Council that precipitated his Milan Decrees. In January 1810, according to both the British and the French, no shipping would be considered neutral. In this letter, Napoleon laid out the responsibilities that Americans would have to take to guarantee freedom of the seas. As American shipping became more vulnerable to confiscation, the result was the War of 1812 between the United States and Great Britain. Source: *Napoleon's Letters: Selected, Translated and Edited by J. M. Thompson* (London: Prion, 1998), 228–29. Reprinted by permission of Prion Books, Ltd.

I enclose a report from the Minister of Finance, and another from the Minister for Home Affairs, upon the important subject of our present relations with America. I want you to make me a report on the history of our relations with the United States since the treaty of Mortefontaine, and to annex to it French translations of all the original documents mentioned by the two ministers.

All the steps I have taken, as I have often remarked before, are mere acts of reprisal. I don't recognize any of the English claims with regard to the neutrals—what they call their maritime code. The English themselves have never pretended that I recognize it. Such a claim would have been pointless, since the code is entirely directed against France. At the same time the English claims have been no more admitted, or admitted only in part, by America and the northern powers. The maritime laws of England, previous to the last few years, were tyrannical, but not quite intolerable. But recently the English have completely altered the situation by arrogating to themselves the right to declare that all the ports of a country, and the whole coastline of an empire, are in a state of blockade. This means that, with respect to the blockaded country, England prohibits all commerce, and refuses to recognize any neutrals. I have said nothing of the influence England claimed to exercise over the neutrals: my Berlin decree was only a reply to the new extension she gave to the right of blockade; and even the Berlin decree cannot be considered as more than a maritime, certainly not as a continental blockade; witness the way in which it was carried out. I regard it simply as a kind of protest—as one act of violence answering another. It was really applied only to Hamburg, the Weser, and the continental coastline, and declarations were made to the neutrals to the effect that its operation would not be extended to the high seas. So far, little harm had been done; neutral ships still entered our ports. But the British Orders in Council necessitated my Milan decree, and thenceforward there were no neutrals. That decree had only one object, namely to protect myself and the neutrals against the intolerable right that England claimed to levy navigation dues upon the commerce and shipping of all nations—a claim which treated the high seas as I might treat the Seine, the Scheldt, or the Rhine. This meant an embargo on all commerce; and in opposing it, all thought of consequences had to be thrown to the winds. I was told today that the English are relaxing their regulations, and no longer impose a tax on shipping: let me know whether there is really an Order to this effect: even if there is not, let me know whether it is true in fact. Once I were sure that England is not going to levy navigation dues, I could relax my regulations in many respects.

I should not be unwilling to sign a treaty with America, by which she undertook (1) never, under any pretext, to allow England to levy dues on her commerce or shipping; (2) never to allow England to prevent her trading with France on the ground of a right of blockade, or any other pretext, it being understood that certain points might be blockaded, but not a whole empire; and (3) never to admit that, in order to reach France, her vessels must first call at some port in British territory. Granted these three conditions, I should be willing to declare, on my side, (1) that my warships and privateers will not exercise the right of search with respect to American ships, except so far as is necessary to make sure that they are really American, and do not belong to an enemy nation, (2) that American ships will be received in my ports, and will not be expected to pay more than the ordinary dues, always provided they come direct from the United States, from another French port, from a country allied to France, or from a neutral; for I refuse to admit American ships coming from English ports.

Document 9
The Diary of a Napoleonic Foot Soldier

The following selection is taken from Jakob Walter's diary, which was never intended for publication. In it, he jotted down his memories and observations of the retreat from Russia in 1813. The passages represent the hardships, pleasantries (finding an old friend), and challenges of the retreat, as seen by a German (Westphalian) conscript in Napoleon's army. It is interesting to note Walter's observations about the Emperor whom he saw as they passed by. As the days wore on, Walter became more and more detached from the suffering of everyone except his closest friends. As he saw the carnage of the retreat, he then turned inward and concentrated solely on his survival. Walter, according to historical records, survived the campaign and lived until 1864. He fathered 10 children, several of whom migrated to the United States. Source: Jakob Walter, *The Diary of a Napoleonic Foot Soldier,* edited by Marc Raeff (New York: Penguin, 1993), 80–89.

It was November 25, 1812, when we reached Borissov. Now the march went toward the Beresina River, where the indescribable horror of all possible plagues awaited us. On the way I met one of my countrymen, by the name of Brenner, who had served with the Light Horse Regiment. He came toward me completely wet and half frozen, and we greeted each other. Brenner said that the night before he and his horse had been caught and plundered but that he had taken to flight again and had come through a river which was not frozen. Now, he said, he was near death from freezing and starvation. This good, noble solider had run into me not far from Smolensk with a little loaf of bread weighing about two pounds and had asked me whether I wanted a piece of bread, saying that this was his last supply. 'However, because you have nothing at all, I will share it with you.' He had dismounted, laid the bread on the ground, and cut it in two with his saber. 'Dear, good friend,' I had replied, 'you treat me like a brother. I will not forget as long as I live this good deed of yours but will rather repay you many times if we live.'

When we came nearer the Beresina River, there was a place where Napoleon ordered his pack horses to be unharnessed and where he ate. He watched his army pass by in the most wretched condition. What he may have felt in his heart is impossible to surmise. His outward appearance seemed indifferent and unconcerned over the wretchedness of his soldiers; only ambition and lost honor may have made themselves felt in his heart; and, although the French and Allies shouted into his ears many oaths and curses about his own guilty person, he was still able to listen to them unmoved.

When I had gone somewhat farther from that place, I met a man who had a sack of raw bran in which there was hardly a dust of flour. I begged him ceaselessly to sell me a little of the bran, pressing a silver ruble into his hand; so he put a few handfuls in my little cloth, although very unwillingly, whereupon I happily continued on my journey.

After a time, from about two till four o'clock in the afternoon, the Russians pressed nearer and nearer from every side and the murdering and torturing seemed about to annihilate everyone. Although our army used a hill, on which what was left of our artillery was placed, and fired at the enemy as much as possible, the question was: what chance was there of rescue? That day we expected that everyone must be captured, killed, or thrown into the water. Everyone thought that his last hour had come, and everyone was expecting it; but since the ridge was held by the French artillery, only cannon and howitzer balls could snatch away a part of the men. There was no hospital for the wounded; they died also of hunger, thirst, cold and despair, uttering complaints and curses with their last breath.

When it became day again, we stood near the stream approximately a thousand paces from the two bridges, which were built of wood near each other. These bridges had the structure of sloping saw-horses suspended like trestles on shallow-sunk piles; on these lay long stringers and across them only bridge ties, which were not fastened down. Everyone crowded together into a solid mass, and nowhere could one see a way out or a means of rescue. From morning till night we stood unprotected from cannonballs and grenades which the Russians hurled at us from two sides. At each blow from three to five men were struck to the ground, and yet no one was able to move a step to get out of the path of the cannonballs.

I could look with indifference at the people falling by the hundreds, although the impact upon the ice bashed their heads. I could look at their rising and falling again, their dull moaning and whining, and the wringing and clenching of hands. The ice and snow sticking in their mouths was frightful. Nevertheless, I had no feeling of pity. Only my friends were in my thoughts.

During this month the cold became worse daily.

Document 10
The Last Will and Testament of Napoleon

Napoleon's *Last Will and Testament* is as much a part of his memoirs and legend as his *Army Bulletins*, published correspondence, and other types of imperial propaganda. In the enumerated list contained in his will, Napoleon left his own response to what others might say about him after his death. First, he stated that he remained a Catholic, although his behavior had been more as an agnostic and the pope had excommunicated him. Second, he publicly stated his wish to be buried in France, although he knew that he would be buried at St. Helena with no recognition or fanfare. In the third and fourth statements, he spun an image of his wife and son. Although Marie Louise had returned to Austria after his defeat at Leipzig and had never visited him at Elba, he characterized her as his special companion. Separated from his son, whom he scarcely knew, he established the image of a French prince. In summary, he had done everything for France—nothing for himself.

In later provisions, he listed by name the men whom he blamed for the unseemly capitulation of France after Waterloo. Generals Augereau and Marmont had refused to field their troops one more time in support of the Emperor; Talleyrand and Lafayette, among others, had led the provisional government against him. If historians failed to note these men, he would make sure that posterity knew who they were. As for his death, he blamed Britain for the selection of St. Helena, its insalubrious climate, and his less-than-acceptable treatment by Sir Hudson Lowe, whom he viewed as his jailor, and whom he did not need to name. In the seventh paragraph, he named his family members, some of whom he had disavowed earlier for their misbehaviors and failures. In his death, they were equal, except for Louis, whose behavior as King of Holland was inexcusable. And, finally, Napoleon stated, one more time, that his execution of the innocent Duc d'Enghien was just. The event had obsessed him throughout most of his life, and in what would seem an unlikely document, he took the opportunity to have his last word.

While the will contains bequests of 5,600,000 francs to named generals and supporters, Napoleon also authorized gifts to those men who had been wounded at Waterloo and to the loyal troops who had joined him on Elba. To men who had been severely wounded, including amputations, he doubled his bequests. Detail by detail, he accounted for his private property, including such items as his furnishings, his library (particularly the four hundred volumes he used the most), and specifics like the three saddles, bridles, and spurs he had used at St. Helena, and even his two watches and a chain made of the Empress's hair. Underlying it all was his admonition that "None of the articles which have been used by me shall be sold."

In his instructions to his executors, he laid out additional suggestions and demands, among them, that his illegitimate son by Maria Walewski should be dissuaded from entering the judiciary, that his executors should continually remind the British king that his ashes should be transported to France, and that his nephews and nieces should never marry into Swedish families. People whom he believed had stolen from him were named, and his executors were charged with retrieving items and wealth from them. Even as he grew ill—detail after detail, codicil after codicil (eight have been identified), Napoleon missed nothing. Following are extracts of Napoleon's *Last Will and Testament.* Source: Emmanuel Dieudonné, comte de Las Cases, *Memoirs of the Life, Exile, and Conversations of the Emperor Napoleon,* 4 vols. (New York: Worthington Company, 1890), 4: 400–12.

This 15th April, 1821, at Longwood, Island of St. Helena. This is my Testament, or act of my last will.

1. I die in the Apostolical Roman religion [Catholic Church], in the bosom of which I was born, more than fifty years since.
2. It is my wish that my ashes may repose on the banks of the Seine, in the midst of the French people, whom I have loved so well.
3. I have always had reason to be pleased with my dearest wife Marie Louisa. I retain for her, to my last moment, the most tender sentiments—I beseech her to watch, in order to preserve my son from the snares which yet environ his infancy.
4. I recommend to my son never to forget that he was born a French prince, and never to allow himself to become an instrument in the hands of the triumvirs who oppress the nations of Europe: he ought never to fight against France, or to injure her in any manner; he ought to adopt my motto: "Every thing [sic] for the French people."
5. I die prematurely, assassinated by the English oligarchy and its * * * [hired assassin]. The English nation will not be slow in avenging me.
6. The two unfortunate results of the invasions of France, when she had still so many resources, are to be attributed to the treason of Marmont, Augereau, Talleyrand, and La Fayette. I forgive them—May the posterity of France forgive them as I do!
7. I thank my good and most excellent mother, the Cardinal [my maternal uncle], my brothers Joseph, Lucien, Jérôme, [my sisters] Pauline, Caroline, [my extended family] Julie, Hortense, Catarine, Eugène, for the interest they have continued to feel for me. I pardon Louis for the libel he published in 1820; it is replete with false assertions and falsi-

fied documents.

8. I disavow the "Manuscript of St. Helena," and other works, under the title of Maxims, Sayings, &c., which persons have been pleased to publish for the last six years. Such are not the rules which have guided my life. I caused the Duc d'Enghien to be arrested and tried, because that step was essential to the safety, interest, and honour of the French people, when the Comte d'Artois was maintaining, by his own confession, sixty assassins at Paris. Under similar circumstances, I should act in the same way.

II.

1. I bequeath to my son the boxes, orders, and other articles such as my plate, field-bed, saddles, spurs, chapel-plate, books, linen which I have been accustomed to wear and use, according to the list annexed (A). It is my wish that this slight bequest may be dear to him, as coming from a father of whom the whole world will remind him.

. . . .

LIST (A).

Annexed to my Will
Longwood, Island of St. Helena,
this 15th April, 1821

. . . .

II.

1. My arms; that is to say, my sword, that which I wore at Austerlitz, the sabre of Sobiesky, my dagger, my broad sword, my hanger, my two pair of Versailles pistols.

2. My gold dressing-case, that which I made use of on the morning of Ulm and of Austerlitz, of Jena, of Eylau, of Friedland, of the Island of Lobau, of the Moskwa, of Montmirail. In this point of view it is my wish that it may be precious in the eyes of my son. (It has been deposited with Count Bertrand since 1814.)

3. I charge Count Bertrand with the care of preserving these objects, and of conveying them to my son when he shall attain the age of sixteen years.

III.

1. Three small mahogany boxes, containing, the first, thirty-three snuff-boxes or comfit-boxes; the second, twelve boxes with the Imperial arms, two small eye-glasses, and four boxes found on the table of Louis XVIII in the Tuileries, on the 20th of March, 1815; the third, three snuff boxes, ornamented with silver medals habitually used by the Emperor; and sundry articles for his use of the toilet [the act of dressing or grooming], according to the lists numbered I. II. III.
2. My field-beds, which I used in all my campaigns.
3. My field-telescope.
4. My dressing-case, one of each of my uniforms, a dozen of shirts, and a complete set of each of my dresses [garments], and generally of every-thing used in my toilet.
5. My wash-hand stand.
6. A small clock which is in my bed-chamber at Longwood.
7. My two watches, and the chain of the Empress's hair.
8. I entrust the care of these articles to Marchand, my principal valet-de-chambre, and direct him to convey them to my son when he shall attain the age of sixteen years.

. . . .

LIST (A).

1. None of the articles which have been used by me shall be sold; the residue shall be divided amongst the executors of my will and my brothers.
2. Marchand shall preserve my hair, and cause a bracelet to be made of it, with a little gold clasp, to be sent to the Empress Marie Louisa, to my mother, and to each of my brothers, sisters, nephews, nieces, the Cardinal; and one of the larger size for my son.

ANNOTATED BIBLIOGRAPHY

Napoleon's Correspondence, Writings, and Memoirs

Letters and Documents of Napoleon. Selected and Translated by John Eldred Howard. New York: Oxford University Press, 1961. Selection of letters and documents from Napoleon's early years through the Peace of Amiens, including family correspondence, *Army Bulletins,* notes, maps, and government documents.

The Military Maxims of Napoleon. Edited by William E. Cairnes. Introduction and Commentary by David Chandler. New York: Da Capo Press, 1995. Seventy-eight tenets on the art of war, tactics, strategy, supply, command, and common soldiering.

The Mind of Napoleon: A Selection from his Written and Spoken Words, Edited and Translated by J. Christopher Herold. New York: Columbia University Press, 1955. A collection of utterances by Napoleon organized topically about politics, history, war, the social order, the arts and sciences, destiny, and the human heart.

Napoleon on the Art of War. Selected, Edited and Translated by Jay Luvaas. New York: The Free Press, 1999. Essays, correspondence, and Napoleon's *Army Bulletins* organized by theme, for example, preparations for war, the operational art, and the composition of the army.

Napoleon on Napoleon: An Autobiography of the Emperor. Edited by Somerset de Chair. London: Cassell, 1992. Topically organized writings and dictations of Napoleon, gleaned from the memoirs of his companions on St. Helena, including Las Cases, Gourgaud, Montholon, and Bertrand.

Napoleon Wrote Fiction. Edited and Translated by Christopher Frayling. Salisbury, U.K.: The Compton Press, Ltd., 1972. Collection of essays including the one novel that Napoleon wrote, preceded by thorough analytical introductions to each of Napoleon's works.

Napoleon's Autobiography: The Personal Memoirs of Bonaparte Compiled from his own Letters and Diaries by Professor F. M. Kircheison. New York: Duffield and Company, 1931. The words of Napoleon and his memoirists, skillfully woven together by one of the preeminent authorities on Napoleon, forming what appears to be an autobiography.

Napoleon's Letters: Selected, Translated, and Edited by J. M. Thompson. London: Prion, 1998. Excellent selection of 292 letters and notes written by Napoleon spanning the period from June 25, 1784 until July 14, 1815.

Napoleon's Letters to Marie Louise. New York: Farrar & Rinehart, 1935. Collection of Napoleon's letters to Marie Louise from 1810 through 1814, reflecting on his family, his affection for her, and his instructions to her about how to be an empress for France and an emissary for the Emperor.

Unpublished Correspondence of Napoleon I, Preserved in the War Archives, 3 vols. Translated by Louise Seymour Houghton. New York: Duffield & Company, 1913. Three-volume addendum to the multivolume original *Correspondance de Napoléon I,* organized chronologically. The collection is composed predominantly of military letters and decisions.

Other Primary Sources

Abrantès, Laure Junot, duchesse d'. *Memoirs of Napoleon, his Court, and Family.* 2 vols. New York: D. Appleton and Company, 1866. Chatty, acerbic, and frequently quoted memoirs of a member of Napoleonic court society who married one of Napoleon's friends and military companions.

Arnold, Eric. *A Documentary Survey of Napoleonic France.* Lanham: University Press of America, 1994. Important collection of primary source documents including Napoleonic constitutions and codes.

Austin, Paul Britten, ed. *1812: The Great Retreat Told by Survivors.* London: Greenhill Books, 1996. A collection of personal narratives of men who returned from the ill-fated Russian campaign that began in 1812.

Bertrand, Henri Gratien. *Napoleon at St. Helena: Memoirs of General Bertrand, Grand Marshal of the Palace, January to May 1821.* London: Cassell and Company, Ltd., 1953. Frank but somewhat impersonal memoirs about Napoleon during his last illness and confinement, interspersed with comments about France, the Revolution, Joséphine, military affairs, and his own health, interests, and friends.

Bourienne, Louis Antoine Fauvelet de. *Memoirs of Napoleon Bonaparte.* 4 vols. New York: Charles Scribner's Sons, 1891. Entertaining, unreliable, and unflattering memoirs by Napoleon's schoolmate at Brienne, private secretary from 1797 to 1802, and plenipotentiary to Hamburg in 1805.

Caulaincourt, Armand Augustin Louis de. *With Napoleon in Russia.* New York: William Morrow and Company, 1935. A very personal and informative memoir from Napoleon's loyal friend and aide-de-camp on the retreat from Russia.

Clauswitz, Carl von. *On War.* Translated by Peter Paret. London: Penguin Books, 1968. First published in 1832 after Clauswitz's death, this treatise on war has become a classic. Clauswitz, who viewed the Napoleonic wars from the Prussian side, saw war as an extension of politics (in a somewhat Machiavellian way).

Denon, Vivant. *Travels in Upper and Lower Egypt.* New York: Arno Press, 1973. Description of Egypt published in 1803 by one of Napoleon's surveyor-artists who traveled with the French armies during the Egyptian campaign.

Gorrequer, Gideon. *St. Helena during Napoleon's Exile: Gorrequer's Diary.* Edited by James Kemble. London: Heinemann, 1969. Disjointed notes from Sir Hudson Lowe's aide-de-camp and acting military secretary at St. Helena from 1817 until 1823. The diary nonetheless sheds light on Napoleon's relations with the governor of St. Helena during Napoleon's captivity.

Jomini, Antoine Henri, baron de. *The Art of War.* London: Greenhill, 1996. An analysis of the art of warfare by one of Napoleon's staff officers. Jomini's analysis of Napoleonic tactics and strategy became a classic that was used by Civil War commanders in the mid-nineteenth century.

Landsdowne, Henry. *The First Napoleon: Some Unpublished Documents from the Bowood Papers.* Boston: Houghton Mifflin Company, 1929. Correspondence from the later Empire, including 1812, the first abdication, Elba, and the Hundred Days, as well as papers from Napoleon's voyage on H.M.S. *Bellerophon* and his exile on St. Helena.

Las Cases, Emmanuel Dieudonné, comte de. *Memoirs of the Life, Exile, and Conversations of the Emperor Napoleon.* 4 vols. New York: Worthington Company, 1890. Memoirs of Napoleon's life, campaigns, and politics that were dictated to Las Cases, who remained with Napoleon on St. Helena from 1815 to 1816.

Lewis, Jon E. *Soldiers at War.* New York: Carroll & Graff Publishers, 2001. A selection of memoirs and documents including the Napoleonic campaigns in Italy, Egypt, Spain, and Russia and the battles of Wagram, Leipzig, and Waterloo.

Méneval, Claude François. *Memoirs Illustrating the History of Napoleon I from 1802 to 1815.* 3 vols. New York: D. Appleton and Company, 1894. Valuable memoirs of the man who served as secretary to Joseph Bonaparte, Napoleon, and Marie Louise.

Restif de la Bretonne, Nicholas. *Les nuits de Paris or the Nocturnal Spectator.* New York: Random House, 1964. A witty, interesting, anecdotal glimpse of Paris during the revolutionary years.

Stewart, John Hall., ed. *Documentary Survey of the French Revolution.* New York: The Macmillan Company, 1951. Collection of proclamations and constitutions of the period of the Revolution and Directory, including Napoleon's Italian Campaign, Egyptian Campaign, coup, and Constitution of 1799.

Secondary Sources

Alexander, R. S. *Napoleon.* New York: Oxford University Press, Inc., 2001. Historiographic study of the Napoleonic era asking questions such as: Hero or villain? Charlatan or true prophet? Sinner or saint? Conqueror or unifier of Europe?

Asprey, Robert. *The Reign of Napoleon Bonaparte.* New York: Basic Books, 2001. Masterful telling of the bloody battles of Napoleon's reign and his exile and death.

—————. *The Rise of Napoleon Bonaparte.* New York: Basic Books, 2000. Evenhanded, though somewhat anecdotal narrative of Napoleon's life until the time of Austerlitz, written in the style of a novel but based extensively on period correspondence.

Blanning, T. C. W., ed. *The Eighteenth Century: Europe, 1688–1815.* London and New York: Oxford University Press, 2000. A series of essays placing the revolutionary and Napoleonic era in the context of the war-ridden eighteenth century.

Blond, Georges, *La Grande Armée.* Translated by Marshall May. London: Arms and Armour Press, 1995. Extensive story of the Grand Army from its creation at Boulogne to the retreat of the Imperial Guard at Waterloo, including information on supply, composition, tactics, and strategy.

Britt III, Albert Sidney. *The Wars of Napoleon.* Wayne, N.J.: Avery Publishing Group, 1985. Well-organized analysis of Napoleon as a commander, stressing the principles of generalship and strategy and the problems that Napoleon encountered with logistics and his staff. The book was written originally for cadets at West Point in 1972.

Bruun, Geoffrey. *Europe and the French Imperium, 1799–1814.* London and New York: Harper & Brothers Publishers, 1938. Classic work on the impact of Napoleon outside of France, including sections on French colonial aspirations, the Oriental mirage, and the International Empire.

Caldwell, Ronald. *The Era of Napoleon: A Bibliography of the History of Western Civilization, 1799–1815.* 2 vols. New York: Garland, 1991. Helpful research tool organized topically.

Chandler, David. *The Campaigns of Napoleon: The Mind and Method of History's Greatest Soldier.* New York: Macmillan Publishing Company, Inc., 1966. One of the most exhaustive analyses of the Napoleonic wars, concluding that Napoleon's success lay in his application of ideas rather than on any new or original plans.

_____. *Dictionary of the Napoleonic Wars: The Soldiers, Strategies, Armaments, Movements and Battles that Shaped Events during Napoleon's Reign.* New York: Macmillan Publishing Company, 1979. Comprehensive collection of short entries on Napoleon's battles, commanders, and military contests as well as the opposition and allied commanders, important civilian personages, and terminology of the day.

_____. *Napoleon's Marshals.* New York: Macmillan Publishing Company, 1987. Engagingly written, comprehensive volume on Napoleon's 26 marshals, detailing their lives, careers, strengths, weaknesses, achievements, and failures.

Connelly, Owen. *Blundering to Glory: Napoleon's Military Campaigns.* Wilmington, Del.: A Scholarly Resources Imprint, 1987. History of Napoleon's campaigns, highlighting his genius and success more as the result of scrambling than planning.

_____. *The Epoch of Napoleon.* Malabar, Fla.: Robert E. Krieger, 1972. Short overview of the Napoleonic period, written as a textbook.

_____. *The French Revolution and Napoleonic Era,* 3rd ed. New York: Wadsworth Publishing Company, 1999. Thoroughly updated, popular, and well-written textbook on the era of the French Revolution and Napoleon.

_____. *Napoleon's Satellite Kingdoms.* New York: The Free Press, 1965. Study of the Kingdoms of Italy, Naples, Holland, Westphalia, and Spain as first governed by members of Napoleon's family and then as Napoleon drew them into greater France. Were they part of a master plan or grand design?

_____, ed., along with Harold Parker, Peter Becker, and June K. Burton, Associate Editors. *Historical Dictionary of Napoleonic France, 1799–1815.* Westport, Conn.: Greenwood Press, 1985. Excellent alphabetical overview of Napoleonic personalities, campaigns, significant events, and terms.

Delorme, Eleanor. *Joséphine: Napoleon's Incomparable Empress.* London: Harry N. Abrams, 2002. Sensitive, romantic, and favorable portrayal of Empress Joséphine, highlighting her sense of style, intellect, and role as Napoleon's *confidante.*

Dowd, David Lloyd. *Napoleon: Was He the Heir of the Revolution?* Hinsdale, Ill.: Dryden Press, 1957. Interpretive, short excursion into the debates on Napoleon using period documents and correspondence.

Dufraisse, Roger. *Napoleon.* Translated by Steven Englund. New York: McGraw-Hill, Inc., 1992. Short history of the Napoleonic era, seen through the eyes of a French author (in translation) and through recent scholarship on the period.

Ellis, Geoffrey James. *Napoleon.* London: Longman, 1997. Chronological examination of how perceptions of Napoleon, including both the heroic and the black legend, survived into the nineteenth century. Part of the series "Profiles in Power."

Elting, John. *Swords Around the Throne: Napoleon's Grande Armée.* New York: The Free Press, 1988. Thorough history of the Grand Army including sections as wide-ranging as rations, pay, mobile hospitals, uniforms, medals, and camp followers.

Esdaille, Charles. *The Wars of Napoleon.* London and New York: Longman, 1995. Very critical study of Napoleon, placing the blame almost exclusively on Napoleon for continuing the continental contest between Great Britain and France.

Esposito, Vincent, and John Elting. *A Military History and Atlas of the Napoleonic Wars.* London: Greenhill, 1999. One of the most comprehensive and detailed campaign-by-campaign histories of the Napoleonic wars, containing superb maps.

Fisher, H. A. L. *Napoleon.* Oxford, U.K.: Oxford University Press, 1967. Well-known, favorable biography of Napoleon, written to focus on his energy and achievements.

Forrest, Alan. *Conscripts and Deserters: The Army and French Society during the Revolution and Empire.* New York: Oxford University Press, 1989. Scholarly examination of French militarization, including issues of conscription, desertion, and policing.

Fregosi, Paul. *Dreams of Empire: Napoleon and the First World War, 1792–1815.* London: Hutchinson, 1989. Narrative of the struggles, wars, and contests that were fought outside of France as part of the global contest of the Napoleonic era, for example, those that took place in the Caribbean, South America, the Philippines, India, the Arab states, South Africa, and Ireland.

Gates, David. *The Napoleonic Wars, 1803–1815.* London: Arnold, 1997. Important, recent work on Napoleon, comparing his military prowess in 1803 against his later years and setting the conflict in the broader context of modern warfare.

Geyl, Pieter. *Napoleon: For or Against.* New Haven, Conn.: Yale University Press, 1963. Classic work interpreting Napoleon, first published in 1949. Based on writings from contemporaries such as Chateaubriand and Mme de Staël, memorists who created the Napoleonic Legend, and French historians from the nineteenth century through Georges Lefebvre, it ends with the poignant, but pointed, truth: "the argument goes on."

Glover, Michael. *The Peninsular War, 1807–1814: A Concise Military History.* Hamden, Conn.: Archon Books, 1974. Good, solid history of the Peninsular War in Spain and Portugal based on Wellington's *Dispatches,* Napoleon's *Correspondance,* and period memoirs. Focuses on the limitations of the armies, conditions of the soldiers, and problems of requisitions.

Godechot, Jacques, Beatrice Hyslop, and David Dowd. *The Napoleonic Era in Europe*. New York: Holt, Rinehart and Winston, 1971. Even-handed text on the Napoleonic era, incorporating scholarship from the bicentennial of Napoleon's birth (1969).

Guerrini, Maurice. *Napoleon and Paris: Thirty Years of History*. London: Cassell, 1970. Excellent study of the city of Paris, highlighting the realities and promises of Napoleonic reconstruction.

Heckscher, Eli F. *The Continental System: An Economic Interpretation*. Oxford: Clarendon Press, 1922. Classic work on the economic blockade, including reproductions of French decrees and British Orders-in-Council.

Herold, J. Christopher. *The Age of Napoleon*. Boston: Houghton Mifflin Company, 1987. Unsympathetic but extensive biography of Napoleon that blends social, political, and military history across the panorama of Europe.

Hibbert, Christopher. *Napoleon: His Wives and Women*. London: HarperCollins, 2002. Chatty but well documented history of Napoleon seen through the Emperor's eyes and the eyes of the women who knew him, including his two empresses and the mothers of the four illegitimate children he acknowledged.

Holtman, Robert. *The Napoleonic Revolution*. New York and Philadelphia: J. B. Lipincott Company, 1967. Study of the gains of the Revolution, rise of the middle class, improvement in the legal status of peasants, and how Napoleon forced France into the modern age.

Horne, Alistair. *How Far from Austerlitz? Napoleon, 1805–1815*. New York: St. Martin's Press, 1996. Well-written, almost conversational coverage of the Napoleonic wars, occasionally comparing Napoleon's successes and failures to contemporary events.

Horward, Donald D., ed. *Napoleonic Military History, a Bibliography*. New York and London: Garland Publishing, Inc., 1986. Extensive bibliography of the Napoleonic era, preceded by an introduction to Napoleonic research and a series of bibliographic essays on each of the campaigns and areas of Napoleonic influence.

Howarth, David. *Waterloo: Day of Battle*. New York: Galahad Books, 1968. Narrative of the battle of Waterloo based on 18 eyewitness accounts, from dawn through the night of June 18, 1815.

Johnson, Paul. *Napoleon*. London: Weidenfield and Nicholson, 2002. Biography of Napoleon, suggesting that the totalitarian states of Russia, Germany, and Italy learned their authoritarianism from Napoleon's myth and reality.

Kafker, Frank A., and James M. Laux. *Napoleon and his Times: Selected Interpretations*. Malabar, Fla.: Krieger Publishing Company, 1989. Series of essays by leading experts on the major events, accomplishments, and challenges of the Napoleonic period.

Lachouque, Henry. *The Anatomy of Glory: Napoleon and his Guard: A Study in Leadership*, 4th ed. London: Greenhill, 1997. Illustrated study of Napoleon's creation and use of the Imperial Guard. Illustrations are drawn from the Anne Brown Collection at Brown University.

Lefebvre, Georges. *Napoleon: From 18 Brumaire to Tilsit, 1799–1807*. New York: Columbia University Press, 1969. Written by one of the leading historians of the French Revolution, traces the legacy of the Revolution through the height of the Napoleonic Empire.

Lyons, Martyn. *Napoleon Bonaparte and the Legacy of the French Revolution*. New York: St. Martin's Press, 1994. Well-written social history of the Napoleonic period through the lens of the Revolution, questioning when the Revolution actually ended.

MacKenzie, Norman. *The Escape from Elba: the Fall & Flight of Napoleon, 1814–1815*. New York and Toronto: Oxford University Press, 1982. History of Napoleon during his reign as Emperor of Elba (1814–1815), viewing his first exile as a miniature of his earlier reorganization of Europe.

Markham, Felix. *The Bonapartes*. New York: Taplinger Publishing Company, 1975. Heavily illustrated story of the Bonaparte family from their Corsican origins throughout the Napoleonic period.

———. *Napoleon*. New York and Toronto: The New American Library, 1963. Thorough, balanced biography of Napoleon based on published sources, memoirs, and correspondence.

———. *Napoleon and the Awakening of Europe*. New York: Collier Books, 1972. Well-written, short narrative of Napoleon from Corsica through the creation of the Napoleonic legend, focusing on the emergence of nationalism.

Markov, Walter. *Grand Empire: Virtue and Vice in the Napoleonic Era*. New York: Hippocrene Books, 1990. Heavily illustrated social history of the Napoleonic period.

Martineau, Gilbert. *Napoleon's Last Journey*. London: John Murray, 1976. Narrative of Napoleon's death, burial at St. Helena, exhumation, and transmission to Paris for burial at Les Invalides, interspersed with elements of the Napoleonic legend.

Nicholls, David. *Napoleon: A Biographical Companion*. Santa Barbara, Calif.: ABC-Clio, 1999. Well-organized and helpful biographical dictionary of the Napoleonic era, including a general introduction, chronology, bibliography, and document section.

Parker, Harold. *Three Napoleonic Battles*. Durham, N.C.: Duke University Press, 1983. Study of the battles of Friedland, Aspern-Essling, and Waterloo, analyzing them for the movement of the armies, amalgamation of troops, leadership, medical care, requisitions and supply, and evidence of Napoleon's imaginative execution. Concludes with an excellent essay on writing military history.

Pinckney, David H. *Napoleon: Historical Enigma.* St. Louis, Mo.: Forum Press, 1969. Historiographic essays questioning whether Napoleon was the defender or destroyer of the Revolution, a military genius or revolutionary general, an enlightened despot or modern dictator.

Roberts, Andrew. *Napoleon and Wellington.* London: Weidenfield and Nicholson, 2001. Dual biography of the two great military rivals of the Napoleonic wars, highlighting their off-the-battlefield rivalry more than their military prowess.

Robiquet, Jean. *Daily Life in France under Napoleon.* Translated by Violet MacDonald. New York: The Macmillan Company, 1963. One of the best portraits of domestic France, dealing with topics as far ranging as everyday consumption, gaming, theatre, fashion, highways, and houses in Paris and the provinces.

Rose, John Holland. *The Personality of Napoleon.* London: G. Bell and Sons, Ltd., 1912. Classic study of Napoleon as "the man, the Jacobin, the warrior, the lawgiver, the emperor, the thinker, the world-ruler, and the exile," noting that Napoleon did not understand the age of nationalism in which he found himself.

Rothenberg, Gunther E. *The Art of Warfare in the Age of Napoleon.* Bloomington: Indiana University Press, 1980. Detailed study of military history, strategy, weaponry, and medicine in the Napoleonic and allied armies.

Schneid, Frederic C. *Napoleon's Italian Campaigns.* Westport, Conn.: Praeger, 2002. Recent, soundly researched study of the early campaigns of Napoleon.

Schom, Alan. *Napoleon Bonaparte.* New York: HarperCollins, 1997. Extensive, anecdotal, and critical revival of the black legend of Napoleon, concentrating on his opportunism.

Schwartz, Berhard. *The Code Napoléon and the Common-law World.* New York: New York University Press, 1956. Collection of essays on the Napoleonic Code, including a good analysis of the major provisions of the Code and the philosophical underpinnings of Napoleonic law.

Thompson, J. M. *Napoleon Bonaparte.* Phoenix Mill, U.K.: Sutton Publishing Ltd., 2001. Reissue of Thompson's excellent, well-documented and correspondence-based 1952 biography of Napoleon Bonaparte.

Tulard, Jean. *Napoleon: The Myth of the Saviour.* London: Weidenfield and Nicolson, 1984. The best study of the Napoleonic legend, tracing it from its birth in the First Italian Campaign, through newspapers, the Napoleonic catechism, and other forms of propaganda, into the period after 1815 when the Emperor became the "Napoleon of the people."

Ward, A. W., G. W. Prothero, and Stanley Leathes. *The Cambridge Modern History: Napoleon.* Vol. 9. Cambridge: Cambridge University Press, 1969. Scholarly, extensively documented study of the Napoleonic period, originally published in 1906 and written by some of the leading European historians at that time.

Weider, Ben, and David Hapgood. *The Murder of Napoleon.* New York: Congdon and Lattès, Inc., 1982. Intriguingly written story and study of Napoleon's death on St. Helena, positing that Napoleon did not die of stomach cancer but was poisoned by his compatriot Montholon. Based on forensic research first conducted by Swedish dentist Sten Forshuvfud.

Woloch, Isser. *Napoleon and his Collaborators: The Making of a Dictatorship.* New York: W. W. Norton, 2001. Carefully researched study of Napoleon's coup, his collaborators, his relationship with the revolutionary legacy, and the balance between creativity and tyranny during the Napoleonic era.

Films

Austerlitz (1959), directed by Abel Gance. Film version of the decisive conflict between the forces of Austria and France in 1805.

The Campaigns of Napoleon (1992–1993) including the *Battle of Waterloo* (1992), and the *Battle of Trafalgar* (1993), *Battle of Borodino* (1993), and *Battle of Austerlitz* (1993) produced by Cromwell Productions. This series of educational videos explores the military genius of Napoleon, his triumphs, and his defeats. Cromwell Productions also produced a short, not well-received *The Campaigns of Napoleon.*

The Duellists (1978), directed by Ridley Scott. A film version of Joseph Conrad's novel of two Napoleonic officers who carry on a duel for two decades. *The Duellists* describes honor as it was known during the Napoleonic period and the condition of the officer corps and common soldiers in the early nineteenth century.

The Emperor's New Clothes (2001), directed by Alan Taylor. A wildly fictional comic tragedy based on Simon Leys' novel of a Napoleonic impostor who returns to France from St. Helena to be mostly ignored (Simon Leys, *Death of Napoleon,* reissued in 2002 by Picador). It is worthwhile viewing, however, for the costumes, locations, and representations of period lifestyles.

Napoleon (1927), directed by Abel Gance. Gance filmed this cinematic marvel, a biography of Napoleon Bonaparte that lasts over three hours and ends only at the First Italian Campaign. Lavishly produced with a huge and well-selected cast, this film can be classed among the epic black and white silent films of the era of the 1920s. Music was composed and conducted by Carmine Coppola. The film has been reissued several times, most recently by MCA Home Video (Universal City, California, 1989).

Napoleon (1955), directed by Sacha Guitry. Biography of Napoleon from his rise to power during the Revolution through his days in exile. The film raises the question of whether or not Napoleon was a hero, tyrant, or madman. Among the stars are Orson Wells and Yves Montand.

Napoleon (1997), video produced by Kultur Films as part of their *Museum Tour* series. Reproduces the world-touring Napoleonic exhibit (Napoleonic furnishings, paintings, nostalgia, and military paraphernalia from 50 museums) that was featured in Memphis, Tennessee in 1993.

Napoleon (2000), produced as part of the Arts and Entertainment *Biography* series for television. Covers Napoleon's entire life, using contemporary prints, maps, and paintings along with interviews with leading military historians to create the portrait of Napoleon and his period.

The Napoleon Murder Mystery (n.d.), produced by Noah Morowitz for Discovery Communications. Made for television historical thriller of two interwoven tales: Napoleon on St. Helena in 1821 and Swedish dentist Sten Forshufvud's search for evidence that Napoleon was murdered by poisoning.

War and Peace (1967), directed by Sergei Bondarchuk. The well-filmed but painfully long Russian-language version of Tolstoy's lengthy, classic novel of the Russian campaign.

Electronic Resources (Web sites)

www.dean.usma.edu/history/dhistorymaps/Napoleonpages/NaptoC.htm. Excellent collection of military maps compiled and posted by the History Department at the United States Military Academy (West Point) showing the European military situation at any time between 1796 and 1815.

www.invalides.org. Site of the Musée de l'Armée in Paris, including a brief history of Napoleon's tomb (and the politics of the return of the ashes) along with photographs of selected collections and personal objects identified with Napoleon.

www.napoleon.org. Omnibus site of the *Fondation Napoléon* including a free weekly information bulletin, detailed imperial genealogy, pictures, a listing of recent books in the field, screen-savers, glossary, and even Napoleonic recipes.

www.napoleonbonaparte.nl. One of the most comprehensive and best Napoleonic Web sites, maintained by Paul Hilferink of Deventer, the Netherlands. The site includes links to primary documents, essays, and pictures.

www.napoleonic-alliance.com. Web site of the Napoleonic Alliance, a membership organization sponsoring annual meetings for scholars and amateurs interested in Napoleon. The site includes on-line articles and information on discount books and annual activities.

www.napoleonic-literature.com. Impressive Web site providing digital texts, an extensive bibliography of the period including fiction, drama and poetry, and one of the best lists of films on the Napoleonic period.

www.napoleonguide.com. Popular mixture of Napoleonic articles, pictures, wargames, movies, and miniseries (e.g., the fictional Richard Sharpe series written by Bernard Cornwell and the Hornblower series), with an extensive set of links to other locations, including museums and scholarly collections. The site is maintained by Richard Moore, editor.

www.napoleonseries.org. All-volunteer educational project created and maintained by amateurs and scholars interested in the Napoleonic period. The site contains articles (usually with some bibliography), translations (including a complete copy of the Code Napoléon in English), reviews, and an extensive list of links to sites throughout the world. Frequently asked questions include how tall Napoleon was, who shot the Sphinx, and what horses Napoleon rode at each battle. Virtual postcards are available.

www.pbs.org/empires/napoleon. Flash-enhanced, easily navigable Web site for the extensive documentary biography of Napoleon produced by Public Broadcasting. Aired first on television in November 2000, the Web site includes lesson plans, an extensive bibliography, and synopses of each of the sections of the production. "Napoleon" is narrated by several dozen leading historians and writers on Napoleon and contains period paintings and engravings and footage of places identified with Napoleon.

wtj.com. Site of the *War Times Journal,* an Internet site of primary source documents related to events in military history (in French and English). It includes an extensive collection of Wellington's *Dispatches* and a limited selection of Napoleonic *Army Bulletins.*

INDEX

About the Author

SUSAN P. CONNER is Professor of History and Vice President for Academic Affairs at Florida Southern College, Lakeland. She has published widely in journals such as *Eighteenth Century Studies*, the *Journal of Social History*, the *Journal of Women's History*, and *Eighteenth Century Life*, and on topics of gender, marginality, crime, and social history in collections, guides, and a historical encyclopedia.